THE BASICS OF
BITCOINS AND BLOCKCHAINS

"A delightful read that cuts the hype, finds the signal in the noise, and fires on all cylinders from front to back."
—John Collins, fintech advisor

"My family asked me to explain what I do, I gave them a copy of this book. Antony explains cryptocurrencies and blockchain technologies clearly and articulately, whilst remaining witty."
—Colin Platt, Co-Host Blockchain Insider Podcast & DLT/ Cryptocurrency Researcher

"One of the few credible books I suggest when people ask 'where can I learn about bitcoin?' It is an excellent, level-headed primary on everything crypto. I've been in the space for quite some time and I still learned from The Basics of Bitcoins and Blockchains."
—Zennon Kapron, Managing Director, Kapronasia

"An engaging, clear, and authoritative guide to the applications and implications of blockchains."
—Greg Wolfson, Head of Business Development at Element Group

"If you want a book that over-sells blockchain, go elsewhere. This explains the fundamentals clearly and cuts through the hype."
—Richard Gendal Brown, CTO, R3

THE BASICS OF

BITCOINS AND BLOCKCHAINS

An Introduction to Cryptocurrencies and the Technology That Powers Them

ANTONY LEWIS

Mango Publishing

CORAL GABLES

For permission requests, please contact the publisher at:
Mango Publishing Group
2850 Douglas Road, 3rd Floor
Coral Gables, FL 33134 USA
info@mango.bz

For special orders, quantity sales, course adoptions and corporate sales, please email the publisher at sales@mango.bz. For trade and wholesale sales, please contact Ingram Publisher Services at:
customer.service@ingramcontent.com or +1.800.509.4887.

The Basics of Bitcoins and Blockchains: An Introduction to Cryptocurrencies and the Technology that Powers Them

Library of Congress Cataloging-in-Publication has been applied for.
ISBN: (paperback) 978-1-63353-800-9, (ebook) 978-1-63353-801-6
BISAC category code:
BUSINESS & ECONOMICS / Investments & Securities / Futures

Printed in the United States of America

To my family, my long-suffering wife Sarah and our progeny-chain Toshi and Tosha.

TABLE OF CONTENTS

Part 0

INTRODUCTION

SOME DEFINITIONS

Bitcoin, blockchains, and cryptocurrencies are fascinating to me because there are so many elements to understand. This multidisciplinary nature is one of the reasons I, and so many others, love the industry—it is easy to get sucked into the rabbit hole, and as you try to understand each element, every answer begets more questions. The journey starts with 'What is Bitcoin?' but the explanations and answers come from the disciplines of economics, law, computer science, finance, civil society, history, geopolitics, and more. You could create a pretty comprehensive high school curriculum around Bitcoin and have plenty of material to spare.

And this is the very reason why it is so hard to explain. This book is an attempt to cover the basics. It is aimed at the thinking person but assumes that the reader doesn't have a detailed background in the various disciplines mentioned previously. Different people will find different parts interesting. I try to use analogies where I think they help explain some concepts, but be gentle with me: all analogies break down if stretched too far. And although I have tried to be accurate, there will still be oversimplifications, errors and omissions. What is true today may not be tomorrow: the pace of change is rapid. I am the first to admit that there are limits to my own technical expertise. Nevertheless, I hope that every reader comes away learning something new.

With that, let's start by defining at a basic level some of the words and concepts we will be exploring later in the book.

Bitcoin[1] and Ether are two of the better-known *cryptocurrencies* or *coins* (note that the coin on the Ethereum network is called Ether, though is often misnamed in the media as 'Ethereum'). These are *assets* or items of value that exist digitally, not physically, and are created by software. They have no issuer as such. No person, company, or entity backs these, and there are no terms of service or guarantees associated with them. Like physical gold, cryptocurrencies simply exist, and are created or destroyed according to the rules articulated in the code that creates and governs them. If you own some cryptocurrency, and we'll see what that actually means later, it is your asset that you control. It has value, and can be exchanged for other cryptocurrencies, US dollars, or other global sovereign (or fiat) currencies. Its value is determined within marketplaces called *exchanges* where buyers and sellers come together to trade at mutually agreed prices.

As well as 'coins,' units of cryptocurrencies may be described as digital assets. That is, unique data items whose ownership can be passed from account to account. These accounts are technically called addresses, and we will explore what addresses are later. When these digital assets move from one account to another they are all recorded on their respective transaction databases known, because of some unique shared characteristics which we will look into later, as blockchains.

Just to confuse everybody, some digital assets are described as tokens, as in 'Is it a cryptocurrency or a

---

1   In this book I try to use 'Bitcoin' (with a capital B) when describing the concept, the idea, or the network, and 'bitcoin' (with a lowercase b) or BTC when describing the units of currency, the coins themselves. So: 'I bought 5 bitcoins (or BTC) and saw the transaction on the Bitcoin blockchain'.

token?'. Cryptocurrencies and tokens are both types of cryptographically secured digital assets, sometimes known as *cryptoassets*. These tokens have different characteristics from cryptocurrencies and from each other. Tokens can be fungible (one token being more or less replaceable by another), or non-fungible (where each token represents something unique). Unlike cryptocurrencies, these newer tokens are usually issued by known issuers who stand behind them, and the tokens can represent legal agreements (like financial assets), physical assets (like gold), or future access to products and services.

Where the underlying item is an asset you could think of the token as a digital version of a cloakroom ticket, issued by a cloakroom clerk and redeemable for your coat. Indeed, these tokens are sometimes called DDRs—Digital Depository Receipts. Where the underlying item is an agreement, product or service, you can think of the token as something like a concert ticket issued by a concert organiser and redeemable for entry to a concert at a later date.

To give some real examples, there are tokens that represent everything from gold bullion sitting in a vault somewhere[2], through to tokens representing unique 'CryptoKitties'— collectable digital cats with specific visual attributes determined by their 'DNA' code.

---

2   See https://tradewindmarkets.com or https://digix.global

A CryptoKitty[3]

What do all of these coins and tokens have in common? All transactions related to them, including their creation, destruction, changes of ownership, and other logic or future obligations, are recorded on *blockchains*: replicated databases that act as the ultimate books and records—the 'golden source' that represents the universal understanding of the current status of all units of the digital asset.

Bitcoin's blockchain is an ever-growing list of every Bitcoin transaction that has ever happened, right from the creation of the very first Bitcoin on 3 January 2009, through to the most recent transfer or payment from one account to another. Ethereum's blockchain is a list of transactions involving the cryptocurrency Ether, a multitude of other tokens (including those representing CryptoKitties) and other related data, all of which is recorded on Ethereum.

Different blockchains have different characteristics, so much so that nowadays it is almost impossible to make a general statement about 'blockchain' without being wrong for some particular example. Some blockchains, like the well-known Bitcoin and Ethereum chains, are *public*, or *permissionless*, meaning that their list of transactions can be written to by anyone, with no gatekeepers to approve or reject parties

---

3   https://www.cryptokitties.co/kitty/234327

who want to create blocks or participate in bookkeeping. Self-identification is not a requirement to create blocks or validate transactions. Other blockchains can be *private* or *permissioned*, in that there is a controlling party who allows participants to read or write to them.

And finally, we need to distinguish between *protocols, code, software, transaction data, coins,* and *blockchains*. Bitcoin is a bunch of *protocols*: rules that define and characterise Bitcoin itself—what it is, how ownership is represented and recorded, what constitutes a valid transaction, how new participants can join the network of operators, how participants should behave if they want to be kept up to date with the latest transactions, and so on. These protocols, or rules, can be described in English or any other human language, but are best articulated in computer *code*, which in turn can be compiled into *software*—Bitcoin software—that enacts those protocols, i.e. makes them operate. When the software is run, Bitcoin *coins* are generated and can be sent from one account to another. These actions are recorded as *transaction data*, and this transaction data is bundled into bundles or *blocks*, and linked together to form the Bitcoin *blockchain*.

So, to recap, Bitcoin *protocols* are written out as Bitcoin *code* which is run as Bitcoin *software* which creates Bitcoin *transactions* containing data about Bitcoin *coins* recorded on Bitcoin's *blockchain*. Got it? Good. Not all other cryptocurrencies or tokens work this way, but it is as good a basis as any to start the journey.

Some people think of Bitcoin as the next evolution of money— it is described as a (crypto) *currency* after all. So we need to understand a little more about money. What is money? Has it always been the same? How successful has money been? Are some forms of money better than others? Can the nature of money ever change, or is what we have going to be the same for evermore? Do cryptocurrencies sit easily alongside today's money, fulfilling a niche or purpose that existing forms of money cannot serve, or are cryptocurrencies competitors to today's money that threaten the status quo of state-issued currency?

This book should give you a good well-rounded education into the basics of bitcoins and blockchains and assumes no specific starting expertise. We start by defining and understanding the nature of money. Then we dive into digital money and how value is really transferred around the world. We then explore a few key concepts from a branch of mathematics called cryptography, so that we can then move to cryptocurrencies themselves. In the cryptocurrencies section, we dive into the Bitcoin and Ethereum networks, and the Bitcoin and Ether digital tokens—what they are, how to buy, store, and sell them, how to explore their blockchains, and the risks in managing them, including the unique challenges in moving this new digital money around the world. Finally, we discuss the types of blockchain technology that are being explored by banks and big businesses to join up their databases and do more efficient business.

Although I have my personal biases and interests, throughout the book I try to maintain a neutral position on the cryptocurrencies, tokens, and blockchain platforms. I try not to neither over-sell them nor be overly critical. I leave it up to readers to conclude for themselves whether these technologies are a trend or a fad, useful or useless, good or bad.

Part 1

MONEY

PHYSICAL AND DIGITAL MONEY

Cash—physical money—is wonderful. You can transfer (or spend or give away) as much of what you have as you want, when you want, without any third parties approving or censoring the transaction or taking a commission for the privilege. Cash doesn't betray valuable identity information that can be stolen or misused. When you receive cash in your hand, you know that the payment can't be 'undone' (or charged back, in industry jargon) at a later date, unlike digital transactions such as credit card payments and some bank transfers, which is a pain point for merchants. Under normal circumstances, once you have cash, it is yours, it is under your control, and you can transfer it again immediately to somebody else. The transfer of physical money immediately extinguishes a financial obligation and leaves nobody waiting for anything else.

But there is a big problem with traditional physical cash: it doesn't work at a distance. Unless you carry it in person, you can't transfer physical cash to someone on the other side of the room, let alone on the other side of the planet. This is where digital money becomes highly useful.

Digital money differs from physical money in that it relies on bookkeepers who are trusted by their customers to keep accurate accounts of balances they hold. To put it another way, you can't own and directly control digital money yourself (well, you couldn't until Bitcoin came along, but more on that later). To own digital money, you must open an account somewhere with someone else—a bank, PayPal, an e-wallet. The 'someone else' is a third party whom you trust to keep books and records of how much money you have with them—or, more specifically, how much they must pay you on demand or transfer to someone else at your request. Your account with a third party is a record of an agreement of trust between you: simultaneously how much you have with them, and how much they owe you.

Without the third party, you would need to keep bilateral records of debts with everyone, even people who you may not trust or who may not trust you, and this is not feasible. For example, if you bought something online, you could attempt to send the merchant an email saying 'I owe you $50, so let's both record this debt'. But the merchant probably wouldn't accept this; firstly, because they probably have no reason to trust you, and secondly, because your email is not very useful to the merchant—they can't use your email to pay their staff or suppliers.

Instead, you instruct your bank to pay the merchant, and your bank does this by reducing how much your bank owes you, and, at the other end, increasing how much the merchant's bank owes them. From the merchant's point of view, this extinguishes your debt to the merchant, and replaces it with a debt from their bank. The merchant is happy, as they trust their bank (well, more than they trust you), and they can use the balance in their bank account to do other useful things.

Unlike cash, which settles using the transfer of physical tokens, digital money settles by increasing and decreasing balances in accounts held by trusted intermediaries. This probably seems obvious, though you may not have thought of it this way. We'll come back to this later, as bitcoins are a form of digital money which share some properties of physical cash.

There is a big difference between *online* card payments, where you type the numbers, and physical card payments, where you tap or swipe the *physical* card. In the industry, an online credit card payment is known as a 'card *not* present' transaction, and swiping your card at the cashier's till in a shop counts as a 'card present' transaction. Online (card not present) transactions have higher rates of fraud, so in an effort to make fraud harder, you need to provide more details—such as your address and the three digits on the back of the card. Merchants are charged higher fees for these types of payments to offset the cost of fraud prevention and the losses from fraud.

Cash is an anonymous bearer asset which does not record or contain identity information, unlike many forms of digital money that by law require personal identification. To open an account with a bank, wallet, or other trusted third party, regulations require that the third party can identify you. This is why you often need to supply information about yourself, with independent evidence to back that up. Usually that means a photo ID to match name and face, and a utility bill or other 'official' registered communication (for example from a government department) to validate your address. Identity information is not just collected when opening accounts. It is also collected and used for validation purposes when some electronic payments are made: when you pay online using a credit or debit card you need to supply your name and address as a first gateway against fraud.

There are exceptions to this identity rule. There are some stored value cards that don't require identity, for example public transport cards in many countries, or low-limit cash cards used in some countries.

Do payments *need* to be linked to identity? Of course not. Cash proves this. But *should* they? This is a big question that raises legal, philosophical and ethical issues that remain subject to ongoing debate. Credit card information is frequently stolen, along with personally identifying information (name, addresses, etc) which creates a cost to society.

Is it a fundamental right to be able to make payments which are shielded from the eyes of the state governments? And should people have the ability to make anonymous digital payments, as they do with physical cash? To what extent should our financial transactions be anonymous or, at the very least, private? And what, if any, are the reasonable limits to that privacy? Should the public sector or the private sector provide the means for electronic payments and financial privacy? Should a nation state be able to block an individual's ability to make digital payments, and with what limits? How can we reconcile financial privacy with the prevention of support for illegal activities, including the funding of terrorism? I won't provide answers to these big questions in this book, but the fundamental questions concerning financial privacy are inevitably raised when understanding the game-changing innovation that is Bitcoin.

HOW DO WE DEFINE MONEY?

We all know what money is, but how might we define it? The generally accepted academic definition of money usually says that money needs to fulfil three functions: A medium of exchange, a store of value, and a unit of account. But what does this really mean?

Medium of exchange means it is a payment mechanism—
you can use it to pay someone for something, or to extinguish
a debt or financial obligation. To be a good medium of
exchange, it doesn't need to be *universally* accepted (nothing
is), but it should be should be widely accepted *in the
particular context* for which it is being used.

Store of value means that in the near term (however
you define this) your money will be worth the same as it is
today. To be a good store of value, you need to be reasonably
confident that your money will buy you more or less the
same amount of goods and services tomorrow, next month,
or next year. When this breaks down, the money's value is
quickly eroded, a process often referred to as hyperinflation.
Individuals quickly develop alternative ways to denominate
value and undertake transactions, for example bartering or
using a 'hard' or more successful and stable currency.

Unit of account means it is something that you can use
to compare the value of two items, or to count up the total
value of your assets. If you record the value of all of your
possessions, you need some unit to price them in, to get a
total. Usually that is your home currency (GBP or USD or
whatever), but you could in theory use any unit. The last time
I counted, I had 0.2 Lamborghinis worth of gadgets in my
study. To be a *good* unit of account, the money needs to have
a well-accepted or understood price against assets, otherwise
it is hard to figure out the total value across all your assets
and, if you need to do so, to convince others of that value.

While some believe that 'good money' should fulfil all of these
functions, others think that the three functions can be fulfilled
by different instruments. For example, there is no real
reason why something used as a medium of exchange (i.e.,

something that can be used to immediately settle a debt) must also be a long term store of value.

Is Today's Money Good Money?

It is debatable how well the forms of money we generally regard as 'good money' stack up against these properties. The US dollar is arguably the most prominent form of money we have today, and can be considered the best, at least for the time being. But how *good* is it? The dollar is generally acceptable for payment, certainly in the USA, and even in other countries, so it is an excellent medium of exchange in those contexts (but less so in Singapore). And it is an excellent unit of account, because many assets are priced in dollars, including global commodities such as crude oil and gold.

But how has it fared as a store of value? According to the St Louis Fed, the purchasing power of the USD from a consumer's perspective has fallen by over 96% since the Federal Reserve System was created in 1913.

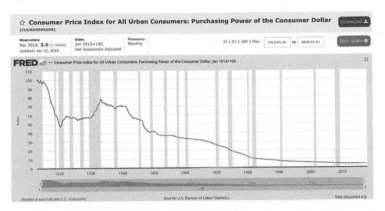

Source: St Louis Fed[4].

Given that purchasing power of the USD over time has decreased significantly, it has been a poor store of value over the long term. Indeed, people don't tend to keep banknotes under their mattress for decades, because they know cash is not a good store of value. And if they did, they would find that the purchasing power has decreased, or worse, that the banknotes have been pulled out of circulation and are no longer accepted in shops. In fact, the dollar, as with almost all government currencies, consistently loses value by design, driven by policy. We can predict, more or less, that the USD will lose its purchasing power by a few percentage points each year. This is known as price inflation (as opposed to currency inflation which is an increase in the number of dollars in circulation). Price inflation is measured by CPI (Consumer Price Inflation)—an index measuring the changes in the price of a theoretical basket of goods that are reportedly chosen to

4   U.S. Bureau of Labor Statistics, Consumer Price Index for All Urban Consumers: Purchasing Power of the Consumer Dollar, 2018, FRED, Federal Reserve Bank of St. Louis, https://fred.stlouisfed.org/series/CUUR0000SA0R

represent typical urban household spending[5]. The makeup of the basket changes over time, and policymakers are not beyond employing various tricks with that basket to bend the rate of inflation to figures they find more convenient[6].

So perhaps 'store of value' is a not a good medium or long term function of money, and perhaps the economists and textbooks don't have it quite right. We certainly need all three 'functions of money,' but perhaps not in the same instrument. Perhaps money fulfils one need (immediate settlement of obligations), whereas the longer-term store of value need can be better achieved through other assets. In terms of the 'store of value' function of money, it is more the short-term predictability of value, or spending power, that is relevant: I need to know that a dollar tomorrow or next month can buy me more or less the same thing as a dollar today and will settle immediate debts. But for long term preservation of value, perhaps housing or land or other assets may be more reliable.

How do cryptocurrencies fare against the standard definitions of money?

Bitcoin as a Medium of Exchange

As a medium of exchange, Bitcoin has some interesting characteristics. It is the very first digital asset of value that can be transferred over the internet without any specific third

---

5   There are other measures of the purchasing power of USD, such as core inflation, which is more or less CPI without the effects of volatile prices such as food and energy.

6   For more information see https://www.bls.gov/cpi/questions-and-answers. htm

party having to approve the transaction or being able to deny it. It is also an asset that is transferred from one owner to another rather than moving via a series of third party debits and credits, for example, through one or more banks. In this respect it is genuinely novel.

This is worth repeating:

> *Bitcoin is the very first digital asset of value that can be transferred over the internet without any specific third party having to approve the transaction or being able to deny it.*

Can you make payments with bitcoins? Yes, absolutely— anytime, anywhere. Is it fast? Sometimes—depending on a number of factors. At a settlement speed varying between seconds and hours, it is certainly faster than some traditional payment methods, but slower than others. Different cryptocurrencies settle transactions at different speeds.

Is Bitcoin widely accepted? Well, among its community it is widely accepted, and some prefer using it to traditional payment mechanisms[7]. But by a global standard, no, it is not widely accepted. Could this change? Could more and more people and businesses accept bitcoins or other cryptocurrencies? Perhaps not in large stable economies, but possibly in unstable smaller economies. There are a number of factors to consider when deciding if bitcoins

---

7   I once paid for a few nights' accommodation in San Francisco by making a bitcoin payment to the landlord. It was much easier, cheaper, and faster than asking for bank details and making an international payment. But then we both use bitcoins. In fact, for international payments within the cryptocurrency community, it's much easier, cheaper, and faster to pay each other in cryptocurrency than with bank wires.

should be used in preference to the domestic currency or existing alternatives.

What about merchant adoption? Every now and again, you might read that a merchant now accepts bitcoins or other cryptocurrencies as payment. What's going on? Doesn't this mean bitcoins are improving as a medium of exchange? Well, yes and no. In reality, most of the companies who say that they accept Bitcoin as payment don't actually accept bitcoins or hold them on their balance sheets. Instead, they use cryptocurrency payment processors that act as an intermediary by quoting a price to the customer in bitcoins (based on current prices of bitcoins to dollars on various cryptocurrency exchanges), accepting the bitcoins from the customer, then wiring an equivalent amount of conventional currency (*fiat* in the jargon) the boring way into the merchant's bank account.

Here is how it works:

1. The customer fills their shopping cart with items, then clicks 'check out'.

2. They are presented with the total value of the goods *in local currency*. 'How would you like to pay?'

3. Customer selects 'Bitcoin'.

4. They are then shown the number of bitcoins that they need to pay. The payment processor calculates this number by using the current exchange rate between Bitcoin and local currency, found on one or more cryptocurrency exchanges.

5. The customer then has a short amount of time to accept the price before the price of Bitcoin changes and the payment processor has to re-price the basket. The

pricing refresh time can be as short as 30 seconds due to Bitcoin's volatility. 30 seconds!

Bitpay[8] is a good example of this kind of cryptocurrency payment processor. In 2013-2015 a number of merchants announced that they now accepted Bitcoin. This was good cheap press for merchants, and many companies did this: Microsoft, Dell, and even—my favourite—Richard Branson for Virgin Galactic trips. Just think—in 2013 you could buy a trip into space and pay in bitcoins! However, since then, many merchants have quietly dropped Bitcoin as a method of payment.

So, in these cases where a merchant says they accept Bitcoin as payment, bitcoins *are* a medium of exchange from the customer's perspective. But these cases are rare, and currently it is not currently a widely used medium of exchange. In July 2017, investment bank Morgan Stanley produced a report on Bitcoin merchant adoption[9] that found that, in 2016, only five of the top 500 online merchants accepted Bitcoin and, in 2017, that number had dropped to three.

Bitcoin as a Store of Value

For now, let's put aside the argument about whether 'store of value' is a valid property of *money*, or if it should be an attribute of an *asset*.

Instead, let's ask the question, what do you want from your store of value? What is its job? Is its job to make you richer

---

8   Bitpay, https://bitpay.com

9   Frank Chaparro, "MORGAN STANLEY: 'Bitcoin acceptance is virtually zero and shrinking," Business Insider Singapore, July 12, 2017, https://www.businessinsider.sg/bitcoin-price-rises-but-retailers-wont-accept-it-7-2017

so you can buy more toys, or is its job to maintain its value
so you can plan your life well? And if the job of the thing
is to make you richer so you can buy more toys, how much
volatility and downside risk are you willing to stomach?
Are we talking about a short-term store of value, perhaps a
speculative investment, or a long-term store of value, often a
lower risk asset?

Bitcoin as a speculative investment has performed amazingly
well. Anything that starts at a price of zero, and is not
currently at a price of zero, is great. Bitcoin started at zero
value in 2009 and now, less than ten years later, each Bitcoin
is worth thousands of dollars. So it has certainly appreciated
in value since its creation. But would you buy it now? Would
you move all your savings into this asset in order to *store*
value (as opposed to gamble and hope for a quick price
appreciation)? Well, due to its price volatility, which is very
high compared to most fiat currencies, the answer is probably
no if you are looking for a stable store of value. As a long-term
store of value I suppose you want, as a minimum, something
that can be used to buy a basket of goods in twenty years' time
roughly identical to the basket you can buy with it now. So, if
you had bought it at the right time, Bitcoin has certainly been
a good *investment*, but its volatility makes it a nauseating
store of value.

Does Bitcoin, or do other cryptocurrencies, have the *potential*
to keep value over the long term, as some people expect
from gold? Possibly. According to its current protocol rules,
bitcoins are created at a known rate (12.5 BTC every 10
minutes or so)—and that rate will decrease over time. So the
supply of it is understood and predictable, capped to almost
21 million BTC and not subject to arbitrary creation, unlike

fiat currencies[10]. Limiting the supply of something can help maintain its value if demand is stable or increases, though the downside of a known, predictable, and completely inelastic supply unrelated to a fluctuating demand results in perpetual price volatility[11], which is not good if you are looking for price stability.

Bitcoin as a Unit of Account

As a unit of account, Bitcoin fails miserably, due to its price volatility against USD and everything else in the world. The fact that there are almost no merchants who are willing to price items in bitcoins (not even merchants who sell cryptocurrency related paraphernalia) is evidence that bitcoins are not a good unit of account.

You wouldn't keep your accounts in BTC. You wouldn't record the price of your laptop in BTC. You certainly wouldn't do your year-end bookkeeping in BTC[12], and if you tried to file mandatory accounts in BTC you would fall foul of accounting standards in all jurisdictions. If you were a masochist, you *could* prepare an inventory and denominate everything in BTC, but first you'd figure out the price of things in USD (say, my laptop is worth about $200), then you'd convert that

---

10   Note though that if the majority of the Bitcoin community agrees, the creation rate and maximum number of BTC can all be changed. As there is no central or formal governance, the rules can be changed according to the community's preferences, though it is hard to push through contentious changes unless there is wide support. See the section on cryptocurrency forks.

11   Robert Sams on Rehypothecation, Deflation, Inelastic Money Supply and Altcoins." Great Wall of Numbers. August 20, 2014. Accessed July 26, 2018. http://www.ofnumbers.com/2014/08/20/robert-sams-on-rehypothecation-deflation-inelastic-money-supply-and-altcoins/

12   Unless you are a BTC trader and have a mandate to increase the number of BTC under management.

number to a Bitcoin number at a 'what is the price of Bitcoin in dollars at this very second?' ratio. So then, very briefly, you could say 'all my worldly possessions are worth 3.0364 BTC'. Within minutes or hours, that BTC number would almost certainly be meaningless as the BTC to USD price fluctuates so rapidly.

Monetary economist JP Koning compared the price volatility of Bitcoin to gold and made the following observation on Twitter[13]:

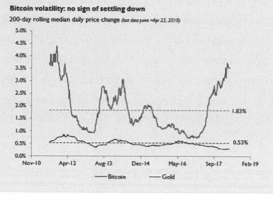

9:27 PM - 24 Apr 2018

37 Retweets 59 Likes

24   37   59

---

13   Koning, JP. Twitter Post. April 24, 2018, 9:27 PM. http://www.jp_koning/status/988771481810186241

Will the price volatility of Bitcoin decrease? It is anyone's guess, but I personally doubt it. One argument I used to hear was, 'When the price of BTC gets really high, the price volatility will decrease because it will take a lot more money to bully the price up and down'. The argument is flawed. A price can be high, but if a market is illiquid, small amounts of money can still push the price around. Stability is determined more by the *liquidity* of a market (how many people are willing to buy and sell at any price point), than the *price* of an asset. But even liquid markets can move quickly if the market's perception of the value of the asset changes suddenly. Also, this argument is predicated on the price of Bitcoin getting really high... There is no good reason why the price of Bitcoin should ever go 'really high'. Furthermore, as discussed earlier, Bitcoin's supply is *inelastic*. If there is a spike in demand, there is no impact on the rate at which bitcoins are generated, unlike normal goods and services, so there is no dampening effect on the price, and this holds true for any price point—*even if* volatility decreased, traders may just take bigger bets, often with leverage, which would then move the price again.

At the time of writing there is a quest for 'stable coins'—cryptocurrencies whose prices are relatively stable compared to some other thing, for example a US dollar. Unless they are backed 1 to 1 with the relevant asset, stable coins are very hard to produce because essentially you are trying to peg the price of something dynamic to something else with a different dynamic, and as we will see in the next section about history of money, no one has ever been successful at this in the long term: Pegs always eventually break. If a successful stable coin *were* to emerge, things could become more interesting[14].

There is one case where BTC may be used as a unit of account: when valuing baskets of other cryptocurrencies. If you are a normal trader trading normal assets like shares, it is a good idea to understand the current value of your assets in your home currency—for example USD, EUR, or GBP. If you are a cryptocurrency trader, you probably still want to understand your total asset value in your home currency, but in this very specific case, you may also want to understand your total balance in BTC as it is the market leader in the cryptocurrency world—you could say BTC is the USD of cryptocurrencies. Perhaps your investors let you manage some bitcoins with the hope that you will turn their bitcoins into more bitcoins. In this case, the value of your assets in BTC is more important than the value in USD. This is a niche case.

The Current State of Cryptocurrencies as Money

Mark Carney, Governor of the Bank of England, summarised the current state of the *moneyness* of Bitcoin during a Q&A session at Regent's University London on 19 February 2018[15]:

---

14   Here I am talking about an independently stable coin, which is different to a coin that is 100% backed by something else (essentially a 'depository receipt' redeemable at par for the backing asset).

15   David Milliken "BoE's Carney says Bitcoin has 'pretty much failed' as currency," Reuters, February 19, 2018, https://www.reuters.com/article/us-britain-boe-carney-currencies/boes-carney-says-bitcoin-has-pretty-much-failed-as-currency-idUSKCN1G320Z

> '[Bitcoin] has pretty much failed thus far on...the traditional
> aspects of money. It is not a store of value because it is all
> over the map. Nobody uses it as a medium of exchange...'

Bitcoin may be suffering growing pains in its infancy, but
this doesn't mean that we should write it off and that the
story must end here. According to the Bitcoin Obituary
website,[16] Bitcoin has been declared dead over 300 times!
But it lives on—at the very least, it still trades on exchanges
with a nonzero price. It seems that people try to fit Bitcoin
into an existing bucket ('It is a currency / asset / property /
digital gold'), and when it exhibits some properties that do
not match others in that bucket, it is declared a failure. Maybe
the answer is to not try to fit it into any existing bucket, but to
design or define a new bucket, and to judge Bitcoin and other
cryptoassets on their own merits.

Also note that central bankers have a potential conflict of
interest when commenting on new forms of money. Central
bankers have a critical role to maintain monetary and
economic stability, and their tools (quantity of money in the
economy and the price of borrowing money) are applied to
their respective fiat currencies. Any new form of money, if
widely adopted and if not under the control of the central
bank, could potentially undermine the ability of the central
bank to fulfil its mandate. New forms of money could be
disruptive and destabilise economies, which, from a central
banker's point of view is not a good thing. So you wouldn't
expect central bankers to warmly embrace new forms of
money that are not under their control.

---

16   https://99Bitcoins.com/Bitcoinobituaries/

A BRIEF HISTORY OF MONEY— DISPELLING THE MYTHS

So far, we have discussed cryptocurrencies and how they measure up as 'money' *as we currently define it*. But has money always been the same? In order to understand where cryptocurrencies might fit in, we should try to understand the history of money itself—its successes, failures, and technological innovations. It is a fascinating topic, as there are so many interesting tidbits and common misunderstandings to straighten out.

The definitive writing on the subject is *A History of Money from Ancient Times to the Present Day* by Glyn Davies[17] who spent nine years researching the book as Emeritus Professor of Banking and Finance at the University of Wales. His work is summarised by his son Roy Davies on the Exeter University website[18]. Much of this section is based on the timeline outlined by Roy, used with his permission. Errors and omissions are mine. I hope you'll find this section as fascinating as I did while researching this book.

Forms of Money

The concepts and eras I want to touch on are:

- Barter (let's exchange valuable things)

- Commodity money (the money *is* the valuable thing)

---

17   Davies, Glyn. *A History of money from ancient times to the present day*. Cardiff: University of Wales Press, 1996

18   http://projects.exeter.ac.uk/RDavies/arian/llyfr.html

- Representative money (the money is a *claim* on the valuable thing)

- Fiat currency (the money is *completely de-linked* from any valuable thing)

Barter

It is common knowledge that before money existed transactions were carried by exchanging goods when both parties agreed on the deal. 'Sir, your five ugly old sheep for my twenty bushels of fine corn'. But barter is difficult. It is very rare that you want something the other person has, and at the same time, they want something you have, and that you're both prepared and able to make a trade. Economists call such a rare situation a 'double coincidence of wants,' and aside from market days in subsistence economies this situation almost never occurs. So, the argument goes, money was invented to lubricate the deal. Money is something that everyone is happy to accept in exchange for other things, so it serves as the intermediary asset for the times when you don't have something that the other person wants. In summary, the inefficiency of barter gave rise to money.

This elegant argument seems intellectually neat. Unfortunately, however, there is not a shred of evidence for it. It is pure fantasy—the textbooks are wrong! When you hear someone talk about money being invented to replace barter, do please educate them or talk to someone else.

Money solving the inefficiencies of barter is a myth popularised in 1776 by Adam Smith in *The Wealth of Nations*. Ilana E Strauss discusses this in an amusing and eye-opening read, 'The Myth of the Barter Economy' published in *The*

40

Atlantic[19], in which she quotes Cambridge Anthropology
Professor Caroline Humphrey in a 1985 paper, '*Barter and
Economic Disintegration*'[20]:

> '*No example of a barter economy, pure and simple, has ever
> been described, let alone the emergence from it of money, ...
> All available ethnography suggests that there never has been
> such a thing*'.

Economies developed based on mutual trust, gifts and debt or
social obligations—'Have a chicken now, but please remember
this for later'. Early communities were small and stable, and
individuals tended to grow up with each other and know each
other well. Reputation within a community was crucially
important, so people didn't tend to renege on their word.
But people still had to keep some sort of record of debts or
favours owed. Trading (the simultaneous exchange of non-
monetary goods) did exist, but mainly occurred where there
was a lack of trust, for example with strangers or enemies,
or where there was a strong possibility that debt wouldn't
be remembered or couldn't easily be repaid, such as with
travelling merchants.

The emergence of money to solve the problem of repaying
a debt or favour makes more sense than the emergence of
money as a solution to the *double coincidence of wants*.
Indeed, David Graeber details the existence of debt and credit
systems before money, which itself appeared *before* barter,

19   https://www.theatlantic.com/business/archive/2016/02/barter-society-
myth/471051/

20   https://www.academia.edu/3621994/Barter_and_Economic_
Disintegration

in his fascinating and influential book *Debt: The First 5,000 Years*[21].

Commodity Money

With commodity money the physical token that is transacted is *itself* valuable, for example grain, which has intrinsic value, or precious metals, which have extrinsic value.

Good forms of commodity money have a stable and known value and are relatively easy to keep and exchange, or 'spend'. They also need to be consistent, and a standardised unit makes things easier. Examples are standardised quantities of grain or cattle, which have intrinsic value by being edible, and precious metals or shells, which have extrinsic value by being both scarce and beautiful.

Note: An argument that cryptocurrency proponents like to use is that the tokens should be valuable because they are *scarce* ('There will only be 21 million bitcoins ever, so that is what makes them valuable!'). This is not a solid argument. Something may be scarce, but that doesn't mean it is, or should be, valuable. There must be one or more underlying factors that make it desirable—beauty, utility, something else. And these underlying factors must create demand for the item. The two underlying factors in Bitcoin that create demand are:

1. It is the most recognised instrument of value that can be transmitted across the internet without needing permission from specific intermediaries.

2. It is censorship resistant.

---

21   Graeber, David. *Debt: The First 5000 Years. Melville House Publishing*, 2011

Representative Money

Representative money is a form of money whose value
is derived by being a *claim* on some underlying item, for
example a receipt from a goldsmith for some gold they are
safekeeping. The receipt may be passed to another party to
transfer that value. You could say that the value of the token
is *backed by* the value of the underlying asset. Warehouse
accounts or receipts (or 'tokens') are backed by the value of
the goods contained in the warehouse and are good examples
of representative money.

Representative money differs from commodity money in that
it relies on a third party (e.g., the manager of the warehouse
or the goldsmith) to be able to supply the underlying item on
redemption of the tokens, so there is some counterparty risk:
What if the third party fails?

Representative money tokens were similar to bearer bonds,
where the person holding a piece of paper was entitled to
reclaim the value of the underlying asset (sometimes on
demand, sometimes on a due date). These tokens were
used as we use cash today to settle transactions, and were
a stepping stone between use of commodity money (e.g.,
precious metal coins) and fiat currency.

Fiat Currency

Commodity money was gradually replaced by representative
money which in turn has now almost entirely been replaced
by 'fiat money'. All major recognisable sovereign currencies
now are fiat. Fiat (pronounced fee-at, Latin for 'let it be done')
is money because legislation says so, rather than because
it has a fundamental or intrinsic value. Fiat money neither

has intrinsic value nor is it convertible[22]. Statements on banknotes often say something along the lines of 'I promise to pay the bearer on demand the sum of ...' but you won't get very far if you go to the issuer of the fiat currency—usually the central bank—and say, 'Hey, give me some of the underlying asset back for this'. At best you will get a new banknote.

So how and why are fiat currencies valuable? Two main reasons:

1. They are declared by law as *legal tender*, meaning that in that legal jurisdiction it must be accepted as valid payment for a debt. Therefore people use it.

2. Governments accept only their own fiat for tax payments. This gives fiat currencies a fundamental usefulness, as everyone needs to pay tax[23].

The Economist newspaper has described cryptocurrencies as having fiat characteristics[24] as it is simply declared so, but to date, cryptocurrencies have not been declared legal tender in any nation. We will discuss legal tender later in the book.

Money Through the Ages

Here I have tried to pick out interesting events in the history of money that help to form a picture of how we got to where we are now.

---

22   Central banks do hold gold, financial assets, and foreign currencies; it's just that they just don't promise to give it to you when you turn up on their doorstep waving a banknote.

23   Well, except very rich people and corporations, it seems ☺

24   https://www.economist.com/free-exchange/2017/09/22/bitcoin-is-fiat-money-too

9,000 BCE: Cattle—Commodity Money

The earliest forms of commodity money were livestock, particularly cattle, and plant products such as grain. Cattle have been used as commodity money from c.9,000 BCE. As such, the cow is probably the most enduring, if not successful, form of money. They are still used today in some parts of the world. For example, in March 2018, 100 cattle stolen in Kenya were believed to be used for paying a dowry[25].

Would a cow pass the three 'is it money' questions that economists like to use? History tells us that cows are a medium of exchange, so it ticks that box. You would assume that if it is used for buying and selling things, people might have some sort of idea of the price of other objects *in cows*. If so, that would make a cow a decent unit of account. But is it a store of value? Hmm, there are some complexities—the price of cows varies by breed and age and individuals can drop down dead. On the other hand, cows have a kind of interest rate, in that they are able to reproduce. So, while any single cow may not be a very good store of value, a herd arguably is. Monetary economists enjoy arguing about things like this.

3,000 BCE: Banks

Between about 3,000 and 2,000 BCE, banks were created in Babylon, Mesopotamia, the land now roughly equating to Iraq, Kuwait, and Syria. Banks evolved from the warehouses that were places for the safekeeping of commodities such as grain, cattle, and precious metals.

---

25   https://www.the-star.co.ke/news/2018/03/21/baringo-stolen-cattle-suspected-to-be-used-for-paying-dowry_c1733135

2,200 BCE: Lumps of Silver

Around 2,250-2,150 BCE silver, ingots were standardised
and guaranteed by the state in Cappadocia (in present day
Turkey), and this helped their acceptance as money. Silver
was the 'gold standard' of precious metal money. This notes
an interesting shift from using commodities that clearly
have an intrinsic value (cattle and grain that you can eat) to
commodities that have an extrinsic value because of their
scarcity and durability. During this shift, you can imagine
people then having the same arguments as we do today with
Bitcoin. 'Yes, but silver doesn't have *intrinsic* value—I can't
feed my family with it'. At the next dinner party if 'intrinsic
value' is brought up, you can say 'Come on guys, we've been
having this argument since 2,200 BCE...'

1,800 BCE: Regulation!

If you want to blame someone for regulation, blame
Hammurabi, sixth King of Babylon, who reigned between
1792 and 1,750 BCE and developed the *Code of Hammurabi*.
This set of laws was once considered the earliest written
legislation in human history, and the 282 case laws include
economic provisions (prices, tariffs, trade, and commerce),
family law (marriage and divorce), as well as criminal law
(assault, theft), and civil law (slavery, debt). It included the
very first laws for banking operations.

Hammurabi code on a clay tablet. Source: Wikimedia[26].

Just think—those libertarians who proclaim that regulation is unnecessary, but then demand that something must be done when they lose money in cryptocurrency scams, are just discovering the value of regulations that have existed ever since laws were first written down!

1,200 BCE: Shell Money

In 1,200 BCE, cowry shells were used as money in China. Cowries are sea snails, most commonly found on the shores of the Indian Ocean and the waters of Southeast Asia. Wikipedia describes cowries as:

> *a group of small to large sea snails, marine gastropod molluscs in the family Cypraeidae, the cowries. The word*

26   By Marie-Lan Nguyen - Own work, Public Domain, https://commons.
wikimedia.org/w/index.php?curid=884154

cowry is also often used to refer only to the shells of these snails, which overall are often shaped more or less like an egg, except that they are rather flat on the underside.

A living cowry. Source: Wikipedia[27]

According to the World Register of Marine Species[28] (WORMS), the zoological name for cowries is *Monetaria Moneta* (Linnaeus, 1758). This sea snail is so 'money' the scientists named it 'money money!'

In fact, the Chinese named these creatures as 'money' well before the West did—the radical 貝(贝 in simplified Chinese and pronounced bèi), means shell or currency, and it even looks like one of the cowries. Chinese words and characters related to money, property, or wealth often use this radical.

---

27   https://en.wikipedia.org/wiki/Cowry

28   http://www.marinespecies.org/aphia.php?p=taxdetails&id=216838

Cowry shells. Source: Wikipedia[29]

As with cattle, the practice of using cowry shells as money survived until as recently as the 1950s in parts of Africa.

700-600 BCE: Mixed Metal Coins

In 640-630 BCE, we see the earliest examples of coins in Lydia (now Turkey), which was a trading hub with large gold supplies. The first coins were made of a naturally occurring mixture of gold and silver called electrum. It is no coincidence that one of the earliest popular Bitcoin wallets, created in 2011 by Thomas Voegtlin, is also called Electrum[30]!

---

29   https://en.wikipedia.org/wiki/Shell_money

30   https://electrum.org

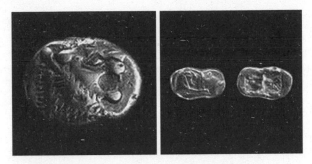

Lydian coins. Source: britishmuseum.org[31]

According to the British Museum, these coins were not consistently round, but were created to various standard weights. It is thought that the coins were weighed rather than counted for many transactions.

600-300 BCE: Round Coins

The first round coins emerged in China, made of base (non-precious) metals. These were still commodity money, so their value was the value of the metal, which was low. Their low value meant that the coins were useful for daily transactions.

c. 550 BCE: Pure Precious Metal Coins

Lydia, which must have been the Silicon Valley of the Iron Age world, continued to innovate, producing separate silver and gold coins, and usage of these started to spread. I suppose this is one of the earliest examples of 'FinTech' (financial technology): using technology to invent new financial instruments. Next time a banker effuses that they

---

31   http://britishmuseum.org/explore/themes/money/the_origins_of_coinage. aspx

are pioneers of FinTech, you can tell them that Lydians got there first in 550 BCE!

According to Amelia Dowler, curator at the British Museum,

> *Silver was more widely available than gold and with a lower value could be used for smaller transactions and was therefore better in the marketplace. So, it was silver coinage which gained rapidly in popularity and, during the sixth century BC, mints opened in Greek cities across the Mediterranean.*

> Source: bbc.co.uk[32]

405 BCE: First Example of Gresham's Law

In 405 BCE, Aristophanes' famous political satire *The Frogs* was produced. It tells of the adventures of Dionysus and his slave in their quest to bring witty poet Euripides back from the underworld to Athens, which had become boring. The play contains the first known example of Gresham's Law, that *bad money drives out good*. What this means is that you'd rather hold on to good/more valuable money and spend the bad/less valuable money if others will accept it. So if you have the choice between spending a *pure* gold coin or a *debased* gold coin (with other base metals mixed in), and they both have the same face value, then you will of course spend the debased one, and the good money disappears from circulation.

---

32   http://www.bbc.co.uk/ahistoryoftheworld/objects/7cEz771FSeOLptGlElaquA

Here is the Chorus lamenting that they now use new ugly
copper coins instead of old gold coins—and with a bit of anti-
immigrant sentiment thrown in for good measure:

> *The freedom of the city has often appeared to us to be*
> *similarly circumstanced with regard to the good and*
> *honourable citizens, as to the old coin and the new gold.*
> **For neither do we employ these at all, which are not**
> **adulterated**, *but the most excellent, as it appears, of all*
> *coins, and alone correctly struck, and proved by ringing every*
> *where, both among the Greeks and the barbarians, **but this***
> ***vile copper coin, struck but yesterday and lately with the***
> ***vilest stamp**; and we insult those of the citizens whom we*
> *know to be well-born, and discreet, and just, and good, and*
> *honourable men, and who have been trained in palæstras,*
> *and choruses, and music; while we use for every purpose*
> *the brazen, foreigners, and slaves, rascals, and sprung from*
> *rascals, who are the latest come; whom the city before this*
> *would not heedlessly and readily have used even as scape-*
> *goats.*

Translation source: libertyfund.org[33]

345 BCE: Origins of the Words Mint and Money

In the centre of Rome a temple was built, dedicated to
goddess Juno Moneta. Juno was the goddess of protection
and Moneta is derived from the Latin *monere*, which means
'to warn or advise'. It is said that Goddess Juno gave warnings
or advice on at least a couple of occasions. First, when the
Gauls sacked Rome in 390 BCE, Juno's sacred geese gave

---

33   http://oll.libertyfund.org/pages/mises-on-gresham-s-law-and-ancient-
greek-silver-coins

Roman commander Marcus Manlius Capitolinus a heads
up that the Gauls were coming, allowing him to protect the
Capitol. Second, during an earthquake when a voice from the
temple advised the Romans to sacrifice a pregnant sow[34].

From 269 BCE, the Roman mint was located at this temple,
and lasted some centuries. The English words 'mint' and
'money' are derived from Juno Moneta.

336–323 BCE: Gold to Silver Peg

Alexander the Great simplified the silver to gold exchange
rate by declaring a fixed exchange rate of ten units of silver
equal to one unit of gold. This peg eventually failed.

The Americans effectively tried the same thing in the
eighteenth century at rates of 15:1 and 16:1. Later, we will
discuss what currency pegs are, how they are managed, and
how difficult they are to maintain. This is relevant today
because there are a number of attempts to create a 'stable
coin' cryptocurrency, some of which rely on an entity or
automated smart contract to defend a peg by buying when the
price is too low and selling when the price is too high.

323–30 BCE: Warehouse Receipts— Representative Money

Ptolemy, a Greek bodyguard of Alexander the Great,
established himself as ruler of Egypt. He created a dynasty
which ruled Egypt until the demise of Cleopatra with the

---

34   NB This particular story is not universally accepted by academics and
historians, but as it involves the history of the words mint and money, I thought
it was worth including. See http://penelope.uchicago.edu/Thayer/E/Gazetteer/
Places/Europe/Italy/Lazio/Roma/Rome/_Texts/PLATOP*/Aedes_Junonis_
Monetae.html

Roman conquest of 30 BCE. The Ptolemies, as the rulers were known, established a system of warehouse accounts where debts could be repaid by transferring the title to grain from one owner to another without physically moving the grain stored within.

118 BCE: Leather Banknotes

Square white deerskin leather with colourful borders was used as money in China. This is possibly the first documented type of banknote. China would later experiment with paper-based banknotes, then stop using them for a few hundred years before reintroducing them.

30 BCE–14 CE: Tax reform!

Augustus Caesar, adopted son of Julius Caesar, expanded Rome's taxation of the provinces, regularising tax levies which, until then, had been decentralised to the provinces. He introduced sales, land, and poll taxes. These taxes weren't universally unpopular, especially in the provinces, where taxes until then had been somewhat arbitrary. If you hate paying taxes, you probably hate paying arbitrary taxes at arbitrary frequencies even more. Augustus Caesar also issued new, almost pure, gold, silver, brass, and copper coins.

To 270 CE: Debasement and Inflation

Over the next 300 years, the silver content of Roman coins fell from 100% to 4%. Talk about debasement! But as we saw earlier, the US dollar has fallen in value by 96% in a third of the time[35]. Attempts by leaders such as Emperor Aurelian to purify coinage failed, as Gresham's Law kicked in and people circulated their debased coins and hoarded the pure ones.

306–337 CE: Gold for the Rich, Debased Coins for the Poor

Constantine, the first Christian Roman emperor, issued a new gold coin, the Solidus, which was used successfully and without debasement for the next 700 years. That is quite some achievement. However he also produced debased silver and copper coins. So the rich got to use nice shiny gold coins that retained value while the poor got coins that steadily decreased in value. Is that surprising?

c. 435 CE: No More Coins for Brits for 200 Years

Anglo-Saxons invaded Britain and coins were no longer used as money for 200 years! Money, it turns out, can come in and out of fashion, depending on the politics at the time. Just because we grow up with one form of money, it doesn't mean it will last forever.

806–821 CE: Fiat Money in China

Due to a shortage of copper, Chinese emperor Hien Tsung issued paper money notes for merchants who wanted to make large payments without the inconvenience of heavy coins. Over the next few hundred years there was much overprinting and inflation, causing paper money to depreciate against metals. This is a theme we hear over and over again.

---

35   This is not a like-for-like comparison, as we do not know how the purchasing power of those coins changed in the period.

Paper money spread to Europe via Marco Polo, a Venetian who travelled extensively and learnt of paper money from his travels in China from 1275–1292.

Paper money was only used in China for a few hundred years, during which time inflation soared due to uncontrolled printing of paper money. In the 1400s, they seem to have stopped using paper money for a few hundred years.

1300s: British Pennies Shrink Twice

In 1344 and 1351, on two separate occasions, King Edward III reduced the size and quality of the penny. The King owned the mints, so a smaller and less fine penny meant that the King could issue more pennies from the same amount of metal, meaning more profits or *seigniorage* for the King.

The debasement of all forms of money that is not commodity money seems to be a common theme in the history of money.

1560: Gresham's Law!

Another year, another currency reform: this time Queen Elizabeth I recalled and melted coins, separating the base metals from the precious metals. Thomas Gresham became an advisor to the Queen and noticed that bad money drives out good.

1600s: The Rise of the Goldsmiths

Goldsmiths in Britain became bankers, as their vaults were used for coin storage, and their notes and receipts became a convenient method of payment.

1660s: Central Banking

The world's oldest central bank, Sveriges Riksbank, was
created in Sweden. Initially, the Bank was forbidden to issue
banknotes due to lessons learnt from Stockholms Banco,
Sweden's first bank. Stockholms Banco issued Europe's first
banknotes but got carried away and issued more than could
be redeemed, a money creation technique known as fractional
reserve banking. Stockholms Banco failed when banknote
holders wanted the underlying metal coins back. In 1668,
Sveriges Riksbank was founded and later, in 1701, it was
allowed to issue banknotes, then called credit notes. It gained
exclusivity over banknote printing 200 years later in 1897
with the first Riksbank Act.

The home of the Riksbank at Järntorget in the old town of
Stockholm. Source: Riksbank[36]

---

36   https://www.riksbank.se/en-gb/about-the-riksbank/history/1600-1699/
first-building-of-its-own/

The Riksbank is noted for its attitude towards innovation: in July 2009, it was the first central bank to charge money from commercial banks to maintain overnight deposits, rather than paying interest, pushing the overnight deposit rate down to -0.25% (annualised). It deepened this interest rate, as well as other associated rates, in 2014 and 2015. This was an effort to stimulate the economy by encouraging the lending and spending of money rather than hoarding, when quantitative easing was not having the desired effect.

1727: Overdrafts!

The Royal Bank of Scotland was founded, introducing an overdraft facility where certain applicants were able to borrow money up to a certain limit and were charged interest only on the amount drawn, rather than on the full amount. This was a form of FinTech.

1800-1860: Cowrie Depreciation

Here is a powerful example of how the supply of money causes price inflation: When cowrie shells were first introduced to Uganda around 1800, a woman could typically be bought for two shells. Over the next 60 years, as more shells were imported at scale, prices rose, and by 1860 a woman commanded a price of one thousand shells.

Rai Stones

No history of money would be complete without mentioning the Rai (sometimes called Fei) stones still in use on the island of Yap.

STONE MONEY OF UAP, WESTERN CAROLINE ISLANDS.
(From the paper by Dr. W. H. Furness, 3rd, in Transactions, Department of Archæology, University of Pennsylvania, Vol. I., No. 1, p. 51, Fig. 3, 1904.)

Yap is a small island in the Federated States of Micronesia, approximately 2,000km east of Manila, Philippines. It is known for its superb SCUBA diving and its Rai stones. Rai stones are large, circular stone discs with holes in the middle, to help transportation. They are made with stone quarried from Palau island, about 400 km away, brought back by canoe with some effort, and still are used as money today.

John Tharngan, Historical Preservation Officer of Yap, in an interview with the BBC[37], explains the origin of the Rai stones:

Several hundred years ago, some people from Yap went on a fishing trip and got lost and arrived accidentally in Palau. They saw the limestone structures that occur naturally on that island and thought they looked great. They broke off a piece of stone and did a bit of carving on it with shell tools. They brought home a stone that was shaped like a whale, which is called 'Rai' in Yapese and that is where the word comes from.

---

37   http://news.bbc.co.uk/hi/english/static/road_to_riches/prog2/tharngan.
stm

Rai stones come in all sorts of sizes, from a few hand spans to over 3 metres in diameter, and have a value mainly based on their history, but also on their size and finish. According to monetary economist JP Koning's excellent blog *Moneyness*[38], W.H. Furness, who spent a year on the island, wrote in his 1910 book *The Island of Stone Money, Uap of the Carolines*:

> A rai spanning a length of three hands and of good whiteness and shape ought to purchase fifty 'baskets'; of food—a basket is about eighteen inches long and ten inches deep, and the food is taro roots, husked coconuts, yams, and bananas;– or, it is worth an eighty or a hundred pound pig, or a thousand coconuts, or a pearl shell measuring the length of the hand plus the width of three fingers up the wrist. I exchanged a small short handled axe for a good white rai, fifty centimeters in diameter. For another Rai, a little larger, I gave a fifty pound bag of rise... I was told that a well-finished rai, about four feet in diameter, is the price usually paid either to the parents or to the headman of the village as a compensation of the theft of a mispil [a woman].

In terms of recording the of ownership changes of these unwieldy pieces, Tharngan comments:

> There's no problem in knowing who owns which piece because all the pieces next to a dwelling tend to belong to that house. All those which are found on dancing grounds— their ownership does shift from time to time, but the shift is always done publicly in front of chiefs or elders, so everyone remembers what belongs to whom.

---

38   https://jpkoning.blogspot.sg/2013/01/yap-stones-and-myth-of-fiat-money.html

There is also the case of a large stone that was lost at sea, recorded by Furness who heard the legend recounted by a local fortune teller and exorcist. The fortune teller told Furness that a few generations ago a large stone was lost at sea, and even though it is not physically present and no one can see it, claims on the stone continue to have value.

This particular Rai stone is used by some economists as an example of fiat money existing in primitive societies. However, Dror Goldberg argues in a 2005 paper, *Famous Myths of Fiat Money*[39] that this is not fiat. There was no evidence of this stone being used in trade, as ownership remained in the family, and the value of the lost stone was agreed by the community, not by any legal decree. Goldberg argues that Rai stones have legal, historical, religious, aesthetic, and sentimental value, and are therefore not fiat, and furthermore, there are no good examples of fiat money existing in primitive societies.

1913: Birth of the US Federal Reserve System

In 1913, the Federal Reserve Act was passed into law in the USA. This created the Federal Reserve System, the central banking system of the USA. The act was drafted by influential commercial bankers and gave the central bank the monopoly on the price and quantity of money, and had the mandate to maximise employment and ensure price stability. The system has public and private sector components, and the regional Federal Reserve Banks are owned by large US private

---

39   https://www.scribd.com/document/149418119/Famous-Myths-of-Fiat-Money

banks. The Federal Reserve is discussed in greater detail in the Appendix.

The US dollar remained on a gold standard for a period of time under the Federal Reserve System, as we will see in the section about gold standards.

1999: The Euro

On 1 Jan 1999, the Euro officially became the currency of the member states of the European Union: Belgium, Germany, Spain, France, Ireland, Italy, Luxembourg, the Netherlands, Austria, Portugal, and Finland. Euro notes and coins came into circulation in 2002. The currency is now the official currency of nineteen of the current twenty-eight EU states, six non-EU jurisdictions, and a number of other non-sovereign entities.

2009: Bitcoin!

On 3 January 2009, the first Bitcoin was brought, or 'mined,' into existence. How does Bitcoin relate to money? We'll discuss Bitcoin in a lot more depth later on, but it was first commonly described as a 'cryptocurrency'. And simply because of the word 'currency' people start thinking... *Is it money? Does it fulfil the traditional three functions of money? What is money anyway? Does Bitcoin count?*

Defining Bitcoin is a popular activity for regulators and policymakers who need to determine if bitcoins fall under their purview or not. I suspect things would have worked out differently had Bitcoin been originally described as a 'cryptocommodity' or a 'cryptoasset'. It turns out that Bitcoin is hard to shoehorn into existing categories, so perhaps it, along with other crypto-things, belongs in a new asset class.

That fact is, for our purposes, the definition of Bitcoin doesn't matter. It doesn't matter how you define money, it doesn't matter it Bitcoin fits the bill or not. Bitcoin has some properties that make it appear from one angle like money, and from another angle like a commodity such as gold.

Money is in the eye of the beholder. Nowadays, we have so many different forms of money, all with slightly different characteristics and trade-offs, that Bitcoin and its siblings can, and will, sit alongside the other forms.

Good Enough Money

I like to use the concept of 'good enough money'. If the money you want to use is good enough for your purposes, then that is ok. For example, when I borrow cash from my colleagues to buy my lunch, sometimes I pay them back in *Grab credits*.

Grab is a ride-hailing app similar to Uber, but localized for Asia, and it also has a wallet function which you top up with your credit or debit card. The credits are denominated in local currency and can be used to pay for journeys, sent to other users, or used to pay for goods in some shops. Some of my colleagues use Grab for their taxis, so paying them back in Grab credits is fine for me and fine for them. So, Grab credits are 'good enough money' as far as we are concerned for that particular small denomination use. But I wouldn't buy a house with Grab credits, nor would a company settle a large invoice with it. It wouldn't be 'good enough money' in those situations.

It seems that people and companies will accept a wide range of forms of money so long as they can do *the next thing* with it—whether that is paying for a taxi, settling invoices, or saving it for long term value appreciation.

Gold Standards

Some people talk about The Gold Standard. In fact, there is no such thing as *the* gold standard. There are a few *types* of gold standard:

1. **Gold specie standard.** Coins are made of gold and are a certain weight and purity in convenient standard units instead of random shapes, sizes, and weights. This is called a *gold specie standard*. Specie is a Latin word for 'the actual form'. This is commodity money.

2. **Gold bullion standard.** Notes (bits of paper) are redeemable or *convertible* at the issuer (usually the central bank) for gold—usually in the form of gold bullion (this means bars of gold of certain standard weights and purities). This is called a *gold bullion standard*. This is representative money.

3. **Non-convertible gold bullion standard.** This is where the issuer declares that their currency is worth a certain amount of gold, but doesn't allow you to redeem your money for gold. This is starting to blur the lines between representative and fiat money.

When people talk about the gold standard, they usually mean a *gold bullion standard* where a note represents some defined amount of gold and can be redeemed for it. The issuer of the currency, usually a central bank, pegs their currency to a fixed weight in pure or fine gold and tells the world that they will exchange one unit of currency for a certain amount of gold stored in their vaults. This is a currency peg, which we discussed earlier, and means they need to have the gold in their vaults in order to remain credible *and* promise to let people redeem their notes for gold. The amount of gold you have in your vaults is largely irrelevant if you don't let people redeem their notes.

When a few countries adopt a gold standard, the exchange rates between their respective currencies become effectively pegged. In theory, you can always sell one currency for gold, and then buy a known amount of another 'gold standard' currency with it. So the gold peg rates also determine the currency-to-currency exchange rates. Before the First World War, the effective exchange rate between the US dollar and the pound sterling was $4.8665 to £1 because both currencies were on a gold standard. Of course, there are costs and risks involved in the transactions and the storage and transport of the gold, so that is why it is an *effective* peg with some wiggle room, rather than an absolute peg.

Before we look at an example of a gold standard, let's clear up some terminology. Gold and silver are measured by weight (or mass, to be pedantic). The units are *grains* and *troy ounces*. There are 480 grains to one troy ounce, and twelve troy ounces to one troy pound. In standard terms, this means one troy ounce is 31.10 grams, which is about 10% heavier than one 'normal' (or *avoirdupois*) ounce of 28.35 grams. Old habits die hard—the troy ounce is still the measure used today when pricing gold and other precious metals.

The small golden disk close to the 5 cm marker is a piece of pure gold
weighing one troy grain. Source: Wikipedia[40]

Gold Standards in the USA

Although many countries have attempted to peg their
currencies to gold, the USA has had an interesting history.
According to *Brief History of the Gold Standard in the United
States*[41] published by the Congressional Research Service,
the USA went through a number of periods with multiple
attempts at pegging the US dollar to gold. They all eventually
failed. Let's look at what happened.

1792–1834—Bimetallic specie standard: Standardised
gold coins ($10 eagles, and $2.50 quarter-eagles) and silver
coins existed, minted by the government. The definition of
one dollar was based on a certain weight of silver or a certain
weight of gold which valued the metals in the ratio 15:1.
World markets valued gold a little more than implied by the

---

40   https://en.wikipedia.org/wiki/Grain_(unit)

41   https://fas.org/sgp/crs/misc/R41887.pdf

USA's peg, so gold coins left the USA, leaving the USA mainly using silver coins.

1834–1862—Silver flees the USA: The USA changed their ratio to 16:1 by minting the gold coins with slightly less gold. World markets now silver a little more than implied by this new ratio. Thus, the silver coins left the USA, leaving the USA mainly using the new, less-goldy gold coins. It is hard to peg things that trade in markets abroad!

1862—Civil War chaos and fiat paper money: The USA government issued notes called 'greenbacks'. Greenbacks were notes that were declared as legal tender, but were not convertible into gold or silver. This took the USA off any metallic standard and onto fiat paper money. The dollar lost value in the marketplace, and people preferred to hold 23.22 grains of gold more than one dollar.

1879–1933—A true gold standard: A dollar was re-defined in terms of the pre-war weight of gold (but not silver) at $20.67 per troy ounce. The treasury issued gold coins and convertible (redeemable) gold notes, and greenbacks were once again redeemable in gold. The Federal Reserve System was created in 1913.

Allow me to digress just for a bit of fun. This was a difficult political period that coincided with the birth of populism in the US. Indeed, L. Frank Baum's book *The Wonderful Wizard of Oz* is regarded by some as a clever political satire, a parable on populism, and a commentary on monetary policy. References are numerous. Yellow brick road? Gold. Ruby slippers? In the book, they were silver, and a reference to a populist demand for 'free and unlimited coinage of silver and gold' at the 16:1 ratio. Scarecrow? Farmers who weren't as dim as first thought. Tin Man? Industrial workers. Flying monkeys? Plains Indians. The Cowardly Lion? William Jennings Bryan, Nebraska representative in Congress and later the democratic presidential candidate. Emerald City, where the Wizard lives? Washington DC. The Wizard, an old man whose power is achieved through acts of deception? Well, pick any politician in Washington. Now can you guess what 'Oz' is a reference to? Yes, the unit for precious metals. These parallels are discussed in more detail by Quentin P. Taylor, Professor of History, Rogers State College in a fascinating essay "Money and Politics in the Land of Oz."[42]

1934–1973: The New Deal and the end of the true gold standard. The 1934 Gold Reserve Act devalued the dollar from $20.67 to $35 per troy ounce, and ended convertibility for citizens. 'The free circulation of gold coins is unnecessary,' President Franklin Roosevelt told Congress, insisting that the transfer of gold 'is essential only for the payment of international trade balances'. The Gold Reserve Act outlawed most private possession of gold, forcing individuals to sell it to the treasury. Those found hoarding gold in coin or bullion could be punished by a fine of up to $10,000 and/or jail time. According to Wikipedia[43]:

> *A year earlier, in 1933, Executive Order 6102 had made it a criminal offense for U.S. citizens to own or trade gold anywhere in the world, with exceptions for some jewellery and collector's coins. These prohibitions were relaxed starting in 1964—gold certificates were again allowed for private investors on April 24, 1964, although the obligation to pay*

---

42   http://www.independent.org/publications/tir/article.asp?id=504

43   https://en.wikipedia.org/wiki/Gold_Reserve_Act

the certificate holder on demand in gold specie would not be honored. By 1975 Americans could again freely own and trade gold.

This quasi-gold standard was maintained under the Bretton Woods international monetary agreement of 1944. The Bretton Woods agreement is explained in greater detail later.

1971: The Nixon administration stopped freely converting dollars at their official exchange rate of $35 per troy ounce. This effectively ended the Bretton Woods agreement.

1972: The dollar was devalued from $35 to $38 per troy ounce.

1973: The dollar was devalued from $38 to $42.22 per troy ounce.

1974: President Gerald Ford permitted private gold ownership again in the USA.

1976: The gold standard was abandoned in the USA: The US dollar became pure fiat money.

So people talk about the gold standard, but let's be realistic: It is not really a gold standard if (a) people can't redeem their dollars for gold, and (b) you keep changing the rate. It turns out that implementing a gold standard is difficult, even if you can put people in prison for owning gold!

Fiat Currency and Intrinsic Value

'Yes, but Bitcoin has no *intrinsic* value,' is a comment I hear a lot from people trying to understand why Bitcoin has a price.

However, it is not a very good argument against Bitcoin. Fiat currencies—USD, GBP, EUR, etc—have no intrinsic value either. In fact, fiat currencies are *defined* by not having intrinsic value.

That is worth repeating. *Fiat currency has no intrinsic value.*

But that is ok! On the European Central Bank's (ECB) website[44] you can read:

Euro banknotes and coins are money but so is the balance on a bank account. What actually is money? How is it created and what is the ECB's role?

The changing essence of money

*The nature of money has evolved over time. Early money was usually commodity money—an object made of something that had a market value, such as a gold coin. Later on, representative money consisted of banknotes that could be swapped against a certain amount of gold or silver. Modern economies, including the Euro area, are based on fiat money. This is money that is declared legal tender and issued by a central bank but, unlike representative money, cannot be converted into, for example, a fixed weight of gold. **It has no intrinsic value—the paper used for banknotes is in principle worthless**—yet is still accepted in exchange for goods and services because people trust the central bank to keep the value of money stable over time. If central banks were to fail in this endeavour, fiat money would lose its general acceptability as a medium of exchange and its attractiveness as a store of value.*

---

44   https://www.ecb.europa.eu/explainers/tell-me-more/html/what_is_money.en.html

The St Louis Fed, in episode nine of a podcast series called *Functions of Money—The Economic Lowdown Podcast Series*, says:

> *Fiat money is money that does not have intrinsic value and does not represent an asset in a vault somewhere. Its value comes from being declared 'legal tender'—an acceptable form of payment—by the government of the issuing country.*

So next time someone brings up intrinsic value, try to be patient and explain that intrinsic value doesn't really matter. What matters is if there is *utility* in the asset. How useful is it? Well, fiat currency is useful, at the very least because it is the settlement instrument with which you pay your taxes to the state, and more broadly because it is legal tender and must be accepted by merchants.

If you don't pay your taxes you go to prison, or worse. So some people argue that fiat currency is backed by the threat of state violence. Other people say that fiat currency is backed by the trust and confidence in state institutions—which is a *little* bit vague, don't you think? But at least it sort of makes sense, unlike the cryptocurrency favourite: 'Bitcoin is backed by math'—which is entirely nonsensical. Although at first it sounds kind of profound, don't stop to think about what that means. Mathematics is used to determine which transactions are valid or not, and is used to control the speed at which bitcoins are created, but this is not a 'backing' in the sense that a bond is backed by the issuing company, or a US dollar is backed by the assets on the Federal Reserve's balance sheet, or a startup is backed by a venture capitalist.

Legal Tender

When a currency is declared legal tender, it means that by statute (law), people must accept it as a settlement mechanism to meet a financial obligation, and that you can pay your tax bills with it[45].

Not all notes and coins are legal tender in all circumstances. Currencies are, in general, not legal tender outside of their home jurisdiction. For example, someone in the UK can refuse to accept Russian roubles as repayment of a debt. This doesn't stop a recipient accepting roubles if they want; it just stops someone being able to force a recipient to accept them.

Also, in many countries you can't force a recipient to accept payment in an antisocial amount of loose change: there are specific rules as to what counts as legal tender. In Singapore, according to the 2002 Currency Act[46], you can't force someone to accept more than $2 in any combination of 5c, 10c, 20c coins, and you can't force someone to accept more than $10 in 50c coins. Currently there are no limits for payment in one dollar coins, but after a series of high profile incidents in 2014 where people and merchants made payments in large amounts of loose change[47], the Currency Act is being reconsidered to a more memorable uniform legal tender limit of ten coins per denomination, across all denominations, per transaction. This means that

---

45   For the sake of completeness, I should add that there are exceptions and provisions to accommodate private transactions provided they are bilaterally agreed.

46   https://sso.agc.gov.sg/Act/CA1967

47   For example, https://www.straitstimes.com/singapore/courts-crime/jover-chew-former-boss-of-mobile-air-jailed-33-months-for-conning-customers

a payer would legally be able to use up to ten pieces each of 5-cent, 10c, 20c, 50c, and one dollar coins, but no more, per transaction.

Also in Singapore, under the 1967 Currency Interchangeability Agreement, the Brunei dollar is acceptable as 'customary tender' on a 1:1 basis. You can pay for a coffee in Singapore by handing over the same amount in Brunei dollars. Banks in each country will accept the other currency at par[48].

Zimbabwe uses USD as the main currency for pricing goods and for government transactions, but lists the following currencies as legal tender: Euro, United States dollar, Pound sterling, South African rand, Botswana pula, Australian dollar, Chinese yuan, and Japanese yen. Its own currency, the Zimbabwe dollar, is not on that list. There are also multiple versions of the Zimbabwe dollar (with different pricing) and the country is a fascinating case study for how not to do currency. It is a mess for shopkeepers, but a delight for monetary economists!

Currency Pegs

A *currency peg* is when someone in charge declares that one currency is worth a fixed amount of another currency and then attempts to maintain that exchange rate by matching the supply of either currency with the demand. If people think that you have got your peg wrong, a black market can emerge

---

48   This is actually quite interesting. See https://www.bullionstar.com/blogs/bullionstar/singapore-brunei-and-the-10000-banknote/ for more on this arrangement.

where people trade the currencies at what they perceive to be a more accurate exchange rate.

How do you maintain a peg? Firstly, you threaten. You announce the pegged rate, and then declare penalties for people found deviating from it. This may mean fines, prison, or perhaps something worse. But you also need to be credible and try to prevent black markets from emerging. Credibility comes from having enough of both currencies to match whatever a trader might want to exchange.

For example, let's say you are the king of a country and you declare a peg of one apple = one orange. If one year for whatever reason people really want apples, the demand for apples will exceed the demand for oranges. So people might be prepared to pay two oranges for one apple. But you've declared a peg, so everyone will come to you with the oranges that they don't want and demand one apple for each orange they bring you. So to keep the peg, you better have a lot of apples to give out. If you don't have them, then a black market will emerge that excludes you, and people will start trading one apple for more than one orange, making a mockery of your peg. So you need to have at least as many apples in reserve as there are oranges in circulation.

And vice versa. If, on the other hand, people really want oranges, you're going to need a lot of oranges to hand out, and you'll be receiving apples (which no one wants) in return.

So to maintain a peg to the very end, you need as many apples in reserve as there are oranges in circulation, and you need as many oranges in reserve as there are apples in circulation. Or in the fiat world, you need to back your fiat currency 100%

with the currency you are pegging to, at the peg rate—an arrangement known as a 'currency board'.

While central banks can prevent their currencies from going up in value by creating as much fiat currency as they want and therefore capping the value of their currency, it is harder for them to prevent their currencies from going down in value, because they need other currencies with which to buy their own currency back in order to prop its price up.

This is essentially how George Soros broke the Bank of England: He had more ammo than the Bank.

George Soros and the Bank of England

Rohin Dhar details the story on priceonomics.com[49]: in October 1990, the Bank of England joined the European Exchange Rate Mechanism (ERM) and committed to keep the exchange rate of Deutsche marks and pounds sterling to between 2.78 and 3.13 marks per pound. By 1992, it had become obvious to the market that sterling was valued too highly, even at the floor of 2.78 marks per pound, and the real price of sterling should have been lower.

In the months leading up to September 1992, Soros, via his Quantum hedge fund, borrowed pounds from anyone he could, and sold them to anyone who would buy them. Borrowing something to sell it with an intention to buy it back later as a lower price is known as 'going short'. According to an article in *The Atlantic*[50], Soros built up a short position

---

49   https://priceonomics.com/the-trade-of-the-century-when-george-soros-broke/

50   https://www.theatlantic.com/business/archive/2010/06/go-for-the-jugular/57696/

of \$1.5bn worth of pounds. On the night of Tuesday, 15 September, the fund accelerated its bet and sold more, extending the fund's short position from \$1.5bn worth to \$10bn worth, and pushing the price of sterling lower and lower overnight while the Bank of England was absent from the markets.

The following morning, the Bank of England had to buy sterling in order to prop up the value of the pound and maintain the peg they committed to. But what can the Bank of England buy pounds with? Their reserves—other currencies or borrowed money. The Bank of England announced that they would borrow up to \$15bn in order to buy pounds. And Soros was prepared to sell that amount to neutralise the demand created by the Bank of England... it was a game of brinkmanship. So, the Bank bought £1bn of sterling over several batches, and raised short term interest rates by two percentage points to make Soros' loans expensive (remember, Soros was borrowing sterling in order to sell it, and had to pay interest on the pounds he was borrowing). But it was too late. The markets didn't react, and the price of sterling didn't rise. At 7.30pm that evening the Bank of England was forced to exit from the ERM and let sterling float. Over the next month the price of sterling fell from 2.78 marks to 2.40 marks per pound. That critical Wednesday was known as Black Wednesday, and Soros became known as the man who broke the Bank of England.

Bretton Woods

The Bretton Woods meeting was all about currency pegs. On 1 July 1944, during World War II, delegates from forty-four countries met in Bretton Woods, New Hampshire, USA, for twenty-one days of discussion to normalise commercial and financial relations.

The outcome was a kind of international gold standard agreement where the US dollar was pegged to gold at $35 per troy ounce and other currencies were pegged to the dollar (with 1% wiggle room) and could be redeemed for gold at the US Treasury. The International Monetary Fund was established, as was the International Bank for Reconstruction and Development (IBRD, which would eventually become part of the World Bank). At that time, ordinary Americans were still banned from owning non-jewellery gold.

Prior to this, in 1931 Britain, most of the Commonwealth, except Canada, and many other countries had abandoned the gold standard. Bretton Woods therefore marked a return to some kind of gold standard.

The Bretton Woods Agreement didn't work very well. Countries frequently devalued their currencies with respect to the dollar and gold. For example, in 1949, Britain devalued the pound by about 30% from $4.30 to $2.80, and many other countries followed suit.

In 1971 the Bretton Woods agreement broke down after the US stopped honouring the convertibility of dollars to gold. This coincided with a big drop in US gold reserves and increase in foreign claims on US dollars.

Quantitative Easing

Quantitative Easing (QE) often comes up in conversations about fiat currencies, and people describe it as 'printing money,' but it is not that simple. QE is a euphemism for an issuing authority (generally a central bank) increasing the amount of fiat money in circulation in order to stimulate a flagging economy. So people worry that this additional money 'dilutes' the value of existing money, and this makes people worry about the sustainability of the fiat system.

'Printing money' is a poor description for QE. Think about it— if the central bank really 'printed money' whether physically or digitally, who would it give it to, and how?

So how does QE work? The central bank buys assets, usually bonds, from the private sector (commercial banks, asset managers, hedge funds, etc) in the secondary market. These are bonds that have already been issued and are now traded by financial market participants. Central banks broadly think of the private sector as having a balance of two things: money, and non-money (other financial assets). And central banks can, to some extent, control that balance by buying financial assets from the private sector to add money, or by selling financial assets to the private sector to remove money.

Why bonds? Because we take comfort that our central banks only own safe assets, and bonds are generally regarded as safe—or at least *safer* than other financial instruments. Their value is also affected by interest rates, something that a central bank has some degree of control over.

Who can central banks buy bonds from? Certainly not you or me directly because we don't have that kind of relationship with central banks. As we will see in the next section, central banks have financial relationships with certain commercial banks called clearing banks, who have accounts called reserve accounts with the central bank. So central banks buy bonds from clearing banks, and they pay by crediting the banks' reserve account with new money. Clearing banks can also act as an agent for other bondholders who wish to sell bonds to the central bank through the clearing banks.

Central banks start the QE journey by buying government bonds (US treasuries, etc) because they are considered the least risky bonds. When they run out of those to buy, they then move to more risky bonds, such as those issued by corporations. The problem is that the central bank ends up with a bunch of risky bonds on its balance sheet—and remember that, from a balance sheet perspective, it is the bonds that 'back' the currency.

There are two worries with QE:

1. With excessive QE, the value of money will go down as there is more of it sloshing around in the private sector, which is not great for savers, and could also cause price inflation (though we haven't seen this yet).

2. A central bank owns risky financial assets that could go down in value, damaging the central bank's balance sheet when the value of the assets it owns falls.

We can see the impact that QE has had on central bank balance sheets since the most recent global financial crisis:

Chart 1 Recent growth in central bank balance sheets

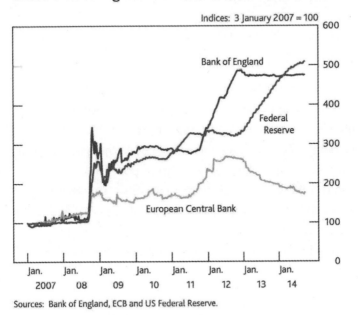

Indices: 3 January 2007 = 100

Sources: Bank of England, ECB and US Federal Reserve.

Source: Bank of England[51]

Summary

The history of money is characterised by its failures. Inflation, dilution, debasement, clipping, re-coining, and creation of new tokens worth less and less all appear frequently. The theme with money seems to be that whatever form it takes, it gets watered down either through debasement or by excessive creation until a certain limit, then there is a reform.

---

51   https://www.bankofengland.co.uk/-/media/boe/files/ccbs/resources/
understanding-the-central-bank-balance-sheet.pdf

The rate of monetary debasement seems to have increased, and the latest experiment in debasing is that of QE. Currency pegs are difficult to manage unless backed 100% with reserves, and although they can be successful for some time, they mostly eventually fail.

Is fiat currency the best solution to money? Will fiat money, backed by the full faith and confidence that people have in today's governments, continue to survive? Who knows. Some believe that we have some new challengers in the form of cryptocurrencies. The narrative from policymakers has shifted from ignoring cryptocurrencies, to stating that they are not a threat to economic stability, to discussing a potential threat. A chapter in the BIS Annual Economic Report[52] published by the Bank of International Settlements in Jun 2018 reads:

> *A third, longer-term challenge concerns the stability of the financial system. It remains to be seen whether widespread use of cryptocurrencies and related self-executing financial products will give rise to new financial vulnerabilities and systemic risks. Close monitoring of developments will be required.*

Although we have arguably better tools and technology now than at any previous point in time, humans are still humans and will still do what they can to gain, and hold on to power and wealth—often making the same mistakes as their predecessors.

---

52   https://www.bis.org/publ/arpdf/ar2018e5.pdf

Part 2

DIGITAL MONEY

It is worth understanding how digital money is currently used to settle debts. In my career, I have spent time with people with a wide range of experience, from new graduates through to seasoned professionals who wear ties and work in banks and management consultancies, yet I rarely come across people who really understand how a payment is made, and who can articulate clearly how money moves around the financial system.

How Are Interbank Payments Made?

Banks need to pay each other all the time, sometimes because a customer has instructed the bank to make a payment on their behalf, sometimes because a bank needs to pay another bank as a result of its own trading or lending activity. Here we are going to look at the bank to bank payment that arises when a customer wishes to make a payment to someone else who banks elsewhere.

We easily understand *physical* payments that are made directly when you pay in cash for something without a third-party intermediary. This can be described as 'peer-to-peer' as you simply hand over cash to the other person. There's no one in the middle, you don't need to instruct or pay a third party, and no one can stop the payment. The cash payment is also resistant to censorship. If you are the recipient, you can be reasonably confident, upon inspection, that the banknote or coins are unique (i.e., not counterfeit copies), otherwise you should not accept them and there is no transaction. It is also obvious that the payer hasn't spent that same cash already (else they wouldn't have it to give to you), and furthermore,

they can't use the same cash to simultaneously pay you and
someone else (because physical cash can't exist in two places
at once). Of course—this is all intuitive.

As soon as you move into the digital world, things become a
little more complex. Digital assets are easy to copy. Unlike
physical cash you can't give a digital asset (e.g., a file) to
someone as a currency payment. Well, you can, but they
won't value it because they can't tell if it is unique. They can't
be sure that you will delete it once you have sent it to them,
and they can't tell if you have sent, or will send, a copy of the
file to a different person[53]. This problem with digital assets is
called the 'double spend' problem.

Wikipedia[54] describes double spending as:

> *...a potential flaw in a digital cash scheme in which the same
> single digital token can be spent more than once. This is
> possible because a digital token consists of a digital file that
> can be duplicated or falsified.*

The digital money world deals with this by using a
bookkeeper who is an independent third party, who, because
they are regulated, can be trusted to maintain accurate books
and records and abide by certain rules. For example, you
trust that PayPal is not creating PayPal dollars out of thin air
because each PayPal balance must be backed by an equivalent
balance in its bank, and you trust that the regulators will

---

53   I am reminded of films where a baddie is selling data, perhaps a list of
secret agents, to another baddie and promises that this is the only copy of the
data. Baddies are very trusting, it seems.

54   https://en.wikipedia.org/wiki/Double-spending

do their job and shut PayPal down if they are not behaving. You also trust that when you instruct your bank to make a payment, the amount of money leaving your account is the same as the amount that is entering the recipient's account (less fees, of course).

So, with any form of digital asset, you need a trusted bookkeeper to maintain a list of who owns what and who plays by some well understood and trusted rules. They often have a licence from an authority that gives them some credibility and increases your confidence that they are carrying out their activities according to certain standards.

Now, let's dive into how the movement of bits and bytes and debits and credits produces the effect of money moving instantly from one person to another.

How are Payments Made?

How does digital money move from one bank account to another? When Alice wants to pay $10 to Bob, does Alice's bank simply subtract $10 from her account and tell Bob's bank to add that $10 to Bob's account? And then how do the banks settle that $10 up between them?

It can be complex. Let's build this up by looking at the following scenarios:

1. Same bank

2. Different banks

3. Cross border (same currency)

4. Foreign exchange

Same Bank

If Alice is trying to pay $10 to Bob and they both have accounts at the same bank, it is relatively straightforward. Alice instructs her bank to make the payment, and they bank then adjusts their records by subtracting $10 from Alice's account and adding $10 Bob's account. In banking jargon some banks call this a 'book transfer' as it is just a transfer from one account to another and no money moves into, or out of, the bank.

If you imagine a bank as managing a giant spreadsheet with a list of account holders in the first column and a list of balances in another column, the bank subtracts ten from Alice's row and adds ten to Bob's row. I refer to this book transfer as a '-10/+10' transaction. Because this accounting entry has been entirely internal to the bank, we can say that the transaction 'settles across the bank's books' or is 'cleared by the bank'.

Before

Bank	
Alice	£ 100
Bob	£ 100

After

Bank	
Alice	£ 90
Bob	£ 110

A book transfer.

It is important to understand that the money in customer accounts is a *liability* of the banks: when you log into your online banking and see $100 in your account, this means the bank *owes* you $100 and should either pay you that money on demand (via a cashier or cash machine), or they need to pay someone else (a coffee shop, a supermarket, or your friend) when you instruct and authorise them to do so.

So while from *your* point of view the money in your account is an asset, from the bank's point of view, the money in your account is an outstanding liability. So the transaction on the bank's balance sheet (where assets and liabilities are recorded) looks more like this:

Before

Bank			
Assets		Liabilities	
		Alice	$ 100
		Bob	$ 100

After

Bank			
Assets		Liabilities	
		Alice	$ 90
		Bob	$ 110

Banks record customer accounts as liabilities.

Although we don't touch the asset side of the balance sheet for transfers between customers of the same bank, we will need it later.

Different Banks

Now consider when Alice wants to pay $10 to Bob, but they bank at different banks, albeit in the same country and currency. Alice instructs her bank, Bank A, to remove $10 from her account and pay it to Bob's account at Bank B. In banking jargon, Alice is the payer and Bob is the beneficiary.

So Bank A reduces Alice's balance, and Bank B increases Bob's balance.

Before

Bank A				Bank B			
Assets		Liabilities		Assets		Liabilities	
		Alice	$100			Bob	$100

After

Bank A				Bank B			
Assets		Liabilities		Assets		Liabilities	
		Alice	$90			Bob	$110

Alice pays Bob.

The Problem

While the customers are happy, can you see the problem from the perspective of the banks?

Bank A now owes Alice $10 less than before and so it is better off, but Bank B now owes Bob $10 more and so is worse off. So that can't be the whole picture. Bank B would be furious!

The Solution

This payment instruction must be balanced by a bank to bank transfer: Bank A needs to pay Bank B $10 to balance out the customer account movements and complete the end to end payment.

How does an interbank payment happen? Bank A could put a bunch of banknotes in a van and send them to Bank B. This would make both banks square:

- Bank A owes Alice $10 less but pays $10 in banknotes to Bank B

- Bank B owes Bob $10 more but receives $10 in banknotes from Bank A

Before

Bank A				Bank B			
Assets		Liabilities		Assets		Liabilities	
Banknotes	$10,000	Alice	$100	Banknotes	$10,000	Bob	$100

After

Bank A					Bank B			
Assets		Liabilities			Assets		Liabilities	
Banknotes	$9,900	Alice	$90		Banknotes	$10,010	Bob	$110

The 'banknotes in a van' solution.

But in most countries, when banks want to transfer money to each other, they don't put bundles of banknotes in vans—they pay each other digitally.

The Digital Solutions

There are two main ways a bank can digitally pay another bank: by using correspondent bank accounts; or by using a central bank payment system.

Correspondent Bank Accounts

If you set up a new business, the first thing you would want to do is open a bank account to let you receive and make payments.

Banks are no different. If you set up a new bank, you still need bank accounts in order to participate in digital payments.

Correspondent bank accounts are industry jargon for the bank accounts that banks open with other banks. These are also called 'nostros' (*nostro* is a Latin word meaning 'our,' as in 'our account'). Correspondent bank*ing* describes activities related to the use of these accounts.

In your new bank's balance sheet, the deposits you hold in your nostros would appear as assets, in the same way as, you (as an individual) consider the deposits you hold in your bank to be your assets. The bank that you opened the account with, your correspondent bank, shows those funds as their liability, in the same way as your own consumer bank regards your individual deposits as its liability.

New Bank

Assets		Liabilities	
Deposits	£ 10,000		

Big Bank

Assets		Liabilities	
		New Bank	£ 10,000

Deposits in my nostro at BigBank

Correspondent banking is just banks holding accounts with each other.

If you google for your bank's name and 'correspondent banks,' you might find a list of accounts where they hold their foreign currency. Here is an example from the Commonwealth Bank of Australia (CBA)[55]:

55   https://www.commbank.com.au/business/international/international-payments/correspondent-banks.html retrieved 25 Feb 2018

Business > International business > International payments > Correspondent banks			
Correspondent Banks			

In order to receive money from overseas, you may be asked to provide details of which banks the Commonwealth Bank maintains accounts with. The names and associated details of the Commonwealth Bank's Correspondent Banks are detailed below:

Currency Name	Currency Code	CBA's Correspondent Bank	Correspondent's SWIFT Code
US Dollar	USD	Bank of New York Mellon, New York	IRVTUS3N
Euro	EUR	Societe Generale, Paris	SOGEFRPP
Great British Pound	GBP	National Westminster Bank Plc, London	NWBKGB2L
New Zealand Dollar	NZD	ASB Bank Ltd, Auckland	ASBBNZ2A
Canadian Dollar	CAD	Royal Bank of Canada, Toronto	ROYCCAT2

You can see that CBA has opened a US dollar account at the Bank of New York Mellon and a Euro account at Societe Generale. The SWIFT codes are identifiers for those specific banks.

So, back to our example. If Bank A had an account at Bank B, it could instruct Bank B to transfer the $10 from its account to Bob's account:

Before

Bank A			
Assets		Liabilities	
		Alice	$100
Bank B acc	$10,000		

Bank B			
Assets		Liabilities	
		Bob	$100
		Bank A	$10,000

After

Bank A				Bank B			
Assets		Liabilities		Assets		Liabilities	
		Alice	$90			Bob	$110
Bank B acc	$9,900					Bank A	$9,900

Bank A pays from its nostro.

In this way, the banks are neatly squared off:

- Bank A owes Alice $10 less but has $10 less in its account with Bank B

- Bank B owes Bob $10 more but owes Bank A $10 less

The Problem with Correspondent Bank Accounts

Although correspondent bank accounts allow payments to flow, they can also present difficulties for the banks themselves. Imagine running a bank and having to maintain accounts at every single other bank that your customers might want to transfer money to. You'd need to open accounts at every single bank in the world, just in case you have a customer who wants to transfer to someone who banks there. This would be an operational nightmare.

Nightmare

Bank A			
Assets		Liabilities	
Bank B acc	$10,000		
Bank C acc	$10,000		
Bank D acc	$10,000		
Bank ...	$10,000		
Bank ZZ acc	$10,000		

The correspondent banking problem.

And it would be expensive, as you'd need to have a positive balance at each of these banks in anticipation of payment instructions, and as we all know, money sitting in current accounts doesn't earn much interest. You'd prefer to put that capital to work elsewhere. And it is risky, too! What if any of your correspondent banks went bankrupt? You'd lose your money.

Central bank accounts provide a more efficient way.

Central Bank Accounts

One of the roles of a central bank is to enable banks in its jurisdiction to pay each other electronically without each of them having to maintain accounts with one another. The idea is that the central bank acts as a bank for the banks in its currency zone. This allows payments to be made between any of the banks in the jurisdiction, each needs to only maintain one account at the central bank instead of accounts with all the others in the jurisdiction. Money held at the central bank is called *reserves*.

Central Bank: A banker's bank

Central Bank		
Assets	Liabilities	
	Bank A	£ 10,000
	Bank B	£ 10,000
	Bank C	£ 10,000

Bank A	
Assets	
Reserves	$10,000

Bank B	
Assets	
Reserves	$10,000

Bank C	
Assets	
Reserves	$10,000

Each bank holds an account with the central bank.

Banks can have multiple accounts with central banks each for different purposes, in the same way that you can have multiple savings pots—a deposit for the home you hope to buy, a holiday, a new car, a wedding, provision for a rainy day, etc. Here, we care about the accounts that are used for interbank payments.

We call the systems that manage these records *interbank settlement systems*. There are broadly two types:

- Deferred Net Settlement (DNS) systems

- Real Time Gross Settlement (RTGS) systems

DNS Systems

DNS systems are systems that queue up payments due between banks then make a single payment at the end of a given period of time, for example at the end of every day. Payments in both directions are 'netted off,' and one single payment of the outstanding balance, in whichever direction it is due, is made at the end of the period. For example, throughout the day Bank A will accumulate payments to make to Bank B, and Bank B will accumulate payments to Bank A. At the end of each day, these payments will be added up against each other and only one single payment will be made representing the net total owed, either by Bank A to Bank B or by Bank B to Bank A, depending on the day's transactions.

DNS systems are capital efficient. Banks need to set aside only the forecast *net* amount of outflow in a given period, taking into account the expected inflow. You do the same when you set aside money for next month's expenses but 'net off' your expected income (e.g., your salary) in that period.

But there is a *credit risk* that builds up during each period, which describes the risk that the forecast inflow doesn't come in or, in the worst case, a bank becomes bankrupt mid-period. This risk can have a systemic impact, as one failed obligation can impact the recipient's ability to make their payments. There needs to be a mechanism to ensure least disruption to the remaining participants.

RTGS Systems

With RTGS systems the -10/+10 adjustments on the central bank's books are made in 'real time' during the day as soon as a payment instruction is made by a customer. Each payment instruction is settled independently and not grouped, batched, or netted off against any other instructions. This is known as 'gross settlement,' the opposite of 'net settlement'.

DNS systems used to be popular, but nowadays most central banks also operate some kind of RTGS system to settle immediate payment instructions, and customers increasingly expect payments to be made in real time. These RTGS systems operate at least during office hours, and many systems now operate 24x7, at least for small transactions. The trade-off is that banks need to set aside more capital to make sure all payments can be made immediately.

So, back to the example. How does Alice pay Bob if both of their banks are on a RTGS system?

As both Bank A and Bank B are on the central bank's RTGS system, the central bank performs the -$10/+$10 to remove money from Bank A's account and add it to Bank B's account. This is the settlement between the two banks, and in industry terminology, it is said that the central bank 'clears' the transaction. The account which each bank holds with the central bank for this purpose is sometimes called their clearing account.

Before

Central Bank			
Assets		Liabilities	
		Bank A	$10,000
		Bank B	$10,000

Bank A			
Assets		Liabilities	
Reserves	$10,000	Alice	$100

Bank B			
Assets		Liabilities	
Reserves	$10,000	Bob	$100

After

Central Bank			
Assets		Liabilities	
		Bank A	$9,990
		Bank B	$10,010

Bank A			
Assets		Liabilities	
Reserves	$9,900	Alice	$90

Bank B			
Assets		Liabilities	
Reserves	$10,010	Bob	$110

Interbank payment via RTGS.

So to recap, and remember, here we are dealing with a single currency only:

- If both customers bank with the same bank, then that bank itself clears the transaction.

- If two banks have a 'correspondent banking' relationship, then the receiving bank clears the transaction.

- If there is a central bank system—a RTGS or DNS—then the central bank clears the transaction.

Clearing

Unfortunately, the word *clearing* is used to mean different things in different contexts. As we have just seen, clearing in *payments* refers to the final -$10/+$10 transaction. It is not to be confused with clearing in *securities trading*, which means something else.

In securities trading (for example, shares), two parties strike a deal, say on a stock exchange: one buys from or sells to the other in return for electronic cash. But they do not exchange the cash and shares directly with each other: they settle against a central clearing party instead. So once a trade between parties A and B is agreed, A and B actually both settle up with C, the central clearing party.

C, the central clearing counterparty (CCP), acts as the legal trading counterparty to each side. So where, for example, A buys shares from B, A sends the cash or funds to C[56], and B sends the shares to C[57]. Once C has received the right amount of funds and shares from the respective sides, it then reassigns the funds and the shares respectively, i.e., it gives the shares to A and the funds to B. This setup removes the credit risk between A and B: A and B no longer have credit

---

56   Or more precisely, C's cash custodian.

57   Or more precisely, C's asset custodian.

risk with each other; instead, they both have credit risk with C, whom they both trust for this purpose, at least more than they trust each other.

Clearing Banks

Back to payments, in some countries only certain banks get to have accounts with the central bank. These are called 'clearing banks,' because they can clear payments, as we have seen above, through the central bank. Smaller banks, or foreign banks with a local presence who are not able to access the central bank, need to open accounts with a clearing bank instead. The clearing banks get to make fees from their privileged position.

Thus, you get a pyramid, a hierarchy of relationships, with the central bank sitting at the top, the clearing banks sitting a layer below, and finally smaller banks, or non-clearers, who don't have an account at the central bank. They use a clearing bank to make payments in the same way a clearing bank uses a central bank, knowing that the clearing bank can call upon the central bank to clear its own payments when it needs to.

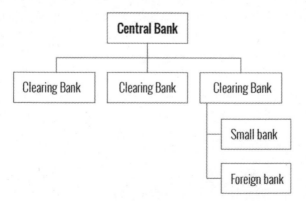

Hierarchy of banks.

Different jurisdictions operate differently. The UK's RTGS system, for example, known as CHAPS, is highly tiered. Only a small number of banks[58] have accounts at the UK's central bank, the Bank of England; whereas in Hong Kong all licensed banks operating in the jurisdiction are required to have an account at its central bank, the Hong Kong Monetary Authority[59].

Although a central set of books run by a central bank is much more efficient than each bank maintaining lots of accounts (or 'nostros') with every other bank, the system works only within one jurisdiction and in one currency. So while most economically developed jurisdictions will have a centrally cleared RTGS or DNS system for clearing interbank payments within that country for their respective domestic currency, there is no 'central bank' of the world[60], not even the World Bank, however grand and ambitious its name.

International Payments

What do we mean by international payments? Well, there are two main types.

---

58   29 participants as at 19 May 2018: https://www.bankofengland.co.uk/payment-and-settlement/chaps although this is changing and the Bank of England will be allowing more participants to access its payment systems.

59   154 participants as at 30 April 2018: http://www.hkicl.com.hk/clientbrowse.do?docID=7195&lang=en

60   Actually, there is an entity called the Bank of International Settlements (BIS), which is a kind of Central Bank's Central Bank, but it facilitates country to country sovereign payments such as war reparation payments (money paid by the loser to the winner to cover damage caused during the war), rather than commercial payments arising from the private sector.

Firstly, there is the payment of a *single currency* across a border. The receiver receives units of the same currency that the sender sends. For example, someone sends USD across a border and someone else receives USD. This means the USD is either *leaving* its domestic currency zone (in this case the USA), or it is *returning* to its domestic currency zone, or it is *moving between* two countries outside its domestic currency zone (e.g., between the UK and Singapore).

Secondly, there is the transfer of value across borders, *with foreign exchange*, where the sender and receiver are working in different currencies. For example, the sender has GBP removed from her GBP account in the UK and the receiver has SGD added to her SGD account in Singapore.

By exploring these concepts separately we will see that money, in general, does not leave its domestic currency zone.

As we have seen, there is no central bank of the world to clear international commercial payments, so we have to fall back to the less efficient correspondent banking systems where banks maintain accounts with each other.

Single Currency Transfers Across a Border

Have you ever thought about how your bank can offer you a current account in a currency from a jurisdiction where your bank doesn't have a banking licence? How does it do that? How does it receive and make payments?

The answer, as you might have guessed by now, is that the bank has an account with a correspondent bank licensed in the country of the currency. For example, a Singapore bank may not have a banking licence in the UK. If it wishes to offer to hold GBP for its customers, it will maintain a GBP denominated account (a nostro) with a major bank in the UK, preferably a clearing bank, and it will then use that as a mega-account (called an 'omnibus' account) for all its customers' GBP currency.

SG Bank			
Assets		Liabilities	
UK Bank acc	£ 600	Alice	£ 200
		Bob	£ 400

Note: These are GBP (£) accounts at the Singapore bank

UK Bank			
Assets		Liabilities	
		SG Bank	£ 600

Foreign currency accounts.

So, a Singapore bank customer, Alice (a new Alice), might log in to her Singapore bank website and see that she has £200 in her GBP account, but the £200 is actually sitting in a UK bank under the name of the Singapore bank, alongside any other GBP which the Singapore bank is holding for its other customers. Alice thinks she has £200 in her Singapore bank, but really the money is sitting in a UK bank, and her Singapore bank just shows her her share of a larger account they are holding on behalf of all their GBP customers.

Sending GBP from UK to Singapore

So let's see what happens when Bob (a new Bob), Alice's British friend wants to send £10 to Alice's sterling account in her Singapore bank. Let's assume Bob banks in the UK with a different bank from the bank that Alice's Singapore bank uses as its correspondent bank.

Before

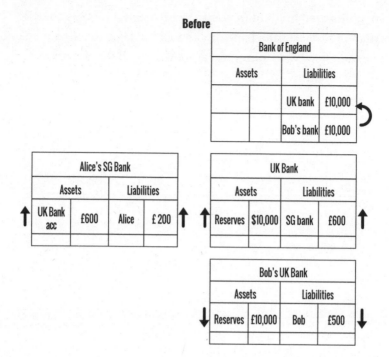

Bank of England			
Assets		Liabilities	
		UK bank	£10,000
		Bob's bank	£10,000

Alice's SG Bank			
Assets		Liabilities	
UK Bank acc	£600	Alice	£ 200

UK Bank			
Assets		Liabilities	
Reserves	$10,000	SG bank	£600

Bob's UK Bank			
Assets		Liabilities	
Reserves	£10,000	Bob	£500

After

Bank of England			
Assets		Liabilities	
		UK bank	£10,010
		Bob's bank	£9,990

Alice's SG Bank			
Assets		Liabilities	
UK Bank acc	£610	Alice	£210

UK Bank			
Assets		Liabilities	
Reserves	$10,010	SG bank	£610

Bob's UK Bank			
Assets		Liabilities	
Reserves	£9,900	Bob	£490

Bob sends £10 from his GBP account at his UK bank to Alice's GBP account at her SG bank.

When Alice in Singapore receives GBP from Bob, the money is actually moving across the Bank of England's RTGS system and arriving in the Singapore bank's nostro at its correspondent bank in the UK. The GBP is not moving in or out of the country... it is simply changing ownership within the UK.

Where banks (often larger ones) have subsidiaries with banking licences in other jurisdictions, they will preferentially use their subsidiaries for their nostros. For example, a US bank, Citibank N.A., has a subsidiary bank in the UK called

'Citibank N.A. London Branch'[61] which is a clearing bank in the UK. So Citibank N.A. would use Citibank N.A. London Branch as its GBP nostro. So if Alice and Bob opened GBP accounts with Citibank N.A., the funds would really be held by Citibank N.A. London Branch:

Global banks often use their subsidaries as correspondents

Citibank N.A. (a US Bank)					Citibank N.A. London Branch (A UK bank)			
Assets		Liabilities			Assets		Liabilities	
UK sub	£600	Alice	£200				US parent	£600
		Bob	£400					

That is what happens if one of the banks is in the country of the currency being moved.

Sending USD from UK to Singapore

We have seen what happens if one of the banks is operating in the domestic zone of the currency being moved. But what if both banks are outside that zone? For example, what if Bob, in the UK, wants to pay Alice, in Singapore, USD $10?

Bob and Alice both have USD 'foreign currency' accounts at their respective banks in their respective countries. Neither bank may have banking licences in the USA, so they must have correspondent bank accounts—their respective nostros—

---

61   Note: There is a difference between a *branch* and a *subsidiary*. A branch is a foreign company operating in a country (not locally incorporated) whereas a subsidiary is a local incorporated company that is owned by a foreign company. Really confusingly, 'Citibank N.A. London Branch' is a *subsidiary* of Citibank N.A., not a *branch*, even though it has 'London Branch' in its name. This is presumably because of historical reasons.

with a US correspondent bank. In the simplest case, if they both use the same correspondent, then the USD is cleared by that correspondent, who does a -$10/+$10 book entry between the banks' nostros.

If the banks have USD nostros at *different* correspondent banks, then the USD is cleared by the central bank, the Federal Reserve, who, as we have seen above, records the -$10/+$10 movement between the accounts of the correspondent banks.

Note that the USD moves in the USA, not in the UK or in Singapore. Currencies (in electronic form) stay inside their domestic zone[62]!

And that is the happy scenario where Alice's and Bob's banks are lucky enough to have nostros at USD clearing banks (who in turn have accounts with the central bank). Sometimes smaller banks or banks licensed in less well-regulated environments might not be able to establish banking relationships in major banking jurisdictions abroad: the big clearing banks see the small banks as not worth the effort, risk, and paperwork required to establish and maintain a high-confidence working relationship. The banks perceived as more risky need to open accounts with local banks perceived as less risky, who could have correspondent accounts at small US banks who might in turn have correspondent accounts at major US clearing banks...

So payments take longer, there is more operational risk, there is less transparency, and fees accumulate. The effect of this, in practice, is a form of financial exclusion. Some small

---

62   Of course, physical cash can move across borders.

banks and financial institutions in less stable regions are practically excluded from the major financial system, and this is detrimental to their growth and the growth of their customers' businesses and other economic activity within their local economies.

This form of financial exclusion is increasing. For example, the World Bank conducted a survey in 2015[63] of 110 banking authorities, twenty large banks and 170 smaller local and regional banks. It found that roughly half of those surveyed experienced a decline in correspondent banking relationships, directly reducing their ability to conduct foreign currency transactions. Money Transfer Operators (MTOs, non-banks) were also surveyed and it was found that of the MTOs surveyed, 28% of MTO principals and 45% of their agents could no longer access banking services. Of those, 25% were no longer able to operate and 75% had to find alternative channels for foreign currency transactions.

Large banks have been actively closing down the nostros of foreign banks, especially banks from those jurisdictions which are deemed higher risk. The large banks cite the risk of being fined or suffering reputational risk if the banks for whom they open nostros are found to be using those nostros for, or are otherwise associated with, illegal or unethical activities.

This has affected the cryptocurrency industry too. In 2015, there were rumours that the big US banks would threaten to cut off smaller banks if the smaller banks continued to bank Bitcoin exchanges. This 'de-risking,' as it is euphemistically known, is serving to cut off the parties who need their services

---

63   http://pubdocs.worldbank.org/en/953551457638381169/remittances-GRWG-Corazza-De-risking-Presentation-Jan2016.pdf

the most, and is creating a moat around the larger economies, disabling smaller economies from flourishing. My favourite financial columnist, Matt Levine, made some comments about big banks threatening to cut off smaller banks who bank cryptocurrency exchanges in his Bloomberg column "Money Stuff"[64]:

> The concern here is that JPMorgan might transfer money for another bank, and that other bank might transfer money for a Bitcoin exchange, and that Bitcoin exchange might transfer money for a drug dealer. Which, in the eyes of the law, means that JPMorgan might as well be dealing drugs itself.
>
> I sometimes think about the analogy between banks and airlines: If a drug dealer uses a bank to move money, that bank is held responsible, but if he just gets on a plane with a bag of money, no one thinks to hold the airline responsible.
>
> But this is much further removed. This is like, a taxi driver flies on United Airlines from New York to Miami, and in Miami he picks up a guy who owns a boat and drives him to the marina, and then the guy with boat transports bags of cash for a drug dealer, and you hold United responsible.
>
> Vast swathes of legitimate financial transactions will be cut off if you punish banks for dealing with people who deal with people who deal with people who commit crimes.

Euro-currencies

Reality is always more complicated than theory, especially in banking. Currencies *can* actually be created and exist outside

---

64   https://www.bloomberg.com/view/articles/2017-04-27/fund-conflicts-and-tax-napkins

of their domestic zones or home jurisdictions. Examples are 'Euro-currencies,' e.g., Euro-dollar, Euro-euro, Euro-sterling. The Euro- prefix originated from Europe the region, and should not be confused with:

- the Euro currency (€) itself, or

- the terminology used in the foreign exchange (FX) trading, e.g., 'Euro/dollar' which refers to the exchange rate between euros and dollars.

In this context, the prefix 'Euro' indicates that the currency exists outside of its home zone. It was first used when the first USD loan was created outside of the USA, in Europe. So, Euro-dollar, Euro-sterling, and Euro-euro mean, respectively, a US dollar that exists outside the USA, a British pound that exists outside the UK, and a Euro that exists outside the Eurozone.

How are Euro-currencies created? When a bank writes a loan in the currency outside its domestic currency zone (e.g., a British bank issuing a loan in USD), it creates money that exists outside its currency zone (i.e., USD deposits existing outside the USA). This is allowed and is normal business practice, fairly common in fact, but complicates the financial world, especially when countries are trying to count how much of their own currency exists in the world. So it is not the case that all currency is directly controlled by its respective central bank.

At this stage, it is worth busting a common myth. It is commonly believed that banks take money from one customer and lend it to another. This is a sloppy way of thinking about banking and leads to incorrect conclusions. Banks *create* money, in the form of deposits, when they write loans. These new deposits are new money, sometimes called 'fountain pen money' because bankers used to approve loans by signing a document with a fountain pen. If you take out an unsecured loan from a bank, the bank adds deposits to your account (increasing their total liabilities) and adds a loan to their balance sheet (increasing their total assets). New money has been created; it hasn't been 'borrowed' from another depositor. The Bank of England explains this in a research piece entitled 'Money creation in the modern economy'[65].

Foreign Exchange

Now that we've dealt with single currency payments (that is, the movement across borders of value denominated in a single currency), what about foreign exchange? What about Alice wanting to send GBP from her sterling account for it to arrive as USD in Bob's US dollar account?

Money doesn't simply 'become' other money, just because of 'banks'. Pounds sterling cannot become US dollars any more than a pint of milk can become a litre of beer, or a lump of silver can become a lump of gold. 1 pound is not 1.2 dollars. 1 pound is not even 'the same as' 1.2 dollars. Sterling is a completely different asset from US dollars, and assets and currencies *cannot*, and *do not*, magically morph from one type to another. You always need a third party who is prepared to accept one currency and give you the other.

---

65   https://www.bankofengland.co.uk/quarterly-bulletin/2014/q1/money-creation-in-the-modern-economy

No, pounds don't magically become dollars

You have to find someone to exchange it with

In a payment involving two currencies, someone somewhere is acting as a third party willing to accept some of your currency in return for some of the other currency. When Alice pays GBP to end up as USD in Bob's account, the role of exchanger may be fulfilled by Alice's bank, who will deduct GBP from Alice's account, and credit USD to Bob's bank, or by Bob's bank, who will accept GBP from Alice's bank, and credit USD into Bob's account. Or Alice could use a specific third party, an MTO such as Transferwise. Transferwise, and other similar MTOs, have local currency accounts in banks in many countries, and they will receive GBP from Alice into their GBP account in London, and they will instruct their USD bank in New York to send some USD from their USD account to Bob's account. Transferwise has therefore changed the balance of currencies it holds by holding more GBP and less USD. This in turn changes its risk arising from foreign exchange fluctuations—that is, movements in the value of those currencies relative to each other. To maintain its original risk profile, Transferwise will then hope that someone will want to send money the other way, helping to square up its books, or it may try to sell those extra GBP to another agent for USD.

Option 1: Alice's (sending) bank does the FX by deducting pounds from Alice and crediting Bob with their dollars

Before

UK Bank			
Assets		Liabilities	
		Alice	£200
US Nostro	$10,000		

US Bank			
Assets		Liabilities	
		Bob	$500
		UK Bank	$10,000

After

UK Bank			
Assets		Liabilities	
		Alice	£100
US Nostro	$9,880		

US Bank			
Assets		Liabilities	
		Bob	$620
		UK Bank	$9,880

Option 2: Bob's (receiving) bank does the FX by receiving pounds and crediting Bob with dollars

Before

UK Bank			
Assets		Liabilities	
		Alice	£200
		US Bank	£10,000

US Bank			
Assets		Liabilities	
		Bob	$500
US Nostro	£10,000		

After

UK Bank			
Assets		Liabilities	
		Alice	£100
		US Bank	£10,100

US Bank			
Assets		Liabilities	
		Bob	$620
UK Nostro	£10,100		

Option 3: 3rd party e.g., Transferwise does the FX by receiving Alice's pounds and sending their dollars to Bob

Before

UK Bank			
Assets		Liabilities	
		Alice	£200
		Transferwise	£10,000

US Bank			
Assets		Liabilities	
		Bob	$500
		Transferwise	$10,000

Transferwise			
Assets		Liabilities	
UK Nostro	£10,000		
US Nostro	$10,000		

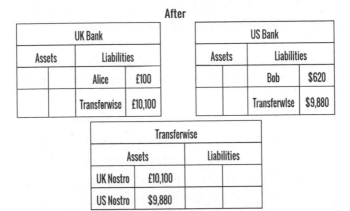

Cross border transactions with foreign exchange.

E-Money Wallets

In recent years, digital wallets have become more popular, and the industry landscape continues to evolve quickly. Digital wallets are usually smartphone apps that allow customers to open accounts. Customers fund their wallets using a credit or debit card, a bank payment, or by paying physical cash to an agent, usually in a convenience store. Once money has been transferred from the customer to the wallet operator, the customer sees a balance in their wallet, which can then be used. Depending on the services provided by the wallet, it can be used to temporarily store value or to send money to other customers, pay bills, buy tickets, shop at various merchants, pay for taxis, pay for groceries at the checkout, and even pay speeding tickets. Many providers offer a 'virtual' credit or debit card number that is connected to the customer's digital wallet. This allows customers who may not have otherwise be able to get a credit or debit card to make payments anywhere that those cards are accepted, and sometimes even make ATM cash withdrawals.

PayPal, Venmo (owned by PayPal), and Starbucks are popular digital wallets in the USA. In India, Paytm and Oxigen are the leading providers. GoPay, owned by Indonesian ride-sharing app GoJek, is popular in Indonesia and is gaining traction in the rest of Southeast Asia, where the dominant ride-sharing app Grab also has a wallet. In China, Alipay and WeChat Pay are used extensively to store value and make payments. The rate of customer growth of these wallets is astonishing: Alipay alone has over 500 million registered users and 100 million daily active users.

Early wallets were provided by telecommunications companies (telcos), who were already dealing in pre-paid airtime, a different type of digital currency. It was a small step to allow customers to move money into a wallet denominated in fiat currency rather than in 'minutes,' especially as the wallet would exist on a device that the customer had likely bought from the telco (do you remember when handsets were branded with the telco's logo?). However, telcos were unable to maintain their early lead due to their 'walled-garden' approach, so this first wave of digital wallets was not, on the whole, successful.

Today's wallets have either developed from private companies who could navigate the airtime-to-wallet path well (PayTM), or ridesharing companies who, due to their popularity, have gigantic scale (Grab, GoJek), or companies that started as social messaging apps and added payments (WeChat).

These businesses operate under different licences in different jurisdictions. The names of the regulatory licences used

by these wallet businesses differ by jurisdiction. Examples
include: e-Money; Money Transmitter; Stored Value Card;
Remittance; Wallet; Money Transfer, and so on. These
licences tend to be easier to obtain than banking licences,
but the permitted activities are more limited. In most
jurisdictions, licensees are usually forbidden to write loans
or create money, a privilege granted to lenders and banks.
Every dollar or unit of currency that a customer sees in their
app must be backed by an equivalent dollar in the company's
bank account.

E-Money wallets are easy to understand from a payments
perspective. Each operator has a bank account that is ring-
fenced to contain only customer money. This account must
not be used for company operations such as receiving income
or paying salaries. When customers fund their wallets,
transfers are made into this bank account. When customers
of one operator move money between each other, there is
no change to the money in the bank account, but the wallet
operator records a debit to one customer and a credit to
another—a -$10/+$10 in its books. If a customer withdraws
money from their account, then the wallet operator makes a
corresponding bank transfer to the customer's bank account.
Customers are not limited to individuals. Merchants, minicab
drivers, utilities companies, and public-sector entities are
often customers of wallets, and wallets are becoming a
convenient and common way to pay bills in some countries.

The rise of wallets, due in part to their focus on delivering
a superior user experience, has caused some concern from
banks. In some jurisdictions banks are losing relevance with
their customers and losing data and revenue from payments.

Wallets are increasingly sitting between the customers and their respective banks.

In Europe, one of the most successful 'challenger banks,' Revolut, uses an e-money wallet licence, so is not technically a bank. Despite this, it offers a full suite of payments, savings, insurance, pensions, loans and investments. Revolut is the customer-facing front-end through which licensed providers offer their services. This dynamic raises interesting questions as to the future of licensed banks.

Banks need to make a tough decision: They should either try to re-engage with their customers and become more relevant by providing better user experiences, or they should focus on becoming extremely efficient financial pipes in the background. Both models are viable if executed well.

Part 3

CRYPTOGRAPHY

CRYPTOGRAPHY

It is time to take a deep breath. To really understand Bitcoin and cryptocurrencies at more than just a superficial cocktail party level you will have to understand a few concepts from a branch of mathematics called cryptography. The section on cryptocurrencies will assume you are familiar with the concepts discussed here.

Don't skip this chapter—it'll be fun. Cryptography is, among other things, about sending secret messages that can be read only by the intended recipient. It is the stuff that spies use. We will cover encryption and decryption (the encoding and decoding of messages), hashing (turning data into fingerprint *digests*), and digital signatures (proofs that you have created or approved a message).

Cryptography is, however, not *just* for spies, criminals, and terrorists. It is now used extensively to protect data that travels across the internet. The 's' in 'https' stands for *secure*. It means that cryptography is being used to guarantee that the website you think you are visiting is in fact the genuine website. It also means that the data in flight between you and that website is encrypted or jumbled up, so snoopers can't easily read the communications between your device and the website that you are accessing.

ENCRYPTION AND DECRYPTION

Although cryptography is used for many more purposes than simply encrypting and decrypting secret messages, encryption is the most well-known use of cryptography, so let's start with this. Blockchains are not generally encrypted, but understanding encryption provides a good background to cryptography which *is* used extensively in blockchains.

Encryption is the process of turning a *plaintext* (i.e., readable) human message into *cyphertext* (a jumble, gobbledegook), so that if the encrypted message is intercepted a snooper can't understand it. *Decryption* is the process of turning the gobbledegook cyphertext back into readable plaintext. 'Breaking' the cyphertext means working out how to decrypt cyphertext without being given the 'key' (see below).

Let's say Alice wants to send a message to Bob, so that only Bob can read it (it is always Alice and Bob, and we will see why later). Alice and Bob first agree on a scheme. Let's use a very simple scheme where they encrypt the text by shifting each letter a set number of places later in the alphabet. They agree to use '+1' as the 'key,' meaning that each letter is moved one place later in the alphabet. So A becomes B, B becomes C, C becomes D etc. This scheme is called the *Caesar cipher*.

Alice writes the plaintext note 'Let's meet, Bob'.

Alice encrypts it by shifting each letter once to the right: 'Mfu't nffu, Cpc'.

Alice sends the cyphertext to Bob.

Bob decrypts the cyphertext by shifting each letter back by one position and gets back the plaintext: 'Let's meet, Bob'.

This type of encryption is part of a family called 'symmetric encryption,' because the same key (+1 in this case) is used in both the encryption and decryption stages.

This method of encryption is not used in real life nowadays. Firstly, because it is too easy to spot and break using techniques such as letter frequency analysis. Secondly, and more importantly, Alice and Bob first had to communicate to agree what key to use for the scheme. They had to agree on the '+1' in the first place. How do they know that someone wasn't snooping when they agreed that?

Perhaps Alice and Bob met physically earlier and agreed on the '+1' in person, but if they suspect at any stage that a snooper has compromised them, either in that meeting or during the course of their conversations, how would they then agree on a new key without the snooper being aware of *that* new communication?

In a world where our devices are constantly initiating connections with new websites, any initial 'handshake' where a symmetric key is agreed and shared between your device and the website is a weak point, and any eavesdropper who snoops on that initial exchange can decrypt the secret messages for the rest of the conversation. So later we will explore *asymmetric* cryptography, a much more commonly used form of encryption.

How is encryption relevant to blockchains? Actually, it is not very relevant. Many journalists and management consultants talk about encrypted blockchains, but they are confusing *encrypted data*, not used in first generation blockchains[66], with *cryptography* which is used extensively in blockchains for hashing and digital signatures, as we will see later.

---

66   In some newer blockchain platforms there are some additional 'privacy' layers where encrypted data is broadcast to a wide audience or a subset, and can only be decrypted by parties who hold the decryption key.

Nothing on the Bitcoin network is encrypted by default. The *whole point* is that plain text transaction data is replicated across the network so that anyone can read and validate it.

However, other cryptographic schemes such as public key schemes, discussed next, are used extensively in Bitcoin, as are cryptographic hashes.

Public Key Cryptography

The Caesar cypher just described is known as a *symmetric* cypher because the same key is used to encrypt and decrypt the message. In public key cryptography, the key used to decrypt a message is different (but mathematically linked) to the key used to encrypt the message. Public key cryptography is described as an asymmetric scheme, because the key used to decrypt the message is *not* the same as the key used to encrypt it. This makes it more secure.

Using asymmetric cryptography, if you want to receive encrypted messages you create *two* mathematically linked keys: a public key and a private key. Together they are called a key pair. You can share your *public* key with the world, and anyone can use it to encrypt messages for you. You use your *private* key, known only to you, to decrypt those messages. Anyone who sends you encrypted messages using your public key knows that *only you* can decrypt them.

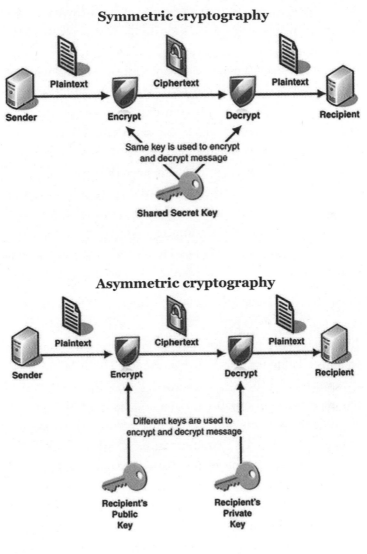

Source: Sachi Mani's blog[67]

---

67   https://sachi73blog.wordpress.com/2013/11/21/symmetric-encryption-vs-asymmetric-encryption/

As we have seen, one of the biggest problems of symmetric cryptography is how to share a key in the first place when all forms of communication are tapped. It is hard to be sure that you can share a decryption key with your friend without the eavesdroppers also getting that key. With public key cryptography, you broadcast your public key to everyone, not caring if the eavesdroppers can see it or not. Your friend then encrypts the message and sends it to you. Only you can decrypt it because only you have the private key. If an eavesdropper gets the encrypted message, they can't decrypt it because they don't have your private key. It is a beautiful system and a huge improvement over symmetric schemes because you never need to communicate a shared or common key.

What do keys look like? There are number of different schemes. PGP (Pretty Good Privacy) is a scheme originally developed in the 1990's for encrypting, decrypting and digitally signing messages such as emails. This scheme was so powerful that the US Government didn't like it and had it classified as Munitions, an 'Auxiliary Military Equipment,' meaning that anyone found exporting it from the US would be in deep trouble. Phil Zimmermann, the creator of PGP, found a way around this by publishing the source code as a hardback book using First Amendment protection of the export of books[68]. This marked the height of tensions between the US Government and individuals who are passionate, quite rightly so, about privacy. To learn about this story in depth, I recommend Steven Levy's book *Crypto* which documents the history of PGP and the revolution of cryptography.

---

68   https://en.wikipedia.org/wiki/Pretty_Good_Privacy

Back to public and private keys. I downloaded GPG Suite[69], an open source and free set of tools that conforms to the OpenPGP standards, and I created a new keypair. Here is what the public and private keys look like:

```
-----BEGIN PGP PUBLIC KEY BLOCK-----

mQINBFrPqNgBEACtXSKabvi7Tecyk1BLSPBcafGjpht-
JD+OIiA47yzo4NBRKB8o+q8IHSxHy9dxJXpBMxkX-
qgaIwUc1aaR0AMccqbeqWS0MYroB5qteCC5ithnAyTh-
3BaNkAuWLgFOte4QgJ+Jql8VF+c1hpYxmITgPwYr++rCp/
h4DAuSIKO4I1arc8BSTcP/foZjV1zgDrE0EV9lrX/
iNWU3S9Y3DVoDFTe4TlnS6ar0t4TLo9TqZtPSpLLzgc-
TR4C00jZ0CcCj4AjXAv8zTdswDLsFuL7khf6xYzF-
h4ZohmHM3qaXqnyHAfuwUh2LdE2a8bzjahu9hHuL-
r8mD7jTyP715G2u92ODHKD05HD2mBBlglhLR2cz0d-
C6p4MyTX7Fju93PHuvpdDxlxNTwWEWUDYrUDGG-
D9TzgSoaaSiyxr4dbTeinaGeGF1TRRtFSOSuMacX-
kdipt8gwdgZ7OcSvjhDXqPWHjZnmukisk60YK/
zsdxBFSviIM0GJ7f/JyBJUJEtzJY0sFxWoUtb-
wHV4MW7u8rCfc74keKfolwleUhtwFr3rd2RQw-
7nAgRoOvEXZ46Ir/+QNIl4sxafHnG7J8LR5w5B+Lk-
JGUs9lLq48APEsXyiCp9CntychzgHsYIQdaJb-
G84kcJx84Ujg2hbwD1W5k+0CCtdhzhXwLP+7M-
Jblt/8Z8BtnguxTwARAQABtCRBbnRvbnkgTGV3aXMg-
PGFudG9ueWxld2lzQGdtYWlsLmNvbT6JAlQEEwEIAD-
4WIQTQh5ifhrStiPdOmBZyTnh3vakkFgUCWs+o2AI-
bAwUJB4YfgAULCQgHAgYVCAkKCwIEFgIDAQIeAQIX-
gAAKCRByTnh3vakkFgsMD/9Chi/7I16nIhIQwlF90juF-
d++mGGBabw17rUmhykhn9P3B7FriBGBK5kViLfjDlI-
JxAPm5anqLiia2SCBhqRXgAOkDs1UCmSr0QP-
GoVTjcoMpznretSB5yzJU6NZUvoL2m6f2Xlyt7/
Hx2xZQPCZD3F4YCqG7BqFvbC31h7PR5mSNPiyW0siIK-
F3b7CuqSSZe3kA6N92hJz42yfpFdahq0gXgZaRHzoIy-
```

---

oFAfxpIUTASq37VP8oyNWIBZl46pasGPZZemz8DGcN-
p09vrxC3FnpcbgCzmzQFaJ0rpPtpV2m2pTSg2au/
HdQRc7/ZVJVkAgAboURUAEzB41SXuGAt9txB81ebM-
0bgG7/hphVerfrZRiQ/ae9xfCms+Q/LgIVX-
M/4+MqrvMkxD98Bx1J9NhSk3Ybt7CyLGUr95S/
ctwH0H8SdN+gz+82TGa1TSbZdqPw9HXmwXNFa9d2dcN-
MGRp+5Dx2fW1RGo4IFy1PFThz9re0psUxt2SGaWOqf-
9bg2HxvckGNx1JOKPdvNC96bEOBV6v1Ns1jSAC6S-
BakQBsh71czmfzMG32Kvn15nckdJ3pWIXRkk1iB/
aXEQAEHvCtoJVYqBgFlRohwcRjZjkxywh8ToR-
rq6T2rqyBTTWU8dq3CJ0yMT1vZoYqeioC+bFJztEsu+oG9T-
4toergRkO2LeJrkCDQRaz6jYARAA1038+djsObvbWS4O5OK-
K2z0xeVZZ37NRGfN1orTKnNgN+YWbo5Ii0eK8AhxEYOs/
J8nTo7iSPo6COyOxo54+ku0tAhBjSR4ExAKO+4fzX-
M/34+nMRQKt8OlmHhJsv+vg7lplr/hEQ3np9QsaMLM-
S8PfhF62XcyGqJ8burAFp13pg4oPckAw8n9fHDS9e+B-
GQU6ks+B6c6YcG1wH+vfFP7YswG0afvo59YKFPyxUan9O-
J4hJLDIConWpS5QTgMmGHUDDTJMXjAZMuPK9v1HIL744-
luabi+rIX7eKfIifu5zTSim2O65n-
2MWa8esmPqglIL2OR9COQtxbrSPrjANDVxGP0WetL-
wq27kWAn+zjTPQaEn7W/imoWxFFBHCVgZghnn/
hN6xlM83IXY1GHbdJR4cilVa3BSmvqe3J7e5l3+ppS-
B9z/exHg1pgCtZjGqFXBViqiSQIfKIbIZ2uT-
bJEAEnwSTqJMdsDz+waNyyxCeFdkASOEkgnVs/
S8KPv6YH6Tb7puizvWA04TX17Kdy5qz4e6yBp9SbzE-
HGLbxgEsKUztI5dRQkR1MDU2i6tJVjAIT2RUafcIT-
60S3H4d6Mu3+mwFfT+qD79nEbJw/CvNq1cqKunMIb-
NJi7ZcS+DyybFfYCaKswTkQuyXLU7ko7fWxbCceg-
sY2RHl1i0iLY1Ru40AEQEAAYkCPAQYAQgAJhYhBNCHm-
J+GtK2I906YFnJOeHe9qSQWBQJaz6jYAhsMBQkHhh+AAAo-
JEHJOeHe9qSQWC2gP/3qMme7I6j8VsXT9sPqc36MQoMtFS/
PSNmpA5NQ+V9Ffuepg91Y3VDLz5HV8tz9xw+JaeHS1T-
469DucoIKAAPouk/umVKn/dfGnf/tq44XKyd30VJ/
kJo+mv/LcQmFcwHbwElrlA7qttjJs/iXsr3Ly5ztgM-
mpgYOXk48IISq3sisEaj03Ph7+H5ylPG3FHiMcjef-
g20vAZ3kXZ9kGVnXtjFOOJ9k2UFfWRSLpq8KDW8pz/
Rp5s0a16MlKFaX8HytL1NKu+gtq26NfYP8P/EGjeMf/
AJFZNQv+oq46PH8fqPXxLSp4IWbQTdQXvc12o9uYut-

jfSEqEaWw6UmL01NuPBZYjIb49M3EJSkgl33+8U-
9JnI3p9+H9iRYW/Mnjb0nBZGPw+SwdzSqEvjcI-
67BaL6SfqPrAAqrKsdNtsbr4tL3ssDtcqTOkv211P+W-
zbSfCl783a+oQUsoggvCb5oOcPO5cwbTrrSebcSf/
KFBQzGxxhzoYp1TKzB127efG/Rwz05GrsFKvtH-
plrj5jGab7Hn8YuYPBtZB77EvYB86NMFQTFn2gUvrA2R/
Rf/r5vyeigP27ClnEvAofTgpUQg3mwTzSB6bMBIst-
k3OYpfy4qNMLluxVA3YaXUC8Lf8jCuQBi+XUDhMKEc-
MtYRJ91YJ/ePA3ZU8iTQ00mYTj0r/VYIy=ieAB

-----END PGP PUBLIC KEY BLOCK-----

-----BEGIN PGP PRIVATE KEY BLOCK-----

lQcYBFrPqNgBEACtXSKabvi7Tecyk1BLSPBcafGjpht-
JD+OIiA47yzo4NBRKB8o+q8IHSxHy9dxJXpBMxkX-
qgaIwUc1aaR0AMccqbeqWS0MYroB5qteCC5ithnAyTh-
3BaNkAuWLgFOte4QgJ+Jql8VF+c1hpYxmITgPwYr++rCp/
h4DAuSIKO4I1arc8BSTcP/foZjV1zgDrE0EV91rX/
iNWU3S9Y3DVoDFTe4TlnS6ar0t4TLo9TqZtPEpLLnge-
TR4C00jZ0CcCj4AjXAv8zTdswDLsFuL7khf6xYzF-
h4ZohmHM3qaXqnyHAfuwUh2LdE2a8bzjahu9hHuL-
r8mD7jTyP715G2u92ODHKD05HD2mBBlglhLR2cz0d-
C6p4MyTX7Fju93PHuvpdDxlxNTwWEWUDYrUDGG-
D9TzgSoaaSiyxr4dbTeinaGeGFlTRRtFSOSuMacX-
kdipt8gwdgZ7OcSvjhDXqPWHjZnmukisk60YK/
zsdxBFSviIM0GJ7f/JyBJUJEtzJY0sFxWoUtb-
wHV4MW7u8rCfc74keKfolwleUhtwFr3rd2RQw-
7nAgRoOvEXZ46Ir/+QNIl4sxafHnG7J8LR5w5B+Lk-
JGUs91Lq48APEsXyiCp9CntychzgHsYIQdaJbG84kc-
Jx84Ujg2hbwD1W5k+0CCtdhzhXwLP+7MJblt/8Z8Bt-
nguxTwARAQABAA/9FW3uyhIvks+VZY4KHdQ9Sd8ar-
HTq6IQbRxQyVjfP0YS2gVQnLsoCaO5hoJu9iCA1T-
BgyKkOt7bUe4i8eE5kTmm4N0lgpShK/9Moma3/
Ndp2onr9DNFYmhM1lqHdNhOPiH4FodFy5Cx1s71H9pPiny-
f4a35HeivcP9kKsL4Gdnca8MaIdJVCO7146+33kZSpzIC-

jcn9hdO92DD6oMF4v+rOgWzF86lIpYlN0/JD-
bloZku8i47DFyH+idt2Oa++7ULTNOi87PWRw4W/
VHy6s/rQOdMeFpBRghebHmVNCgxzmpzVx8/
Ya6VrTJ2e9Hw7eNDdkfbbAB08QDqBd9a2RP-
G7QMa7k1SAFmq5wt0oGXhl/rmowem1UQ4mpDb-
yuL43hR8VTtAyG4RsKzj0WWK4jSQEPEeSj6uMyZt4oF-
nrNVTNBEGXCYOaFtj9ufDCUdYuzk7v0eZ4y2G33W-
WI1YXomOkqECd1BA07WTjdKr3HaJiiI+N1UYrmN+d-
NXC6TOvIvCxBX6oc2DSCLHNNRWDFezflCUgbt-
Prn81ieZ10HsugbE7pFT47fgBSzCK8a4zdrXVFpbwtD-
86tOsLcFLpya6ZVWgnahqXnMfM2FLnlweNeB8X6k0U-
toYNL94fazaqm7jceDPtLl65HiTB+bKrLhV8UMyGk/
jwgKXi4VrSm0GzFOyXEIAMSyQKCgl0z2w/xUC6eBlv-
3vhTlJXEHm3jsHVdzwXGd9bfRqrbX3Y6qTSch4a2MNe8e-
ILEZitely+4NSg88xQnwKM4zRChReQeVT0Ug2YdRyJHeZ/
ynPJQfUJrUSIslFOU+hEDThnQaB9Q4czL26DEKV-
fOJghGQ/6xXS5Hifoe8YJWhyUo/RCfuvFCkFWn-
p2qZJaiFW64Md1SY78084W92a3ZQ7wsNPvB2REmok-
fAApXnpBEboIxExuHRQIGiOfXEfivTdWB-
NwNkTTecpDP3cgFtoYBrfSunSIsgmEZcl-
CUyZ56MFQCpGJHrTi8SamTm+A2TK1C9HU0G20d/
Eem73gkIAOGh/rNI8iiTLwdI6C7huin-
pIJms9n2T9AdyZrciq+GY9f6NWPLyjdgYrjd-
C4esyWOBuSTNVokJ95GFRVgii1TeLjP8YUTAi87/
jlaXpGGjYLdVdvfLDw48iT7UXVE79qkcedTiOqULNBLx-
IP0tTt0zI9IDJGi1VbnJZkk8TrL23mQwcSRKT97sapvp-
jXDH9xzHdJw3bv6tkUYaGQgZE8BtelX7kUzUl4S1qSH/
Xp8Ozs1YyyappCfkEkFwlidcUy5rBaO5UYHtEkq6ZuFp-
Meocss+IFl6b1TG16MUZ+LtxKQRZ7b51b/k8bCs3Qh/5/
FgFPZs7694xZY+MRM5bsapcH/RwT1bkTos3F5dk-
BQ4SDEUAXjLDvssjR33u3HGijC/4y2Q1DN5Nk3npg-
ZGOSwu5/S6oTBWRLX7e+NB31+5b9D+pgotgFK90r0AX-
ZuhZxXYtNgxsNgwLLQDLY1JEiTPfZzPKGwP162/C4cw/
C0Xum48ynHTjFsMNeP4h8n72NsYmWYVUPsclGGw-
GoMKweJkWdgPcRpnW3OT1/lAjY3enikmXRBeZat-
l+Gr0AszGGU9Iudd1bdNKadbx6ADkVEEAFmNkx5ff-
N1vxHvzEx3KvDtrIhYEiApzLBUK4d5sgq844M3gs-
g25aBfaTrb3M2DGbOApxMwIfn0d9yoqkgqKHs+TaY-

txLbQkQW50b255IExld21zIDxhbnRvbn1sZXdpc0Bn-
bWFpbC5jb20+iQJUBBMBCAA+FiEEOleYn4a0rYj3Tp-
gWck54d72pJBYFA1rPqNgCGwMFCQeGH4AFCwkIBwIG-
FQgJCgsCBBYCAwECHgECF4AACgkQck54d72pJBYLDA//
QoYv+yNepyISEMJRfdI7hXfvphhgWm8Je61JocpIZ/
T9wexa4gRgSuZFYi34w5SCcQD5uWp6i4omtkggYak-
V4ADpA7NVApkq9EDxqFU43KDKc563rUgecsyVO-
jWVL6C9pun915cre/x8dsWUDwmQ9xeGAqhuwah-
b2wt5Yez0eZkjT4sltLIiChd2+wrqkkmXt5AO-
jfdoSc+Nsn6RXWoatIF4GWkR86CMqBQH8aSFEwEqt+1T/
KMjViAWZeOqWrBj2WXps/AxnDadPb68QtxZ6XG4As5s0B-
WidK6T7aVdptqU0oNmrvx3UEXO/2VSVZAIAG6FEVABM-
weNUl7hgLfbcQfNXmzNG4Bu/4aYVXq362UYkP2nvcXw-
prPkPy4CFVzP+PjKq7zJMQ/fAcdSfTYUpN2G7ewsixlK/
eUv3LcB9B/EnTfoM/vNkxmtU0m2Xaj8PR15sFzR-
WvXdnXDTBkafuQ8dn1tURqOCBcpTxU4c/a3tKbFMb-
dkhmljqn/W4Nh8b3JBjcdSTij3bzQvemxDgVer5Tb-
NY0gAukgWpEAbIe9XM5n8zBt9ir59eZ3JHSd6Vi-
F0ZJNYgf21xEABB7wraCVWKgYBZUaIcHEY2Y5Mc-
sIfE6Ea6uk9q6sgU01lPHatwidMjE9b2aGKnoqAvmx-
Sc7RLLvqBvU+LaHq4EZDti3iadRxgFWs+o?AFQANdN/
PnY7Dm721kuDuTiits9MXlWWd+zURnzdaK0ypzYDfmFm6OS-
ItIivAIcRGDrPyfJ06O4kj6Ogjsjsa0ePpLtLQIQY0keB-
MQCjvuH81zP9+PpzEUCrfDpZh4SbL/r4O5aZa/4REN-
56fULGjCzEvD34Retl3MhqifG7qwBadd6YOKD3JAMPJ/
Xxw0vXvgRkFOpLPgenOmHBtcB/r3xT+2LMBtGn76Of-
WChT8sVGp/TieISSwyAqJ1qUuUE4DJhh1Aw0yTF4wGTL-
jyvb9RyC++OJbmm4vqyF+3inyIn7uc00optjuuZ9jFm-
vHrJj6oJSC9jkfQjkLcW60j64wDQ1cRj9FnrS8Ktu5FgJ/
s40z0GhJ+1v4pqFsRRQRwlYGYIZ5/4TesZTPNyF2NRh-
23SUeHIpVWtwUpr6ntye3uZd/qaUgfc/3sR4NaYAr-
WYxqhVwVYqokkCHyiGyGdrk2yRABJ8Ek6iTHbA8/
sGjcssQnhXZAEjhJIJIbP0vCj7+mB+k2+6bos-
71gNOE15eyncuas+HusgafUm8xBxi28YBLClM7SOX-
UUJEdTA1NourSVYwCE9kVGn3CE+tEtx+HejLt/psBX0/
qg+/ZxGycPwrzatXKirpzCGzSYu2XEvg8smxX2Amir-
ME5ELsly1O5KO31sWwnHoLGNkR5dYtIi2NUbuNABE-
BAAEAD/4sS3wvPsSiwBZJi6M+zai5oCZMi0pkLnUR/

LeH6OACUqTVX/p8NXV6bsY1PPGIav2MRwaGmVNlE-
VaTqilCtyyyd58Z3JtAkK90T/5wmzCjOJoMRq5iyEFW-
3f3HVA0RkwqsnuZqxI3uv+c1JbqWqFDOSIED-
qRAOfK+QDWpO8t9+mEvUbkJzVEEotXDbMpK8QIjL3XNF/
K5VkRUEKQHqu/mwqkEUa3wz7Qa4WZeb9VSL6y5j11W-
fVdzaveQd/9nMI6p+Af1+hEPGsCwECifcsjXoa/
sw7bem0fsAUu5gTYzl/kUOe6m6qOswkK1YKZ2n-
4s76COcfLi34rPttAUiwg0ZnBzRBD-
Jp4nB48T1wXBTenbN4lwhLdET6bhhL/Qkzad-
cCFIsYBchDYz80XHr4Mzd3gZqrYFuNf4Ne+Ob/
V1tLNiWC8MTTdE3NaDVy8LGNorRSgDM7oGjjSvSCYE6+N-
JzqRt7PTn1PYtZcYRsyvFTO8Rwp8WedeCNsOsZhH-
vdmEH3ilP3loFV3pdcJtEcBhjqQo7h9t39DDfQOwe-
hHSNXi+b9Wc5kLlPRx6ZeeRPulp9+0RuCGZux-
QLuzsH5UkWznpb0CkmtkMJpvMuzTB7xV9s/
ldtzMFrfwyVWXg0BedgI6mVZF7S/r+eHGzEGvwaYu-
jXan9kOLYvvrlWQZP5N8x+FQgA2Z+2jhDtIbho/
VC492coTf1N2ctGJDQMryMus2kdhQWMpB0Fg-
puglibfPPYGta0ObsgOIQ9j3PtA6kS5yz+-
sUgGXCwY0XIo4O9rWmBrMziLGTtfiFtq90A-
CpEJNM1YkCKDFuGOcZ2023eTQZ3WMQqgak-
gYlmrbIwTCZmfmORpThN8a/zhG+6TUhMqjZ/
M0mWf1mwt4WRhJ8Txojo4U8+G6kZXxmCTOdk2eiIQKl-
CvAvHlhgc8Xf/EKAoxY6gRi/RwXWqVG+3ybAqVT-
JbbIp/9efLjaifCN5MfInRRtMrRtHoSwoKPmt-
McuChkjmZrUyTtTzTevjpz0JIA1y7V9HzqwgA/
UWTpVAnAibOlfvglMy7HKKv2+eGGTJaR+Z/npU9Vm-
J1FjI4xM5k190reMcHwur++Pg+1vZ3dkcZPR6h7t-
18GCiJ2JSB7CU0iFec6C+pxl2CrGZ08qeRKdC9Tk-
4pvhcuXBbjeguv6xo4H8JGSAC8oPOnjCupu3hWUx-
GRFZL5Ig+1PzqpSJedySUW1BZwy0TtHitbyqluU52D-
1wtfdrqSvZjIi+C5Of6MN9Glf3+Si3QY+bW-
cUSebHEDSNTV0Y7aOp2RFOyEhcuEKVLutHDzDkGoltldW/
KsmMz4C3mlmpquZbVYtv5tLMa3gtT2EEc62cm-
fvKrVG1Fe0AXBU9FxVpwf/SgaiW6Q1ddu7NYZMsL-
Mw/YBQiAlcDqlCspRxYRZQLZqxdpCz62IUhI-
1aHd9nIMSWu4ssSvfuU+iBeDiJoL0vRFmnpzmc-
Q4yhV2uLTeVza6BPtHio/qRdtfGHwxIz6x/

```
VQ0fDjIpPGKja6J12eAnOJt5GjYHfSYBuEEHY0+eB-
fU8twQMnFi65IHktOArdrvRq2FsvjjvnvGQXr3wf-
N66d9pMKqcyBtmZMhJDkU8cGTvcMCp1Z3w+GCrLK-
PO5aJXGD5KxrNGkB8vNWdiFynms67KufkalEnBjg/
v3wnWJWfD4Zgavw7KNTbCOMFcMaWra3pOC4FQSq6aqrKQ18b-
g+1NXUNiQI8BBgBCAAmFiEE0IeYn4a0rYj3TpgWck54d-
72pJBYFAlrPqNgCGwwFCQeGH4AACgkQck54d72pJBYLaA//
eoyZ7sjqPxWxdP2w+pzfoxCgy0VL89I2akDk1D5X-
0V+56mD3VjdUMvPkdXy3P3HD41p4dLVPjr0O5yg-
goAA+i6T+6ZUqf918ad/+2rjhcrJ3fRUn+Qmj6a/8tx-
CYVzAdvASWuUDuq22Mmz+JeyvcvLnO2AyamBq5eT-
jwghKreyKwRqPTc+Hv4fnKU8bcUeIxyN5+DbS8B-
neRdn2QZWde2MU44n2TZQV9ZFIumrwoNbynP9Gn-
mzRrXoyUoVpfwfK0vU0q76C2rbo19g/w/8Qa-
N4x/8AkVk1C/6irjo8fx+o9fEtKnghZtBN-
1Be9zXaj25i62N9ISoRpbDpSYvTU248F1iMhv-
j0zcQlKSCXff7xT0mcjen34f2JFhb8yeNvScFkY/
D5LB3NKoS+NwjrsFovpJ+o+sACqsqx022xu-
vi0veywO1ypM6S/bWU/5bNtJ8KXvzdr6hBSy-
iCC8Jvmg5w871zBtOutJ5txJ/8oUFDMbHGHO-
h1nVMrMHXbt58b9HDPTkauwUq+0emWuPmMZpvsefx-
i5g8G1kHvsS9gHzo0wVBMWfaBS+sDZH9F/+vm/J6KA/
bsKWcS8Ch9OClRCDebBPNIHpswEiy2Tc5il/Lio0wuW-
7FUDdhpdQLwt/yMK5AGL5dQOEwoRwy1hEn2Vgn948D-
dlTyJNDTSZhOPSv9VgjI==7kkJ

-----END PGP PRIVATE KEY BLOCK-----
```

Of course this specific keypair is useless now, as I have made both keys available to the public.

So that is PGP. Bitcoin uses a different scheme called 'ECDSA'—Elliptic Curve Digital Signature Algorithm. It works like this:

- Pick a random number between 0 and 2256-1 (that, written out, has seventy-eight digits: 115, 792, 089, 237,

316, 195, 423, 570, 985, 008, 687, 907, 853, 269, 984, 665, 640, 564, 039, 457, 584, 007, 913, 129, 639, 935). **This is your private key.**

- Do some ECDSA maths on it to generate a **public key**. The ECDSA algorithms are well known and there are plenty of tools to help with the calculations.

That is it! You now have a randomly chosen private key and you have mathematically generated a public key from it. From your public key you can generate your Bitcoin address to tell the world, but make sure you don't tell anyone your private key. Although it was easy for you to convert your private key into a public key by doing some ECDSA maths on it, it is mathematically impossible for someone to 'work backwards' and derive your private key from your public key.

For a real example, go to www.bitaddress.org and wiggle your mouse a bit to generate some randomness. I did it with the following result:

The Bitcoin address is derived from the public key. By pasting the private key into the 'Wallet Details' section of the website, you can see all of the gory details including the public and private keys in various formats:

Again, of course this keypair is useless now and I wouldn't recommend sending any bitcoins to it!

So there you have it. Bitcoin addresses (accounts) are derivatives of public keys, and when you make a Bitcoin transaction, you use your private key to sign, or authorize, the transaction which moves bitcoins from your account to someone else's. Most blockchain schemes operate this way. Digital assets are held in accounts made from public keys, and the respective private keys are used for signing outbound transactions.

HASHES

A *hash function* is a series of mathematical steps or *algorithms* that you can perform on some *input* data, resulting in a *fingerprint*, or *digest*, or simply, a *hash*. There are *basic* hash functions (not used in blockchains) and *cryptographic* hash functions (used in blockchains).

We'll need to understand *basic* hash functions before moving to cryptographic hash functions.

Basic Hash Function

A really basic hash function might be 'Use the first character of the input'. So using this function you'd get:

Hash('What time is it?') => 'W'

The input to this function is 'What time is it?' and is sometimes called the *preimage* or the *message*.

The output of this function is 'W' and is called the *digest*, the *hash value*, or simply the *hash*.

Hash functions are *deterministic* because the output is *determined* by the input. If a function is deterministic, it always produces the same output for any given input. All mathematical functions are deterministic (adding, multiplying, dividing, etc).

Cryptographic Hash Functions

A *cryptographic* hash function is special and has some characteristics that makes it useful in cryptography and for cryptocurrencies, as we will see later. Wikipedia[70] states that the ideal cryptographic hash function has five main properties (my comments in parentheses):

1. It is deterministic so the same message always results in the same hash

2. It is quick to compute the hash value for any given message (you can easily go 'forwards')

3. It is not feasible to generate a message from its hash value except by trying all possible messages (you can't go 'backwards')

4. A small change to a message should change the hash value so extensively that the new hash value appears uncorrelated with the old hash value (a small change makes a big difference)

5. It is not feasible to find two different messages with the same hash value (it is hard to create a hash clash)

What does this mean? The combination of properties 2 (you can easily go 'forwards') and 3 (you can't go 'backwards') means that cryptographic functions are sometimes called 'trapdoor function'. It is easy to create a hash from a message, but you can't re-create the input from the hash. Nor can you guess or infer what the message may be by looking at the hash (property 4). The only way to go backwards is to try every possible combination of inputs and see if the hash value matches the one you are trying to reverse. This is called a brute force attack.

So would our previous hash function ('Use the first character') be a good *cryptographic* hash function? Let's see:

---

70   https://en.wikipedia.org/wiki/Cryptographic_hash_function

1. Yes, it is deterministic. 'What time is it?' always hashes to 'W'.

2. Yes, it is quick to compute the output, you simply take the first character.

3. Yes, by knowing only 'W' it is not feasible to guess the original sentence (but see 5).

4. No, a small change in the message doesn't necessarily change the output. 'What time is **at**?' also hashes down to 'W'.

5. No, we can easily create loads of inputs that will all hash down to the same output. Anything starting with 'W' will work.

So our earlier hash function is no good as a cryptographic hash function.

So what is a good cryptographic hash function? There are some established industry standard cryptographic hash functions that meet all of these criteria. They have names like MD5[71] (Message Digest) or SHA-256 (Secure Hash Algorithm), and they have an additional benefit in that their output is usually of a fixed length. This means that whatever you use as an input to the hash function, whether it is a sentence, a file, a hard drive, or an entire data centre, you will always get a short digest back.

Here is the kind of output you get:

---

[71] MD5 has been recognised as flawed, failing on collision resistance, but was used extensively for a period of time. Other ones have taken its place, but it is still used where the stakes are low.

```
MD5('What time is it?') -> 67e07d-
17d43ee2e70633123fdaba8181

SHA256('What time is it?') -> 8edb61c4f743e-
be9fdb967171bd3f9c02ee74612ca6e0f6cbc-
9ba38e7d362c4d
```

You can even try this on your computer. If you have a Mac, run the Terminal application and type:

md5 -s "What time is it?"

or

echo "What time is it?" | shasum -a 256

You will see that your results are the same as mine. Of course, that is the whole point in a cryptographic hash—it is deterministic.

If you change the input slightly, you get a very different result:

```
SHA256('What time is it?') -> 8edb61c4f743e-
be9fdb967171bd3f9c02ee74612ca6e0f6cbc-
9ba38e7d362c4d

SHA256('What time is at?') ->
2d6f63aa35c65106d86cc64e18164963a950b-
f21879a87f741a2192979e87e33
```

Hash functions can be used for proving that two things are the same without revealing the two things. For example, let's say that you want to make a prediction and don't want others to know the prediction, but you want to be able to reveal the prediction later. You'd write the prediction down privately, hash it, and display the hash to your audience. People can see that you've committed to a prediction but can't back-calculate what your prediction is. Later, you can reveal the prediction, and others can calculate the hash and see that it matches the hash you published.

Cryptographic hashes, the output from cryptographic hash functions, are used in Bitcoin in a number of places:

- In the mining process

- As identifiers for transactions

- As identifiers for blocks, in order to link them in a chain

- Ensuring that data tampering is immediately evident

DIGITAL SIGNATURES

Digital signatures are used extensively in Bitcoin and blockchains for creating valid transactions 'signing' transaction messages to move coins from your account to someone else's.

What are digital signatures, in a cryptographic sense? Well, we can afford to be a bit pedantic here. *Digital signatures* are a subset of *electronic signatures*, which can take a number of forms.

Only one of these electronic signatures is a digital signature

Writing your name in a box is not a digital signature

A graphic that looks like your handwritten signature is not a digital signature

A digital signature is mathematically linked to the content and to your private key

One form of electronic signature is as simple typing your name into a box:

> **Joe Bloggs**

This is an *electronic* signature but not a *digital* signature.

Another form of electronic signature is a picture that looks like a wet-ink signature, but inserted into a document:

This is also an *electronic* signature, but not a *digital* signature.

So what does a *digital signature* look like? I created a small message containing the text 'Here is a message I want to sign'. and I signed it using the (private) PGP key I generated earlier. Here is what the signature looks like:

-----BEGIN PGP SIGNATURE-----

iQIzBAABCAAdFiEE0IeYn4a0rYj3TpgWck54d72pJBY-
FAlrPq0EACgkQck54d72p

JBakcw//akztOKUDE7h/uAMcqMlj6r7V/
UYsHZ7AR5j2eplX/Nc8sw/CifK6uPQ/

XWanoI85PaOJgq00i4s5NKC/B0GHDaE+mrkjDjYYJj/
U66jHczpBFiMcJHGM8rOB

SJAIlvI3NLRq45zkV9IizrPbGrrIZ15Kiqvqd7AtSsU-
jwelARsZEoqwsXds6EdZA

9oNaz7XN5uNJQ9gVjzxboGP6DXOEdpQWZm0qt6bX-
q8NaPibLB7MqOdHDY0DFLoiY

Q5IdWRQzE0T3iECHG8rSSNbwDPvi6BsBTCie5OdfFr-
1Mice3UZaflehKqUks4uti

cwLKbtwSXApROOV4cVBUm12+Atqlpggq4O/zj0mlpo-
lnKOK16lXKzjhz334iE39u

Pw7pLmnhAcI+kRt4OXD0LOakUhV3iV4/jUo1WEpd2RcB-
zgGRcGn3tTlkMF+fDpZx

8dGNip40glpRUDHWPSRJYM66elQq7gfDkEUo7j34EVB-
PIzIWkDqD2vdqsZaZHFmA

8TGttea0RdouUSsc0RBbF/t0PpI7xbh3uaeiqyJfEw-
FoapWGYPfXwPPg7+zUn+O2

32ZAEOnswzGribliVYgOGSr1ABMhWAPmVwBk0FRbbjd-
vkYwUpZ3dEBG8+6AmKIav

559racy4D6pAiFQ9iYWwoQ1A7BKICY51ErvXVY/2Ci-
E04Q6MCjw=

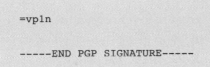

```
=vpln


-----END PGP SIGNATURE-----
```

So that is a digital signature. Looks like gibberish. So what's so special about it? What does it prove?

A digital signature is created by taking the message you want to sign and applying a mathematical formula with your *private* key. Anyone who knows your *public* key can mathematically verify that this signature was indeed created by the holder of the associated private key (but without knowing the private key itself).

So, anyone can independently validate that *this* piece of data was signed by the private key holder of *this* public key.

In essence:

```
Message + Private key -> Digital signature

Message + Digital signature + Public key ->
Valid/Invalid
```

How is this better than a wet-ink-on-paper signature? The problem with a wet-ink signature is that it is independent of the data that is being signed, and this creates two problems:

1. There is no way of knowing if a document has been tampered *after* your signature is applied to the bottom.

2. Your signature can easily be copied and re-used with other documents, without your knowledge.

Your wet-ink-on-paper signature is your signature and doesn't change based on the item being signed: when you sign a cheque, a letter, or a document, *the whole point* is that your signature looks the same. This is easy for other people to copy! This is really terrible security!

In contrast, a digital signature is only valid for that *exact* piece of data, and so it cannot be copied and pasted underneath another piece of data, nor can someone else re-use it for their own purposes. Any tampering with the message will result in the signature being invalidated. The digital signature is a one-time 'proof' that the person with the private key really did approve that exact message. No one else in the world can create that digital signature except you, unless they have your private key.

Now, just to explain one further step, the mathematical process of 'signing' a message with a private key is actually an encryption process. Remember that you encrypt data with a public key, and decrypt it with a private key? With some schemes you can also do it the other way around: you can encrypt data with a private key and decrypt it with a public key. So actually the validation process is taking the digital signature and decrypting it with the well-known public key, and seeing that the decrypted signature matches the message being signed.

But what if the message being signed is really big, like, say, gigabytes of data? Well, you don't want a really long digital signature, as that would be inefficient. So in most signing schemes, it is actually the *hash* (fingerprint) of the message that is signed with the private key to produce a digital signature which is small, irrespective of the size of the data being signed.

There is a good summary on Microsoft's Technet website[72]:

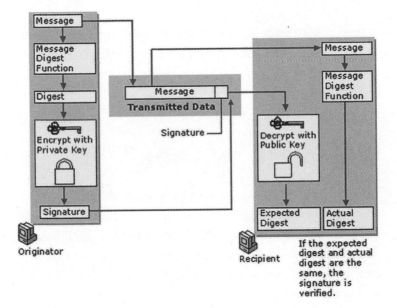

So digital signatures can be used to authenticate a transaction or message, as well as to ensure data integrity of the message. Also, unless a private key has been copied, it is impossible afterwards to say 'it wasn't me'—this property is called 'non-repudiation' and provides comfort for both parties to a transaction.

Digital signatures are used in blockchain transactions because they prove account ownership, and the validity of a digital signature can be proven mathematically and offline, without asking any other party. Compare this to traditional banking: when you instruct your bank to make a payment, you first authenticate yourself by logging in to the bank's

---

72   https://technet.microsoft.com/en-us/library/cc962021.aspx

website, or showing your ID to a bank teller in person. If the bank believes that you are the account holder, then the bank executes your instruction on your behalf. In a blockchain system, where there is deliberately no organisation to provide or maintain accounts for you, your digital signatures are the critical piece of evidence that entitle you to make transactions.

WHY ALICE AND BOB?

In cryptography, it always seems to be Alice and Bob. Why? They are characters first used by Ron Rivest, Adi Shamir, and Leonard Adleman in their 1978 paper 'A method for obtaining digital signatures and public key cryptosystems'[73] instead of a drier 'A' and 'B'. Since then, people use these characters as a nod to the inventors.

But wait, there's more... Wikipedia[74] has a list of commonly used characters, and here are a few I am fond of:

- Craig the password cracker

- Eve the eavesdropper

- Grace the government (generally characterised as anti-cryptography)

- Mallory the malicious man-in-the-middle

---

73   https://dl.acm.org/citation.cfm?doid=359340.359342

74   https://en.wikipedia.org/wiki/Alice_and_Bob

- Sybil the attacker who uses a lot of pseudonyms to overwhelm Alice and Bob

So there you go, that is why it is always Alice and Bob.

Part 4

CRYPTOCURRENCIES

Where do we start? There are so many cryptocurrencies, each working differently with different rules and mechanisms, that is it not particularly easy to make accurate generalisations: however you describe cryptocurrencies, there are bound to be exceptions. For example, Bitcoin uses a mechanism called 'proof-of-work' to ensure that anyone (in theory, at least) can add blocks to the blockchain at a certain cadence without a central actor coordinating access or providing permission. Proof-of-work creates a fair competition between block adders who compete to add blocks. This competition consumes electricity—a lot of it[75]—which is one reason some people describe Bitcoin as wasteful. However not all cryptocurrencies, and certainly not all blockchain technologies, work this way. So it is inaccurate and therefore unhelpful to generalise and say 'cryptocurrencies' or 'blockchains' are energy intensive. Just because Bitcoin works in a certain way, it doesn't mean everything else does.

Bearing this in mind, we will nevertheless start by getting a good grounding in how Bitcoin works, and then later describe some of the differences between Bitcoin and other cryptocurrencies and their respective blockchain protocols (all to be explained—do not fear!).

BITCOIN

People refer to Bitcoin as a digital currency, virtual currency, or cryptocurrency, but it may be easier to think of it as an electronic *asset*. The word *currency* often side-tracks people

---

75   https://www.wired.com/story/Bitcoin-mining-guzzles-energyand-its-carbon-footprint-just-keeps-growing/

when they are trying to understand Bitcoin. They get caught up trying to understand aspects of conventional currencies which do not apply to Bitcoin, for example, what backs it (nothing) and who sets the interest rate (there is none). Bitcoin is also sometimes described as a *digital token*, and in some respects that is accurate; but, alas, the term *token* is now also used to mean something more specific, which we will cover later, so the ambiguity of this term too is best avoided.

What Are Bitcoins?

Bitcoins are digital assets ('coins') whose ownership is recorded on an electronic ledger that is updated (almost) simultaneously on about 10,000 independently operated computers around the world that connect and gossip with each other[76]. This ledger is called Bitcoin's blockchain. Transactions that record transfer of ownership of those coins are created and validated according to a protocol—a list of rules that define how things work and which therefore govern updates to the ledger. The protocol is implemented by software—an app—that participants run on their computers. The machines running the apps are called 'nodes' of the network. Each node independently validates all pending transactions wherever they arise, and updates its own record of the ledger with validated blocks of confirmed transactions. Specialist nodes, called miners, bundle together valid

---

76   This is the number of reachable nodes according to https://bitnodes.earn. com at time of writing. Note that it's not 'millions and millions' of computers as some claim, for instance Don Tapscott said in one of his TED talks 'And when a transaction is conducted, it's posted globally, across millions and millions of computers'. This is an exaggeration of some 100-fold!

transactions into blocks and distribute those blocks to nodes across the network.

Anyone can buy bitcoins, own them, and send them to other people. Every Bitcoin transaction is recorded and shared publicly in plain text on Bitcoin's blockchain. Contrary to many media articles, Bitcoin's blockchain is *not* encrypted. By design, everyone sees all details of all transactions. Anyone can, in theory, create bitcoins for themselves too. This is part of the block creation process, called *mining*, and is described later.

What Is the Point of Bitcoin?

The purpose of Bitcoin is described in its whitepaper—a short document written by a pseudonymous Satoshi Nakamoto, published in October 2008. It describes *why* Bitcoin exists and *how* it should work. It is worth reading the whitepaper in full. It is only nine pages long and available online[77]. The abstract says:

> *A purely peer-to-peer version of electronic cash would allow online payments to be sent directly from one party to another without going through a financial institution. Digital signatures provide part of the solution, but the main benefits are lost if a trusted third party is still required to prevent double spending. We propose a solution to the double spending problem using a peer-to-peer network. The network timestamps transactions by hashing them into an ongoing chain of hash-based proof-of-work, forming a record that cannot be changed without redoing the proof-*

---

[77] https://bitcoin.org/bitcoin.pdf is one place the whitepaper can be found.

of-work. The longest chain not only serves as proof of the sequence of events witnessed, but proof that it came from the largest pool of CPU power. As long as a majority of CPU power is controlled by nodes that are not cooperating to attack the network, they'll generate the longest chain and outpace attackers. The network itself requires minimal structure. Messages are broadcast on a best effort basis, and nodes can leave and rejoin the network at will, accepting the longest proof-of-work chain as proof of what happened while they were gone.

That first sentence says it all. It sets out the purpose of Bitcoin, and how Bitcoin derives both value and utility. For the first time in history, we have a system that can send value from A to B, without the physical movement of items or using specific third-party intermediaries. It is difficult to overstate how important a milestone this is in the evolution of payments. I get shivers down my spine every time I think of Bitcoin like this[78]. As popularised by cryptocurrency

---

78   Censorship resistance is extremely important in a world where nation states are overextending their roles in monitoring and censoring personal activities, including private financial transactions. While some people think it is ok that governments should be able to have insight and control over every single aspect of our private lives, they are fortunate to live in countries where governments are currently benign. Financial privacy and censorship resistance is extremely important, globally. Financial institutions are tools used by governments to enact their policies. One example of this is the weaponising of finance is via financial messaging network SWIFT: although SWIFT claims to be neutral a non-political cooperative based in Belgium, it is routinely pressured by various governments to cut off countries from the global financial network, and it obeys. This is a characteristic of centralised systems—there is always someone to pressure, to throw in prison or exclude if they disobey. While we mostly all agree that terrorism, however you define it, is a bad thing and cutting off terrorists' funds is a good thing, it is possible for regimes to use the same methods to freeze the bank accounts of, say, homosexuals, immigrants, or other groups or individuals out of favour—far less obviously a use of power for the general public good.

industry commentator Tim Swanson[79], Bitcoin is designed as *censorship resistant digital cash.*

There is no mention of a blockchain or 'block chain' at all in the original Bitcoin whitepaper, even though we are constantly reminded by the media that Bitcoin is built on blockchain or that blockchain is the underlying technology of Bitcoin. A chain of blocks was not the purpose of Bitcoin, it is just the design that was developed to achieve the objective— the solution to the business problem.

How Does Bitcoin Work?

The Bitcoin blockchain is managed by software running on computers that communicate with each other forming a network. Although multiple compatible software implementations exist, the most commonly used software is called 'Bitcoin Core' and source code to this software is published on GitHub[80]. This software contains the full range of functionalities needed for the network to exist. It has the ability to perform the following tasks which will be explained in this section:

- Connect with other participants in the Bitcoin network

- Download the blockchain from other participants

- Store the blockchain

- Listen for new transactions

---

79   Tim's blog www.ofnumbers.com is one of the best blogs for data-driven analysis of the cryptocurrency industry.

80   https://github.com/Bitcoin/Bitcoin

- Validate those transactions

- Store those transactions

- Relay valid transactions to other nodes

- Listen for new blocks

- Validate those blocks

- Store those blocks as part of its blockchain

- Relay valid blocks

- Create new blocks

- 'Mine' new blocks

- Manage addresses

- Create and send transactions

However, in practice, the software is usually only used for its bookkeeping function, which will be explained in depth in this section.

To understand how Bitcoin works, and why it works the way it does, it is important to keep in mind the objective: to create an electronic payment system that cannot be censored, and to allow anyone the ability to send payments *directly from one party to another without going through a financial institution*.

Such a system cannot have a central administrator managing the ledger, as that administrator would be the financial institution that Bitcoin is set up to avoid. The system therefore needs to be able to be operated by anyone, without any need to identify themselves or gain permission from a gatekeeper. The moment that parties need to identify themselves, they lose privacy and are vulnerable to interference, coercion, prison, or worse. This goes for both administrators of the system and users themselves. So every single part of the solution needs to work with these constraints in mind.

How did Satoshi go about designing the solution? Let's start with a classic centralised model and then try to decentralise it. In this way, we can build up the design of Bitcoin step by step.

Classic Centralised Model

Let's start with a ledger which keeps tracks of balances, managed by an administrator. You can think of it as a list with two columns: Account, Balance[81].

Classic centralized model

Bookkeeper	
Account	Balance
000001	$100
000002	$50
000003	$240

The administrator assigns account numbers to customers, and customers make payments by instructing the administrator. There is an authentication process where the

---

81   We will start with a generic $ (dollars) as the accounting unit, and later see why we need to move to BTC.

customer proves that they are the account holder before the administrator will carry out the payment instruction. So each customer is named and, for security, has a password linked to their account.

Account mapping

Account	Username	Pin/Password
000001	Alice	1234
000002	Bob	8888
000003	Charlie	9876

The administrator maintains the central record of balances and makes all payments. They are responsible for ensuring that no one spends money they don't have or spends the same money more than once, the 'double spend'.

But if we want resistance to control and censorship, and to allow anyone to be able to transact with anyone else, *we need to remove the administrator.*

First, let's remove the administrator from the *account opening* process, so that anyone can open an account without needing permission from the administrator.

Problem: Accounts Need Permission

Someone has to set up an account and assign it to you. It is the administrator's job to assign you an unused account number then set you up with some sort of username (which may be your own name) and password so that when you ask the administrator to make a payment on your behalf, the administrator knows it is really you making the request.

In setting up your account the administrator has *granted permission* for you to open the account, and may, equally, choose to refuse that permission. Any time you have an entity that can approve or deny something, you have a point of third party control. We are trying to eliminate third party control.

Is there a way you can open an account without having to ask permission? Well, cryptography provides a solution.

Solution: Use Public Keys as Account Numbers

Instead of names or account numbers and passwords, why not use public keys as the account number, and digital signatures instead of passwords?

By using public keys as account numbers, anyone can create their own accounts with their own computer without having to ask an administrator for an account number. Remember, a public key is derived from a private key, which is a number picked at random. So you create an account by picking a random number (your private key) and doing some maths on it to get your public key. In Bitcoin and most other cryptocurrencies, account numbers are mathematically derived from public keys (not public keys themselves), and are called *addresses*.

Using user-generated addresses instead of accounts

Bookkeeper	
Address (derived from public key)	Balance
1mk41QrLLeC9Cwph6UgV4GZ5nRfejQFsS	$100
1LnaIHnAZ5nuGyyTjPWqh34KxERCYLeEM1	$50
1PFZiJCYYaWc1C2FCc2UWXDU197rhyP	$240

You can tell the world this Bitcoin address to allow people
to pay to it[82]. No one can spend anything from it unless they
have the private key, which only you have. You can also create
as many addresses as you want and your wallet software will
manage all of them for you.

Could someone else already be using an address that you
randomly picked? Possible, but unlikely. We saw in the
cryptography section that Bitcoin's scheme uses a random
number between 0 and 115,792,089,237,316,195,423,570,985,
008,687,907,853,269,984,665,640,564,039,457,584,007,913
,129,639,935 as a private key. There are so many private keys
available that the possibility of stumbling across someone
else's account is virtually nil. As one commentator put it, 'Go
back to bed and don't worry about this ever happening'. [83]

Public/private keypairs also solve the authentication problem.
You don't have to log in to prove that you are the account
holder. When sending a payment instruction you digitally
sign the transaction with your private key, and this signature
proves to the administrator that the instruction is indeed
coming from you, the account holder. You can create and
sign the transaction offline without being connected to any
network. When you broadcast the signed transaction to the

---

82   Bitcoin addresses are more secure in some respects than bank accounts.
It is inadvisable to make bank account details known, as Top Gear presenter
Jeremy Clarkson found out in 2008. He printed his bank details in a newspaper
called The Sun to try to make the point that his bank account details could
only be used by others to receive payments, not make them. He was proven
wrong and his details were used to set up a £500 direct debit from his account.
The perpetrator had some ethics and used a charity as the beneficiary. Mr
Clarkson subsequently ate his words (an unusual occurrence) See https://www.
theregister.co.uk/2008/01/07/clarkson_bank_prank_backfires/

83   Miguel Moreno provides some calculations of an address collision on his
blog https://www.miguelmoreno.net/bitcoin-address-collision/.

administrator, all the administrator has to do is check that the digital signature is valid for the respective account number, rather than maintain a list of usernames and passwords for you and all transacting parties.

No more usernames and passwords or account mapping

Account	Username	Pin/Password
000001	~~Al...~~	1234
000002	~~Bob~~	8888
000003	Claire	9876

Problem: Single Central Bookkeeper

We have now eliminated the role of the third-party administrator in *creating* accounts. But we still have the third-party administrator in the role of central bookkeeper— the coordinator who maintains the list of transactions and balances and who both validates and orders the transactions you request against some business and technical rules. This single point of control ultimately decides what is reflected in your account, whether your transaction goes through or not. As a single point of control, it is classified as a financial institution, and has the regulatory burden of having to identify you and all other customers, a process known as Know Your Customer or KYC. It can also be coerced to censor transactions.

So, for a digital cash system resistant to third party influence, including control and censorship, we need to remove that single point of control[84].

Single bookkeeper: Not censorship resistant

Bookkeeper	
Address (derived from public key)	Balance
1mk41QrLLeC9Cwph6UgV4GZ5nRfejQFsS	$100
1Lna1HnAZ5nuGyyTjPWqh34KxERCYLeEM1	$50
1PFZip1iJCYYaWc1C2FCc2UWXDU197rhyP	$240

Solution: Replicate the Books

The more people you have sharing a secure system and its information, the less vulnerable that information is to manipulation. However, a group of 'trusted bookkeepers' would inevitably require their own gatekeeper, so we would be back to the central point of control problem again.
The solution is for *anyone anywhere* to be able to be a bookkeeper without asking permission from anyone else and without hierarchy. And all bookkeepers, wherever they are, maintain the same complete books of record and are *peers* of equal seniority, with checks and balances such that if any single bookkeeper were forced to try to censor a transaction or manipulate the database, the others would ignore or exclude them.

---

84   This was a lesson learnt from Napster, a file sharing system that had a central administrator. It eventually failed and paved the way for Bit Torrent, a file sharing system *without* a central administrator which is harder to shut down.

Replicated bookkeeping

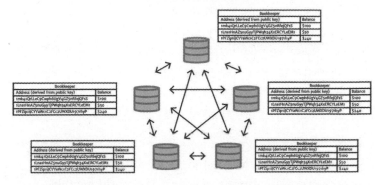

As long as all bookkeepers maintain identical records of which transactions are included and which excluded, we have a more resilient system. If any individual bookkeeper is forced to stop work, the others can continue. Anyone is able to join this network of bookkeepers without needing permission from anyone else. So the network is resilient to anyone joining or leaving at any time.

In Bitcoin, any individual with a computer, adequate storage, and access to internet bandwidth can download some software (or write their own), connect to a few neighbours, and become a bookkeeper.

New transactions are broadcast to all bookkeepers via a gossip network, and each bookkeeper relays new transactions to as many others as they are connected to. This ensures eventual propagation of transactions to all bookkeepers.

Problem: Transaction Ordering

How do multiple bookkeepers stay in sync with each other? Every bookkeeper will have a different idea of the order of transactions. Given that there could be hundreds of transactions being created anywhere in the world, and given that it takes some time for these to fully propagate across the network, if every bookkeeper tried to put these transactions in order, there would be many conflicting versions of the 'correct' order of transactions. What happens if a bookkeeper in China receives transaction A then transaction B, whereas a bookkeeper in the USA receives transaction B first, then A?

Geography, technology, connectivity, internet traffic, servers, and bandwidth all influence the speed and order in which transactions originating anywhere in the world manifest themselves everywhere else. *Your* ordered list of transactions as manifest, say, in London is going to be very different from someone else's list, even next door, let alone in, say, Lagos, New York, Auckland, or Nairobi.

Transaction (Tx) ordering problem in distributed network

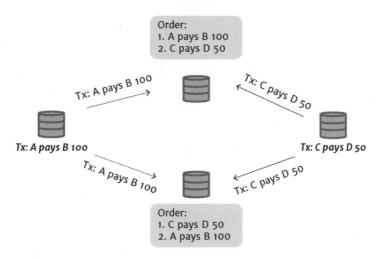

How do we get an agreed ordering of transactions?

Solution: Blocks

We can't control how many transactions can be *created* per second, but we can control the *data entry* into the ledgers. We can do this by recording transactions in batches, *page by page* instead of transaction by transaction. Individual transactions, validated as 'pending' transactions, can be passed around the network, then entered into the books in less frequent batches. We call these batches *blocks*!

Bundle transactions into blocks that are created less frequently

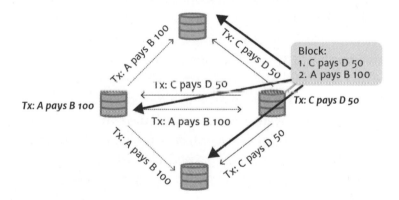

Blocks are created much less frequently than transactions, so it is more likely that a block reaches all bookkeepers in the network before another one is created. This means that a bookkeeper now performs two functions:

1. Validating and propagating 'pending' transactions

2. Validating, storing, and propagating blocks of transactions

By slowing down the 'data entry' process of the bookkeeping system, bookkeepers around the world have more time to agree on the ordering of blocks of transactions. So rather than all bookkeepers needing to agree on the order of *transactions*, they need to agree on the order of *blocks* which are generated less frequently. Because there is more time to agree on the order of blocks, there are fewer differences in opinion about block ordering, and so a greater chance of network-wide consensus. Later we will see how the network deals with conflicting blocks.

Once your transaction is bundled along with other transactions into a valid block, and that block is passed around the network, the transaction is said to be 'confirmed' with one confirmation. When the next block is added, on top of the block with your transaction, your transaction is confirmed with two confirmations. As new blocks arrive on top of the initial block, your transaction is deeper in the ledger and becomes more and more confirmed. This is important because there are situations where the very top of the chain, i.e., the newest blocks, may be replaced by other blocks, kicking out transactions which looked like they have already been confirmed[85]. We will look into the 'longest chain rule' later.

There is a trade-off between the ease with which bookkeepers can agree on the ordering of transactions and the speed at which valid transactions are written into the blockchain. Having blocks created, say, once per day would make it very easy for all bookkeepers to agree on the ordering of those

---

85   And yes, this means that blockchains aren't immutable, contrary to some commentary.

blocks, but this is longer than people want to wait for their transactions to be confirmed.

In Bitcoin, blocks are created every 10 minutes on average. Different cryptocurrencies have different block creation target times.

Problem: Who Can Create Blocks, and How Often?

We have seen that it makes sense to batch pending transactions into blocks that are propagated around the network. Bookkeepers add those blocks to their own ledgers. As we will see later, if there are discrepancies or competing blocks, they use the 'longest chain rule' to decide which block wins.

Firstly, we need to manage the creation and frequency of blocks. How can we do this? If one party gathers up all the pending transactions, puts them into blocks, and sends the blocks to all the bookkeepers then we are back to a single, centralised control point, which we have set out to avoid.

So anyone, without permission, needs to be able to create blocks and send them around the network. But then how do we control the speed at which blocks are created? How do we get a bunch of anonymous block-creators to take it in turns and ensure that they don't create blocks too quickly or too slowly?

Could the bookkeepers themselves have a rule to accept blocks only a minimum ten minutes after the last block they saw, to make it pointless for someone to try to create blocks at more frequent intervals? Due to the latency of the internet, this may create some unfair advantages (we don't know the precise time when any individual bookkeeper received the latest block, and we can't trust timestamps on blocks because these can be easily faked), and we also can't trust the individual bookkeepers who might alter this rule, or their computer's clock, and accept their own blocks sooner than 10 minutes.

Perhaps, we could have a conductor, an entity whose job is to randomly assign the next block-creator, who allows the next block to be created only 10 minutes after the previous one? No, that would not work either, as the conductor would be a central point of control over the network, and we don't want a central point of control.

So perhaps each block-creator could be randomly assigned, like rolling some virtual dice so whoever gets a 'double six' is the next block maker. But that wouldn't work—how could anyone prove they have or haven't cheated? Who would roll the dice? How do we randomise the next block-creator and ensure that everyone agrees that it was a fair process?

Solution: Proof-of-Work

The solution is extremely elegant. The solution is that all block-creators have to play and win at a game of chance, a game that in aggregate, over the whole network, takes some specific amount of time to play (say 10 minutes on average).

The game must give all block-creators an equal chance of winning. The game must not have a barrier to entry, else the gatekeeper would be a central point of control. The game must not have shortcuts, and the game needs to have a publicly displayable proof so that the winner can prove they have won. The game must not be cheatable.

The prize? Being allowed to create the next block.

The game of chance that Bitcoin uses is called 'proof-of-work'. Each block-creator takes a bunch of transactions that they know about, but which have not yet been included in any previous blocks, and builds a block out of them, in a specific format. The creator then calculates a cryptographic hash from the block's data[86]. Remember that a hash is just a number. The rule of Bitcoin's proof-of-work game of chance says, *if the hash of the block is smaller than a target number*, then this block is considered a valid block which all bookkeepers should accept[87].

What if the hash of the block is bigger than this number? Does the specific block-creator bow out for this turn? No. The block-creator needs to alter the data going in to the hash function and try hashing the block again. They *could* do this by removing a transaction from the block, or adding a new transaction, or changing the order of transactions in the block, but these are not elegant and eventually you might run out of permutations. You don't really want to mess around with the transactions in a block.

The solution in Bitcoin is that in every Bitcoin block there is a special part of the block that block-creators can populate with an arbitrary number. Its only purpose is to allow block-creators to fill it with a number, and change the number if the hash block doesn't meet the 'hash is smaller than a target number' rule. So, if the first hash attempt doesn't result in a winning hash, then they can just change the number

---

86   Technically the hash function is performed on a *subset* of the block's data, called the block header, which itself includes hashes of the transactions contained within the block.

87   There are other rules too that determine a 'valid' block, such as its size In bytes, but the proof-of-work hash is what we focus on here.

in this part of the block. This number is called the 'nonce' (number once) and is completely separate from the financial transactions in the block. Its only job is to change the input data for the hash function.

Mining blocks

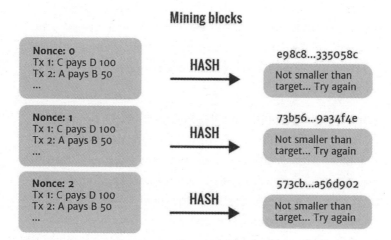

So each block-creator puts together a block and fills the nonce field with the number and hashes the block. If the result meets the 'hash is less than a target number' rule for valid blocks, then they have created a valid block, and can send it to the bookkeepers, and get to work on the next block. If the result doesn't fit the rule, then they change the nonce (e.g., by adding 1) and hash again. They do this repeatedly until they find a valid block. This is a process known as *mining*.

This is elegantly described as a scratch-off puzzle in a paper by Miller et al entitled "Nonoutsourceable Scratch-Off Puzzles to Discourage Bitcoin Mining Coalitions"[88]. Like scratch-off lottery cards, each miner has to expend a bit of effort scratching off a puzzle to see if they have a winning ticket.

So the authority to create a valid block is not given by a third party but is self-assigned by repeating some tedious mathematical algorithms, which all computers can do[89]. Note that mining is a *tedious, repetitive job*. Take some transactions with the nonce, hash it, see if the hash is smaller than a certain number, and if not, repeat with a different nonce. It is not '*solving complex mathematical problems*' as is widely described in the media. Hashing is easy but boring! You can even do it by hand using pencil and paper if you have the patience, though you would be unlikely to win a block with only these tools to power you. Ken Shiriff did a round of hashing by hand with pencil and paper without a calculator, and you can watch him do it on his blog[90].

In this way, anyone can be a block-creator and create valid blocks. They then send the valid blocks to the bookkeepers. The only thing that the bookkeepers have to do is to take the block, including the nonce, and hash it once to verify

---

88   Non-outsourceable Scratch-Off Puzzles to Discourage Bitcoin Mining Coalitions. Andrew Miller, Elaine Shi, Ahmed Kosba, and Jonathan Katz. ACM Computer and Communications Security (CCS), October 2015. http://soc1024. ece.illinois.edu/nonoutsourceable_full.pdf

89   Nowadays, special chips known as ASICs (Application Specific Integrated Circuits) are designed, built, and used specifically for this mining task. ASICs built for this purpose are very efficient at SHA-256 hashing but pretty much useless for anything else. So any comparisons between the amount of (very specific) calculations that Bitcoin miners can do per second, compared with the world's supercomputers (that can do general purpose computing), is not comparing like for like and therefore a false comparison.

90   http://www.righto.com/2014/09/mining-Bitcoin-with-pencil-and-paper. html

for themselves that the hash of the block is less than the target number.

Proof-of-work also avoids another kind of attack, a Sybil attack. A Sybil[91] attack is when a network is overwhelmed by multiple forged identities all under the control of a single actor. Think Facebook or Twitter bots... loads of usernames but all under control of a small number of bad actors.

In Bitcoin, your chance of winning a block is proportional to how much hashing power you control. In the Bitcoin whitepaper this described as 'one-CPU-one-vote'. If Bitcoin had given each *node* (each block-adder) an equal chance of winning a block (one node, one vote), the Sybil attack would be to create unlimited numbers of block adders and try to win all the blocks. Creating multiple identities is very cheap for attackers to do. So proof-of-work works well as a solution to this kind of Sybil attack because proof-of-work is *computationally expensive*, and this in turn means expensive in terms of *electricity* and *hardware* (i.e., cash), which means it is expensive to try to overwhelm the network with hashing power, which in turn increases the attack costs to a bad actor. If you have all of this hashing power available, you might as well put it to work finding blocks and making money (well, bitcoins) instead of trying to subvert the network, so the theory goes.

---

91   These attacks are named after Sybil Dorsett, the pseudonymous subject of a 1973 book *Sybil* by Flora Rheta Schreiber, a case study about Sybil's multiple personality disorder.

Problem: Incentivising Block-Creators

But all of this tedious hashing needs resources: computers, electricity, bandwidth... and this all costs money. Why should anyone bother creating blocks? What's in it for them? How can we incentivise the block-creators to create blocks and keep the system running?

Solution: Transaction Fees

The solution is to pay the block-creators for their time and resources! But who is going to pay them and in what currency? An external payment or incentivisation mechanism, i.e., a third party paying the block-creators, would centralise and gate the process, defeating the purpose of censorship resistance, so that will not work. US dollars or any fiat currency would not work either, as fiat is held in bank accounts and banks can be instructed to freeze accounts.

An *internal* or *intrinsic* incentivisation scheme avoids third party control. This is implemented as a per transaction fee, so the block-creator gets a commission, a small amount of value, from each transaction. This could be specified as a percentage or a flat rate for all transactions and encoded into the rules of the system—a bit like the '10 minutes per block' rule. But it is difficult to establish the right fee. Bitcoin's solution is a market-based approach where people creating transactions add their own voluntary transaction fees, and the block-creators can prioritise those transactions with higher fees over those with lower fees.

Incentivisation via voluntary transaction fees

A pays B 50 (fee for miner: 0.1)
C pays D 500 (fee for miner: 0.08)
E pays F 0.5 (fee for miner: 0.06)
A pays E 50 (fee for miner: 0.02)
E pays G 50 (fee for miner: 0.01)
G pays B 50 (fee for miner: 0)

> Build my block with highest fee transactions

When Alice creates her Bitcoin transaction she can optionally add a fee that is collected by the lucky who mines her transaction[92]. This fee allows miners to prioritise her transaction over others, who are all competing to get in a block. Blocks are limited by network rules, as to how much data can squeeze into a block. In Bitcoin, this limit is nominally 1 MB[93]. Fees tend to go up in times where there are many transactions queuing up to get into blocks, and down again in times with fewer transactions.

Problem: How to Bootstrap?

How were block-creators incentivised to keep creating blocks in the early days or, indeed, now during slack periods when there may be periods where there are no transactions for some hours? The hashing work consumes electricity and costs miners' money.

---

92   The way this works in practice is that when Alice creates a transaction, she can specify that the transaction pays the recipient slightly less than the amount that is deducted from her account. In jargon, her transaction outputs is less than her inputs. This difference is the fee for the miner. The miner adds up the fees from all the transactions in the block and includes it in the 'coinbase' transaction which is a transaction paid to the miner and is described later.

93   But now it is a little more complicated, with innovations such as Segregated Witnesses where part of the data in the block isn't counted towards the block's size.

Solution: Block Rewards

The second, and currently much larger, incentive for block-creators to create blocks is the '*block reward*'. In effect, the block-creator can write a cheque to themselves once per block, for up to a certain amount. The idea is that block rewards can kick start the system, and then be phased out gradually, with transaction fees to replace them.

Bootstrapping the incentive scheme

```
Block                                    MINER'S REWARD
Coinbase Tx: Create 12.5 BTC for me  ◄───────────────
Tx 1: A pays B 50 (fee for miner: 0.1)
Tx 2: C pays D 500 (fee for miner: 0.08)
...
```

The very first transaction in a block is called the *coinbase* transaction[94]. This coinbase transaction is special because it is the only transaction that creates bitcoins. All other transactions move bitcoins between addresses. The block-creator can create a transaction that pays any address (usually themselves) any number of bitcoins, up to a limit specified by the Bitcoin protocol. This limit was 50 BTC per block in 2009 and reduces by half every 210,000 blocks, which at 10 minutes per block, is about every 4 years. Currently (mid-2018) the maximum block reward is 12.5 BTC, with the next reduction to occur on block 630,000, estimated to occur in May 2020[95]. These block rewards have created around 17 million bitcoins to date, and owing to the repeated halving of

94   Not to be confused with a cryptocurrency wallet company based in the USA called Coinbase.

95   http://www.Bitcoinblockhalf.com/

the block reward, the maximum number of bitcoins created
ever will be a sliver under 21 million, the last of which
should be created a little before the year 2140. Unless the
rules change.

This block reward is the mechanism that keeps block-creators
creating blocks. They receive valuable BTC in return for
spending resources doing the tedious hashing to create valid
blocks. Note that block-creators are under no obligation to
include any transactions in their blocks, but they choose to
because the transactions themselves contain transaction fees
and these also accrue to the block-creator.

The beauty of this system is that the payment for creating
blocks comes from the protocol itself rather than from an
external third party.

Problem: More Hashing, Faster Blocks, More Monetary Supply

If anyone can create valid blocks by finding the nonce that
makes the hash of the block meet a certain criterion and get
paid for it, then surely by throwing more computers at the
hashing they can create valid blocks more quickly and get
paid more! By doubling the amount of hashing power, they
can, on average, double the speed at which they can create
valid blocks.

But this, unchecked, would cause havoc. With more people
throwing more hashing power (i.e., computers) at the block
creation process, blocks would be created faster and faster.
Remember, we want blocks to be created slowly, so that the
bookkeepers have a better chance of staying in consensus.

And BTC would be created faster and faster, creating a huge supply and possibly decreasing the value of each unit.

Solution: Difficulty

The network needs to self-correct and slow down if blocks are created more quickly than the target of one block every ten minutes. The answer lies in changing the target number for the hash calculation. Variations in this target number can make it easier or harder for the network, in aggregate, to find hashes that fall below this number. As an analogy, if you have to roll two dice and get a sum total below eight, that is quite easy, but if you have to get a sum total below four then that will take you more rolls. So making the target number smaller slows down the rate at which valid blocks are created.

In Bitcoin, the target number is mathematically calculated from a number called the 'difficulty'. The difficulty changes every 2016 blocks (which takes about two weeks at ten minutes per block), according to a formula that uses the elapsed time it took to mine the previous 2016 blocks. The faster the previous 2016 blocks were created, the more the difficulty increased. The difficulty and the hashing target number are inversely related, so as difficulty increases, the target number becomes smaller, making it harder and therefore slower to find valid blocks.

The network is beautifully self-balancing. If more hashing or mining power is added, then blocks get created faster for a period of time until the next difficulty change, after which it becomes harder to find valid blocks, slowing block creation down. If mining power leaves the network, then blocks take longer to be found, until the next time the difficulty changes, then difficulty decreases, and blocks become easier to find. And this is all done without a central coordinator.

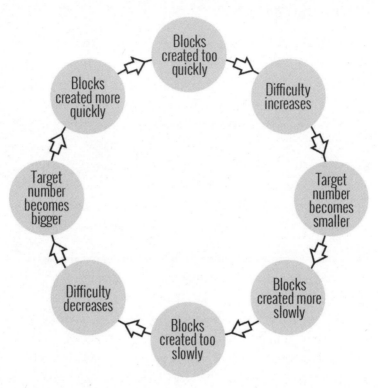

Problem: Block Ordering

Transactions are bundled into blocks which are like pages in a ledger. These blocks are passed around the network at a slower rate than individual pending transactions would be. But how do you know what order the blocks should be? In a book, each page has a unique page number, and you know that the pages follow in ascending order. If the pages fall out, you can put the book back together again in the right order.

Could the same be done for blocks where each block gets
a unique 'block number'? In principle, yes, but remember
that block-creators are competing to mine blocks by hashing
their contents and seeing if the hash is smaller than a target
number determined by the current difficulty. Imagine that
the block 1,000 has just been mined and passed to all the
nodes. The miners start mining block 1,001. Someone super
sneaky might get to work mining block 1,002 and to try to
get ahead of competitors, so that as soon as someone else has
found block 1,001, they can submit block 1,002 and claim the
block reward. Remember, the miner doesn't need to populate
any transactions in the block, they can just hash an empty
block 1,002 that refers to block 1,001 with a coinbase reward
transaction and no other transactions. Hmm, that wouldn't be
a good idea, there'd be all sorts of gamesmanship.

What restricts miners to ensure they mine only the very next
block? How is 'mining ahead' prevented?

Solution: A Block Chain!

Instead of having each block have a 'block number,' each
block refers to the previous block *by its hash*. Miners
must include the previous block's hash in the block they
are creating.

This means that to mine block 1,002, miners need to know
the hash of block 1,001. Until 1,001 has been mined, 1,002
can't be mined. This forces miners to focus on block 1,001,
which in turn includes the hash of block 1,000, and no
miner can skip ahead. Thus a chain of blocks is created, held
together not by block *numbers* (which can be predicted) but
by block *hashes* (which can't). Each block refers to a previous

block by the previous block's hash, rather than by a number that goes up sequentially.

This is the chain of blocks, or *blockchain*.

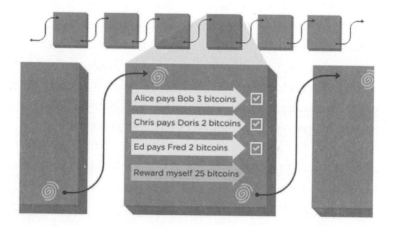

A block chain[96] where each block includes the hash of the previous block, rather than a sequential block number.

An additional benefit of blocks linking through their hashes is that of internal consistency, sometimes described as immutability. Let's say the latest block that has been passed around the network is block 1,000. If a rogue bookkeeper attempts to tamper with a previous block, say, block 990, and attempts to republish that block to other bookkeepers, they could:

1.   Publish block 990 with new data but using the old hash; *or*

---

96   https://bitsonblocks.net/2015/09/09/a-gentle-introduction-to-blockchain-technology/

2. publish block 990 with new data and a new valid hash
    (i.e., 're-mine' the block).

In the first case, the block will be considered invalid by all
other bookkeepers, because it is internally inconsistent (the
block's hash doesn't match the data inside it), and in the
second case, the hash of block 990 won't match the reference
found in block 991. Thus, it is very hard to get away with
tampering with any records that already form part of the
blockchain—it will be immediately obvious to anyone who
you try to convince. This is what is meant when blockchains
are described as *immutable*. Of course, nothing is immutable
(can't be changed), but blockchains are tamper-evident—
that is, it is easy for others to tell if data has been modified,
accidentally or otherwise.

Problem: Block Clashes / Consensus

There is still a chance that blocks are created by different
block-creators at the same time, due to the random process of
hashing. If a bookkeeper receives two valid blocks from two
different block-creators (miners) and they both reference the
hash of the same previous block, how does the bookkeeper
know which one to use and which one to throw away? How
does the network come to *consensus* about which block to
use? And if a miner receives two valid but competing blocks,
how do they know which block to build the next block on?

Solution: Longest Chain Rule

There is another protocol rule called the longest chain rule[97]. If a miner sees two valid blocks at the same block height then they can mine on either block (usually the first seen) and would keep the other one 'in mind'. Others will also make their decisions and eventually one of the blocks will have another block mined on it, then another, and another. So the rule is that the *longest chain* is the chain that should be considered the chain of record, and the block that is discarded is called an *orphan*.

What happens to the transactions in the orphaned block? They are considered as if they have never been part of a valid block and therefore are 'unconfirmed'. They will just be included in later blocks along with other unconfirmed transactions, assuming they don't conflict with the transactions that have already been confirmed in the blockchain.

Problem: Double Spend

Although the longest chain rule seems sensible, it can be used to create mischief in a deliberate double spend. Here is how you could do it:

1.   Create two transactions using the same bitcoins: one payment to an online retailer, the other to yourself (i.e., to another address you control).

---

97   The 'consensus mechanism' in Bitcoin is not proof-of-work (as a lot of people say), it's the longest chain rule (or to be pedantic, it's the chain with the most work done on it, which normally equates to the most blocks). Showing a proof-of-work proof is the Sybl-resistant data entry mechanism, i.e., the entry price of being able to add a block, but the mechanism that is used to determine which chain of blocks commands consensus is the longest chain rule.

2. Only broadcast the transaction that is the payment to the retailer.

3. When the payment gets added in an 'honest' block the retailer sees this and sends you goods.

4. Secretly create a longer chain of blocks which excludes the payment to the retailer, and replaces it with the payment to yourself.

5. Publish the longer chain. If the other nodes are playing by the 'longest chain rule,' then they will reorganise their blockchains, discarding the honest block containing the payment to the retailer, replacing it with the longer chain you published. The honest block is said to be 'orphaned' and, to all intents and purposes, does not exist.

6. The original payment to the retailer will be deemed invalid by the honest nodes because those bitcoins have already been spent in your longer, substituted, chain. You will have received your goods but the payment to the retailer will be rejected by the network.

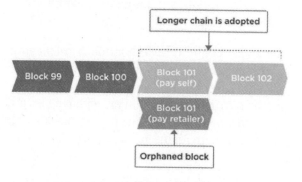

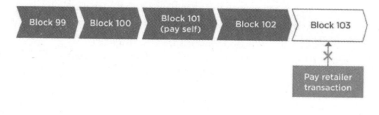

How to double spend.

Solution: Wait About Six Blocks

Therefore, common advice for people receiving bitcoins is to wait for the transaction to be a few blocks deep (i.e., to have a few blocks mined on top of it). This gives comfort that the transaction is settled and can't easily be unwound[98]. At this point the amount of mining that has to be done to create a competing chain longer than the existing chain is enormous,[99] so rational miners would prefer to dedicate their hash power towards creating legitimate blocks, receiving the block reward and transaction fees, rather than trying to subvert the network.

To put it another way, it is deliberately hard to generate a valid block. Therefore, if someone wants to replace blocks, they have to create blocks quickly and overtake the rest of the (presumably honest) network. This is another reason why people say Bitcoin's blockchain is immutable and cannot be changed. However, if more than 50% of the total hash power of the network is used to re-write blocks, then it will be able to do so, because it will create blocks faster than the other, less powerful, half. This is called a 51% attack. Smaller amounts of hash power can also be used to re-write the blockchain, but with a lower probability of success[100]. 51% attacks have been successfully performed on unpopular coins with few miners.

Which Coins?

Earlier, I used the phrase '*using the same bitcoins*'. What does this mean? With physical cash, each coin or banknote is

---

98   In blockchains like bitcoin, transactions are never completely settled. There is a probability that a longer chain exists somewhere and is adopted by the network. This means that cryptocurrency payments are settled probabilistically rather than deterministically. The deeper your transaction in the blockchain, the more probable it is that it won't be usurped by a longer chain.

99   As an extreme precaution, miners have to wait 100 blocks before they can spend the special coinbase block reward they get from mining. This is called the *coinbase maturity*.

100   See http://hackingdistributed.com/2013/11/04/bitcoin-is-broken/

a unique object. You can't pay *the same coin or banknote* to two people. However, digital money doesn't work that way. In a traditional bank account, all your money is mixed up or *co-mingled* in a 'total balance' figure. Your income goes into the bank account and is immediately jumbled up with all the other money that is in there, like adding water to a half-full bath. When you make a payment your total balance is reduced, like removing water from the bath. You cannot specify which dollar you are spending. For example, when you pay $8 for a coffee, you don't say, 'Use $8 from my salary payment that came in on 25 Jan,' you just say, 'Use $8 from the pool of money that is my account balance'. This non-specificity promotes the *fungibility* of digital money, that is, one dollar in an account is exactly the same as another.

Bitcoin is digital, but it works more like physical cash. With cash you open your wallet and take *this specific* $10 note which you received earlier and pay $8 for your coffee and expect $2 change. Bitcoin is similar: for every payment you make, you have to specify exactly *which* coins you are spending—that is, *which specific* bitcoins that you received earlier. You refer to these received bitcoins by the transaction hash[101] that sent the coins to you. In the same way that blocks build on each other by referring to the previous block's hash, transactions also refer to each other using a previous transaction's hash. When you make a Bitcoin payment, you say, 'Take *this* bundle of money that came in to my account in *this* transaction, and pay some of it to *this* account and return the change to me'.

---

101   Actually, because a transaction can contain multiple payments, you need to refer to the transaction's hash and the specific payment into your address.

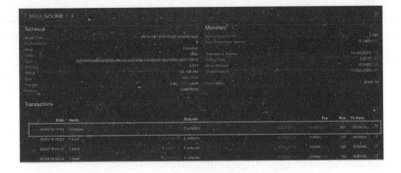

Here is a Bitcoin transaction[102]. You can see that it takes
1.427 bitcoins from address 17tVxts...QM and sends 0.5999
bitcoins into 1Ce2Qzz...wK and returns 0.827 bitcoins back
to 17tVxts...QM. But wait... The two payments add up to less
than the amount spent. 0.5999 + 0.8270 = 1.4269 which is
less than the 1.427 spent. The 0.0001 Bitcoin difference is the
mining fee. The miner can add that 0.0001 to the coinbase
transaction in the block and pay it to themselves.

If we look at the block the transaction is included in,[103] we can
see that the miner paid themselves 12.52723951 bitcoins in
the coinbase transaction, which is the 12.5 BTC block reward
plus the sum of the transaction fees from the transactions in
the block:

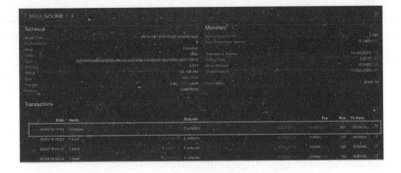

---

102   https://tradeblock.com/bitcoin/
tx/237e0b782a27f83873e781298f13ffae93fd6c274d49b36b015b7c2a814adea3

103   https://tradeblock.com/bitcoin/block/525908

Hence all bitcoins are traceable. You can see the exact composition of every lump of Bitcoin that comes into your account—what it is composed of and where it came from—and you can trace every part of that money via the previous accounts, all the way back to when it was first created in a coinbase transaction.

I say each 'lump of money' specifically, rather than 'each Bitcoin,' because you don't send bitcoins coin by coin, you just send a total amount. Let's see how this works with an example.

Let's start with an empty address and assume that you are friends with a Bitcoin miner who has just created a 'lump' of 12.5 BTC in a coinbase transaction when they successfully mined a block. The 12.5 BTC is like a single banknote in a physical wallet and needs to be spent in its entirety. The miner takes pity on you because you have no bitcoins and wants to give you 1 BTC. So the miner creates a transaction spending those 12.5 BTC to two recipients: 1 BTC to you, and 11.5 BTC back to herself. You now have a 1 BTC 'lump' in your account.

Now it is your lucky day and a few other people give you BTC. In further separate transactions, you receive 'lumps' of 2 BTC and 3 BTC. So now you have 6 BTC in your wallet, in three lumps: 1 BTC, 2 BTC, and 3 BTC.

If you want to give 1.5 BTC to another friend, how would you do that? You could do it in a few different ways:

Option 1: Spend the 2 BTC lump
You'd create a transaction that looks like this:
Spend: 2 BTC lump
Pay: 1.5 BTC to your friend, 0.5 BTC lump as change

back to yourself

Option 2: Spend the 3 BTC lump
You'd create a transaction that looks like this:
Spend: 3 BTC lump
Pay: 1.5 BTC to your friend, 1.5 BTC lump as change
back to yourself

Option 3: Spend the 1 BTC and 2 BTC lumps
You'd create a transaction that looks like this:
Spend: 1 BTC and 2 BTC lumps
Pay: 1.5 BTC to your friend, 1.5 BTC lump as change
back to yourself

Option 4: Spend the 1 BTC and 3 BTC lumps
You'd create a transaction that looks like this:
Spend: 1 BTC and 3 BTC lumps
Pay: 1.5 BTC to your friend, 2.5 BTC lump as change
back to yourself

Option 5: Spend the 1 BTC and 2 BTC and 3 BTC lumps
You'd create a transaction that looks like this:
Spend: 1 BTC and 2 BTC and 3 BTC lumps
Pay: 1.5 BTC to your friend, 4.5 BTC lump as change
back to yourself

Although Option 1 feels like the most obvious and is probably what you would do if you were spending banknotes in a physical wallet, you could in theory choose any of those options. These are all different transactions but all achieve the same thing. The lumps of money that sit in your account are called 'UTXO's which stands for Unspent Transaction Outputs. Most people think in terms of 'account balances' (i.e., my account goes up and down) whereas Bitcoin 'thinks' in transactions (the transaction spends *this* money and puts it *there*). The lumps are the result or *output* of a transaction, and they are *unspent* because you haven't spent them yet. Bitcoin would describe Option 1 as follows:

Option 1: Spend the 2 BTC lump

Transaction *inputs*: (this is money that is being spent)

1.   2 BTC lump

Transaction *outputs*: (this is money that is not yet spent)

1.   1.5 BTC to your friend

2.   0.5 BTC lump as change back to yourself

This whole transaction is hashed, giving it a Transaction ID which can then be used by future transactions. If you later want to spend the 0.5 BTC you returned to yourself, you would say 'take output (2) from this transaction, and spend it like this...'

Now, assuming you did Option 1 described above, what is left in your account? You started with lumps of 1, 2, and 3 BTC. You spent the 2 BTC lump and got 0.5 BTC back. So you're left with three lumps: 1 BTC, 3 BTC, and the new 0.5 BTC lump. The blockchain records that the 0.5 BTC lump came from yourself, so anyone can trace the 0.5 BTC lump back to its original 2 BTC lump, and then further trace it to the account which it came from originally.

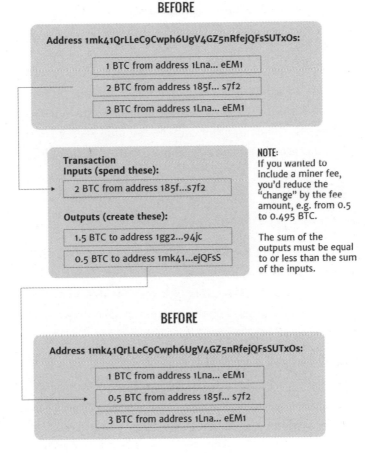

Spending Unspent Transaction Outputs (UTxOs)

BEFORE

Address 1mk41QrLLeC9Cwph6UgV4GZ5nRfejQFsSUTxOs:

1 BTC from address 1Lna... eEM1

2 BTC from address 185f... s7f2

3 BTC from address 1Lna... eEM1

Transaction
Inputs (spend these):

2 BTC from address 185f...s7f2

Outputs (create these):

1.5 BTC to address 1gg2...94jc

0.5 BTC to address 1mk41...ejQFsS

NOTE:
If you wanted to include a miner fee, you'd reduce the "change" by the fee amount, e.g. from 0.5 to 0.495 BTC.

The sum of the outputs must be equal to or less than the sum of the inputs.

BEFORE

Address 1mk41QrLLeC9Cwph6UgV4GZ5nRfejQFsSUTxOs:

1 BTC from address 1Lna... eEM1

0.5 BTC from address 185f... s7f2

3 BTC from address 1Lna... eEM1

What next?

The transaction is created and signed by the sender using their private keys. This signed transaction is then sent to a node (bookkeeper) who validates it according to business rules (e.g., Does this UTXO exist? Has it been spent before?) and technical rules (e.g., How much data does the transaction contain? Is the digital signature valid?), and if found to be valid, the bookkeeper keeps this transaction in a pool of 'unconfirmed transactions' that they have heard about, called a *mempool* or *memory pool*. They then propagate this transaction to their neighbours in the network. Each neighbour follows the same process. Eventually a miner or block-creator picks up this transaction and decides whether they want to pack it into a block, and if so, they start mining the block. If the miner is successful in mining the block, they propagate the block to other miners and bookkeepers and each node records this transaction as confirmed in a block.

Peer-to-Peer

When people say Bitcoin is 'peer-to-peer' what do they mean?

Firstly, *data* is sent between bookkeepers in a peer-to-peer way, i.e., directly and not via a central server. Transactions and blocks are sent between bookkeepers who are each as important in status as each other—that is, they are *peers*. They use the internet to send data between themselves, instead of a 3rd party infrastructure like the SWIFT network used by major banks.

Second, Bitcoin *payments* are often described as peer-to-peer (i.e., with no middle man). But is this really true? Up to a point. A *physical cash* transaction is definitely peer-to-peer as there are no other actors other than the payer and the recipient. But Bitcoin also has intermediaries such as miners and bookkeepers. The difference between Bitcoin payments and bank payments is that, with Bitcoin payments, the intermediaries are *non-specific* and can act in lieu of each other, whereas traditional banks and centralised payment services are *specific* intermediaries. For example, if you have an account with HSBC you can't instruct another bank such as Citibank to move your money, but in Bitcoin any miner can add your transaction to a block they are mining.

Peer-to-peer models of data distribution are like a gossip network where each peer shares updates. Peer-to-peer is in many ways less efficient than client-server, as data is replicated and validated many times, once per machine, and each change to the data creates a lot of noisy gossip. However, each peer is independent and the network can continue operating if some nodes temporarily lose connectivity. And because there is no central server that can be controlled, peer-to-peer networks are more robust and resistant to shutdown, whether accidental or deliberate.

In anonymous, and therefore untrusted, peer-to-peer networks, each peer needs to operate on the basis that any other peer could be a bad actor. So every peer needs to do their own homework and validate transactions and blocks, rather than trusting other peers. The network as a whole acts honestly, if populated by a majority of honest nodes. Next, we examine the limits of bad behaviour and the related costs and incentives.

Miscreants

What can and can't miscreants do?

The impact of a malicious *bookkeeper* is very limited. They can withhold transactions and refuse to pass them to other bookkeepers, or they can present a false view of the state of the blockchain to anyone asking them. A quick check with other bookkeepers will reveal any discrepancies.

Malicious *miners* can cause a little more impact. They can:

- Attempt to create blocks that include or exclude specific transactions of their choosing.

- Create a double spend by attempting to create a 'longer chain' of blocks that make previously accepted blocks become 'orphans' and not part of the main chain. They can realistically only do this if they command a significant proportion of the entire network's hashing power.

But they can't:

- Steal bitcoins from your account, because they can't fake your digital signatures.

- Create bitcoins out of thin air, because no other miners or bookkeepers would accept this transaction.

So the impact of a malicious miner is also actually quite limited. Furthermore, a miner discovered to be enabling double spends could quickly find themselves cut off from the rest of the network if the rest of the network informally agrees to take action. Honest miners might agree not to build on blocks generated by a malicious miner.

Summary

Transactions are payment instructions of specific amounts of Bitcoin (UTXOs) from one user-generated account (address) to another. The transactions are created using wallet software, authenticated with unique digital signatures, then sent to bookkeepers (nodes) who individually validate them according to some well-known business and technical rules. The bookkeepers then add valid transactions to their *mempool* and distribute them to other bookkeepers that they are connected to.

Miners gather these individual transactions into blocks and compete with each other to mine their blocks by tweaking the block contents, specifically the nonce field, until the hash of the block is smaller than some target number. The target number is based on the difficulty setting at the time, which is derived from the time taken to mine the previous set of blocks to achieve a network-wide target frequency of one new mined block every 10 minutes. Miners receive a financial incentive in the form of new BTC and transaction fees which they may credit themselves, to compensate for spending resources to perform the competitive, repetitive hashing needed to create valid blocks.

The blocks link to each other in a unique sequence to form a ledger, the Bitcoin blockchain, that is recorded identically almost simultaneously on thousands of computers around the world that run Bitcoin software. If a Bitcoin transaction is not recorded on this blockchain, it is not a Bitcoin transaction. It doesn't exist. A Bitcoin transaction recorded outside this file does not form part of the ledger.

There is no central authority who controls the ledger or who can censor specific transactions.

Different blockchain platforms or systems work differently. If you relax or change the aims or constraints, the design of the solution can also change. The solution may be simpler, as we will see later with private blockchains where censorship resistance is not a critical factor.

Bitcoin's Ecosystem

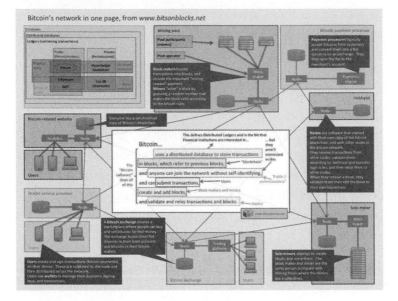

Putting this all together, we can see that the Bitcoin ecosystem consists of parties who perform different roles. Miners and bookkeepers focus on building and maintaining the blockchain itself. Wallets make it easy for people to use cryptocurrencies. Exchanges and cryptocurrency payment processors bridge between the fiat and crypto worlds.

Bitcoin in Practice

While the theory sounds good, Bitcoin in practice is not as decentralised as people might have you believe. By some metrics it is not performing as well as some proponents might lead you to believe.

Bookkeeping Nodes

While there are around 10,000 nodes who perform bookkeeping tasks and who relay transactions and blocks, they are mostly running the same software written, and therefore controlled, by a very small number of people. They are known as the 'Bitcoin Core' developers and the software is known as 'Bitcoin Core'.

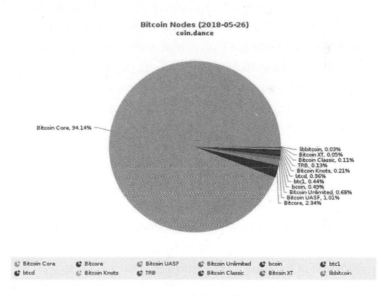

Source: coin.dance[104]

The various versions, or implementations, that are not Bitcoin Core all have slightly different rules but are not different enough to create incompatibilities. Some, for example, may have additional flags to signal that the bookkeepers would be

---

prepared to adopt a rule change if enough participants also
signal the same intention.

Mining

Although anyone can mine, the process has become so
intensive that new hardware and chips are created which
are designed to be exceedingly efficient at performing the
SHA-256 hashing. ASICs (Application Specific Integrated
Chips) became the norm for mining in 2014 and outcompete
all other forms of hardware in terms of energy efficiency for
Bitcoin mining. Dave Hudson explores the effects of ASICs
in his excellent blog *Hashing It*[105]. In the popular media, the
computational power of these specially designed chips is often
compared to the computational power of supercomputers,
but ACICs cannot operate as general-purpose computers, so
comparisons with supercomputers are meaningless. Only a
few entities can mine profitably, usually using special purpose
'mining farms' clustered in areas of cheap electricity. The
chart below shows miners and what proportion of blocks
they have recently mined. The proportion of blocks they
have mined is roughly equivalent to their hashing power as a
proportion of the total hashing power of the network.

---

105   http://hashingit.com/analysis/22-where-next-for-bitcoin-mining-asics

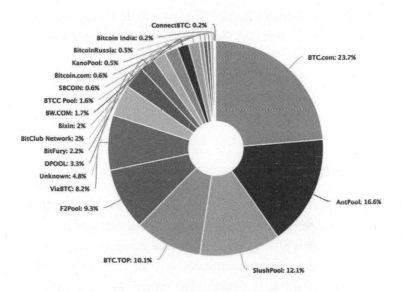

ConnectBTC: 0.2%
Bitcoin India: 0.2%
BitcoinRussia: 0.5%
KanoPool: 0.5%
Bitcoin.com: 0.6%
58COIN: 0.6%
BTCC Pool: 1.6%
BW.COM: 1.7%
Bixin: 2%
BitClub Network: 2%
BitFury: 2.2%
DPOOL: 3.3%
Unknown: 4.8%
ViaBTC: 8.2%
F2Pool: 9.3%
BTC.TOP: 10.1%
SlushPool: 12.1%
BTC.com: 23.7%
AntPool: 16.6%

Bitcoin mining is not that decentralised! Source: blockchain.info[106]

Some of these are single mining entities. Others are syndicates that anyone can join, contribute hash power, and receive rewards in proportion to their contributions. At an estimate, around 80% of the hash power is controlled by Chinese entities. BTC.com, Antpool, BTC.TOP, F2Pool, viaBTC are all Chinese groups[107], and a company called Bitmain owns both BTC.com and Antpool. Hence, if only the top three mining pools collaborate, they can reorganise blocks and arrange double spends, and no one would be able to stop them as they represent more than 50% of the total hashing power. So this is not a well-decentralised system.

---

106   https://blockchain.info/pools?timespan=4days past 4 days of blocks, retrieved 27 May 2018

107   Although the pools are controlled by Chinese entities, the people controlling the hashrate contributing to those pools may not be Chinese and may be free to switch pools at will, in theory.

It is often argued that miners wouldn't do this because it would cause a loss of confidence in Bitcoin and thus cause the price to fall, and their stock of bitcoins would be worth less. However, an enterprising group of miners who carried this out could build a temporary large short trading position just before executing a double spend and profit on the fall in price of BTC.

Mining Hardware

As discussed, miners use special purpose chips called ASICS that are specifically designed and built to be efficient at SHA256 hashing. Commercial chip manufacturers have been slow to design chips that are specifically built to be efficient at SHA256 hashing, so demand has created an alternative specialised industry for supplying Bitcoin ASICs. The main provider of this is Bitmain, the same Chinese company who controls the top two mining pools. It has been estimated that Bitmain produces hardware that mines 70-80% of the total blocks in Bitcoin[108]. Bitcoin hardware manufacturing is not well decentralised.

BTC ownership

The ownership of BTC too shows a concentration in a small number of hands:

---

108   https://www.cnbc.com/2018/02/23/secretive-chinese-bitcoin-mining-company-may-have-made-as-much-money-as-nvidia-last-year.html

Bitcoin distribution

Balance	Addresses	% Addresses (Total)	Coins	$USD	% Coins (Total)
0 - 0.001	10883342	49.38% (100%)	2,171 BTC	15,919,352 USD	0.01% (100%)
0.001 - 0.01	4962026	22.51% (50.62%)	20,194 BTC	148,058,699 USD	0.12% (99.99%)
0.01 - 0.1	3804708	17.26% (28.11%)	122,128 BTC	895,429,283 USD	0.72% (99.87%)
0.1 - 1	1688044	7.66% (10.85%)	544,622 BTC	3,993,117,911 USD	3.22% (99.15%)
1 - 10	554922	2.52% (3.19%)	1,464,218 BTC	10,735,507,983 USD	8.65% (95.93%)
10 - 100	131602	0.6% (0.68%)	4,348,552 BTC	31,883,178,092 USD	25.69% (87.28%)
100 - 1,000	15651	0.07% (0.08%)	3,687,811 BTC	27,038,686,890 USD	21.79% (61.59%)
1,000 - 10,000	1530	0.01% (0.01%)	3,338,428 BTC	24,477,042,089 USD	19.72% (39.8%)
10,000 - 100,000	111	0% (0%)	2,941,590 BTC	21,567,458,295 USD	17.38% (20.08%)
100,000 - 1,000,000	3	0% (0%)	457,218 BTC	3,352,282,885 USD	2.7% (2.7%)

Addresses richer than

1 USD	100 USD	1,000 USD	10,000 USD	100,000 USD	1,000,000 USD	10,000,000 USD
15,451,012	5,125,085	2,014,741	505,564	119,653	10,734	1,033

Source: bitinfocharts.com[109]

According to this analysis, almost 90% of value is owned by fewer than 0.7% of the addresses. Of course, we have to treat this kind of analysis with some caution. Some large wallets are controlled by exchanges who take custody of coins on behalf of a large number of users. So the table might be overstating the centralisation of Bitcoin ownership. Against that, some people might spread out their bitcoins across a large number of wallets in order to not attract attention. This is very easy to do. So the table might be understating the centralisation of Bitcoin ownership. However, it remains highly likely that, just as in the non-crypto world, very few people probably own the vast proportion of the value. Now, there's a surprise.

Upgrades to the Bitcoin Protocol

Upgrades to the Bitcoin network and protocols are also fairly centralised. Changes are suggested in 'Bitcoin Improvement Proposals' (BIPs). These are documents that anyone may

---

109   https://bitinfocharts.com/top-100-richest-bitcoin-addresses.html
retrieved 27 May 2018

write but, but they all end up on a single website: https://
github.com/bitcoin/bips. If it gets written into the Bitcoin
Core software on Github, https://github.com/bitcoin/Bitcoin,
it forms part of an upgrade, the next version of 'Bitcoin Core'
which is the most commonly used software, or 'reference
implementation,' of the protocol. As we have seen, this is run
by the vast majority of participants.

Transaction Fees

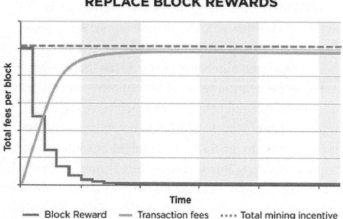

TRANSACTION FEES ARE MEANT TO
REPLACE BLOCK REWARDS

In theory, the transaction fees collected per block is meant to
compensate for the decrease in block reward as the network
gets more popular over time. The reality is that this doesn't
seem to be working out.

Source: tradeblock.com[110]

The chart shows that except for a brief spike at the end of 2017, the total transaction fees have stayed stubbornly low at approximately 200 BTC per week. Compare this with the new 12,600 BTC generated from coinbase rewards per week (12.5 BTC per block x 6 blocks/hour x 24 hours/day x 7 days/week = 12,600 BTC, a figure which reduced by half in 2016, and is estimated to half again in 2020). Without significant increase in transaction fees to compensate, clearly the economics of Bitcoin mining will change.

Bitcoin's Predecessors

Bitcoin, like most innovative innovations, was not created in a vacuum. Bitcoin was built by drawing from previous experiences and piecing together various tried-and-tested concepts in an innovative way to come up with new characteristics for decentralised digital cash.

---

110   https://tradeblock.com/bitcoin/historical/1w-f-tfee_per_tot-01071

Below are some technologies and ideas that may have directly or indirectly inspired Bitcoin:

Digicash

It is hard to overstate the impact that David Chaum had on the movement towards electronic cash, by which he meant a privacy preserving digital asset that could settle financial obligations. Chaum, an early cypherpunk, described this concept in 1983 in a paper entitled '*Blind signatures for untraceable payments*' in the journal *Advances in Cryptology Proceedings*. He wanted a bank to be able to create digitally signed digital lumps of cash for their customers. The customers could spend the digital cash at shops, who would then redeem the digital cash with the bank. When the merchant redeemed the digital cash, the bank would see that the digital cash was good, but it did not know which of its customers the digital cash had originally been assigned to. The individual transactions were therefore anonymous as far as the bank was concerned. Digicash was the Amsterdam based company incorporated to commercialise this technology. The system was called eCash, sometimes *Chaumian* eCash, with the tokens themselves called CyberBucks. Although a few banks did some trials with CyberBucks, Digitcash filed for bankruptcy in 1998, unable to secure a deal to keep it afloat.

b-money

In November 1998, Wei Dai, an American-educated cryptography researcher and cypherpunk, published a short paper[111] describing b-money under two protocols. b-money would operate on an untraceable network where senders and receivers would be identified only by digital pseudonyms (i.e., public keys). Every message would be signed by its sender and encrypted to its receiver. Transactions would be broadcast to a network of servers who would keep track of account balances and update them when they received signed transaction messages. Money creation would be agreed by the participants in a periodic auction.

Hashcash

In 1992, Cynthia Dwork and Moni Naor described a technique for reducing spam (junk email) in their paper,[112] *'Pricing via Processing or Combatting Junk Mail,'* by creating a hoop that email senders would have to jump through before sending emails. Email senders would have to attach a kind of *proof* or receipt to their outbound emails demonstrating that they had incurred a very small 'cost'. Recipients would reject inbound emails without these receipts. The 'costs' incurred by the senders would be tiny at normal email volumes, but add up and discourage spammers who send out millions of emails. The 'cost' wasn't a payment to a third party, but it would be incurred as 'work' in the form of repeated calculations that had to be made, to ensure an email would be accepted. So the receipt would be a 'proof' that repeated calculations, or 'work' had been done, leading to the phrase 'proof-of-work'.

---

111   http://www.weidai.com/bmoney.txt

112   https://link.springer.com/content/pdf/10.1007%2F3-540-48071-4_10.pdf

In 1997, Adam Back proposed a similar idea[113] and described a 'partial hash collision-based postage scheme' which he named 'Hashcash'. Bitcoin mining uses this concept of forcing someone to do some work, and proving they have done it, before allowing them access to a resource. He followed up in 2002 with a paper,[114] *'Hashcash—A Denial of Service Counter-Measure,'* describing improvements and applications of proof-of-work, including hashcash as a minting mechanism for Wei Dai's b-money electronic cash proposal.

e-gold

E-gold was a website opened in 1996 and operated by Gold & Silver Reserve Inc. (G&SR) under the name 'e-gold Ltd' that allowed customers to open accounts and trade units of gold between each other. The digital units were backed by gold stored in a bank safe deposit box in Florida, USA. E-gold didn't ask users to prove their identity, and this made it attractive for the underworld. It became very successful. It was reported to have up to 3.5 million accounts in 165 countries in 2005 with 1,000 new accounts opening every day[115], but the website was eventually shut down due to fraud and allegations of facilitation of crime[116]. Unlike Bitcoin, it had a centralised ledger.

---

113   http://www.hashcash.org/papers/announce.txt

114   http://www.hashcash.org/papers/hashcash.pdf

115   https://www.wired.com/2009/06/e-gold/

116   https://www.justice.gov/usao-md/pr/over-566-million-forfeited-e-gold-accounts-involved-criminal-offenses

Liberty Reserve

Like e-gold, Liberty Reserve, based in Costa Rica, allowed customers to open accounts with few personal details, nothing more than a name, email address, and birth date. Liberty Reserve made no attempts to verify these, even for obviously false accounts named 'Mickey Mouse' and so on. During an investigation[117], a US agent opened a functional account with a username 'ToStealEverything' in the name of 'Joe Bogus' who lived at '123 Fake Main Street' in 'Completely Made Up City, New York' and wrote that it would be used for 'shady things'. As a result of its relaxed controls, Liberty Reserve was used extensively for money laundering and other criminal proceeds, more than $6 billion according to ABC News[118]. It served over 1 million customers before it was shut down in 2013 by the US Government under the Patriot Act.

Napster

Napster was a peer-to-peer filesharing system that was live between 1999 and 2001. It was created by Shawn Fanning and Sean Parker, and was popular with people who liked to share music, particularly in mp3 format, and who didn't like to pay for it. The idea was to allow anyone to copy and share content saved on users' hard drives. At its peak the service had about 80 million registered users. It was eventually shut down because its relaxed approach to the sharing of copyright material wasn't appreciated by those with interests vested in that material.

---

117   https://www.theatlantic.com/magazine/archive/2015/05/bank-of-the-underworld/389555/

118   http://abcnews.go.com/US/black-market-bank-accused-laundering-6b-criminal-proceeds/story?id=19275887

Napster's technical weakness was that it had central servers. When a user searched for a song, their machine would send the search request to Napster's central servers, which would return a list of computers storing that song and would allow the user to connect to one of them (this is the peer-to-peer bit) to download the song. Although Napster itself didn't host the material, it made it easy for users to discover others who did. Centralised services and entities running those services are easy to shut down, and so it was, to have its role replaced by BitTorrent, a *decentralised* peer-to-peer file sharing system.

Mojo Nation

According to CEO Jim McCoy, Mojo Nation was an open source project that was a cross between Napster and eBay. Launched in or around 2000[119], it combined filesharing with microtransactions of a token called Mojo, so that file sharers could be compensated for sharing content. It split files into encrypted chunks and distributed them such that no single computer would host an entire file. Mojo Nation failed to gain traction, but Zooko Wilcox-O'Hearn, who worked on Mojo Nation later founded Zcash, a cryptocurrency focused on transaction privacy.

BitTorrent

BitTorrent is a successful peer-to-peer filesharing protocol that is still in wide use today. It was developed by BitTorrent Inc, a company cofounded by Bram Cohen who worked on Mojo Nation. BitTorrent is popular with those sharing music

---

119   https://www.wired.com/2000/07/get-your-music-mojo-working/

and movies, users who may once have used Napster. It is decentralised: each search request is made from user to user rather than via a central search server. As there is no central point of administration, it is hard to censor and shut down.

As a theme, whether we consider money (e-Gold, Liberty Reserve, Bitcoin etc), or data (Napster, BitTorrent, etc), the evidence shows that decentralised protocols are more resilient to being shut down than services with a central point of control or failure. I expect the trend of decentralisation to continue in the future, driven in part by concerns that authorities are overextending their reach into private social matters.

Bitcoin's Early History

Bitcoin's history is colourful, more colourful than some received wisdom might have it. Some Bitcoin proponents say 'Bitcoin (the protocol) has never been hacked,' but they are wrong. Bitcoin *has* been hacked. Here is a selection of events from historyofBitcoin.org[120] and the Bitcoin Wiki[121] with my personal comments about these events.

2007

A pseudonymous Satoshi Nakamoto began working on Bitcoin.

---

120   http://historyofBitcoin.org/

121   https://en.bitcoin.it/wiki/Category:History

18 Aug 2008

The website bitcoin.org was registered using anonymousspeech.com, a broker that registers domains on behalf of customers who can choose to remain anonymous. This shows how important privacy was to the person or group involved in Bitcoin.

31 Oct 2008

The Bitcoin whitepaper, written under the pseudonym Satoshi Nakamoto, was released on an obscure but fascinating mailing list metzdowd.com that is much loved by cypherpunks. Wikipedia has this to say about cypherpunks:

> *A cypherpunk is any activist advocating widespread use of strong cryptography and privacy–enhancing technologies as a route to social and political change. Originally communicating through the cypherpunks electronic mailing list, informal groups aimed to achieve privacy and security through proactive use of cryptography. Cypherpunks have been engaged in an active movement since the late 1980s.*

This short whitepaper is regarded by Bitcoin believers as sort of bible.

3 Jan 2009

The genesis (first) block was mined. At that moment, the first bitcoins, fifty of them, were created out of thin air and recorded on Bitcoin's blockchain in the first block—block zero. The transaction that contains the mining reward, the so called 'coinbase' transaction, contains the text:

*'The Times 03/Jan/2009 Chancellor on brink of second
bailout for banks'*

The text refers to a headline of the UK newspaper *The Times*.
This is regarded as proof that the block cannot have been
mined significantly earlier than that date, and the headline
was presumably chosen deliberately for its implication: When
banks fail, their losses are socialized; here is Bitcoin—it
doesn't need banks.

Source: thrivemovement.com[122]

---

122   http://www.thrivemovement.com/Bitcoin-lessons-thriving-world.blog

So beware of people who say they were 'in Bitcoin' before 2009! I have been on a number of panels where other panellists try to establish credibility by saying just how early they were involved in Bitcoin. Sometimes, in their enthusiasm, they try to convince eager listeners that they were there before 2009...

An interesting aside: The 50 BTC mined in the first block are unspendable. They sit in address 1A1zP1eP5QGefi2DMPTfTL5SLmv7DivfNa, but the account holder, presumably Satoshi, whoever he, she, or they may be, is unable to transfer them to anyone else due to some quirk in the code.

9 Jan 2009

Version 0.1 of the Bitcoin software was released by Satoshi Nakamoto, along with its source code. This allowed people to review the code, and download and run the software, becoming both bookkeepers and miners. Bitcoin was thus accessible to anyone who wanted to download and use it. Developers were able to scrutinise the code and build on it if they wanted to contribute.

12 Jan 2009

The first Bitcoin payment was made from Satoshi's address to Hal Finney's address in block 170[123], the first recorded movement of bitcoins. Hal Finney was a cryptographer, cypherpunk, and coder, and some people believe he was partly behind the Satoshi pseudonym.

---

123   https://blockchain.info/
block/00000000d1145790a8694403d4063f323d499e655c83426834d4ce2f8dd4a2ee

6 Feb 2010

The first Bitcoin exchange, 'The Bitcoin Market,' was created by bitcointalk.org forum user 'dwdollar'[124].

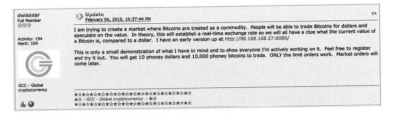

Previously, people traded bitcoins, but in a relatively unstructured way in chat rooms and message boards. An exchange is the first step towards making it easier for people to buy or sell bitcoins and increasing price transparency.

22 May 2010

Pizza day! This was the first documented time bitcoins were used to pay for something in the real world. Laszlo Hanyecz, a programmer in Florida, USA, offered to pay 10,000 BTC for a pizza on the bitcointalk forum[125].

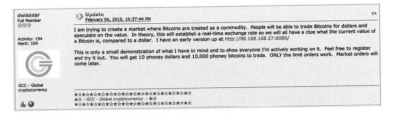

---

124   https://bitcointalk.org/index.php?topic=20.0

125   https://bitcointalk.org/index.php?topic=137.0

Another developer Jeremy Sturdivant ('jercos') took up the offer and called Domino's Pizza (not Papa Johns as frequently reported) and had two pizzas delivered to Laszlo. He received 10,000 BTC[126] from Laszlo.

Here is the transaction[127]:

Laszlo kept the offer open and, over the next month, received a number of pizzas for 10,000 BTC each time, before cancelling the offer:

This is the first transaction where bitcoins were used for economic activity other than a straight buy or sell.

---

126   http://bitcoinwhoswho.com/index/jercosinterview

127   https://blockchain.info/tx/
a1075db55d416d3ca199f55b6084e2115b9345e16c5cf302fc80e9d5fbf5d48d?

17 Jul 2010

Jed McCaleb (who has more recently founded Stellar, a cryptocurrency platform based on Ripple), converted his card trading exchange into a Bitcoin trading exchange. 'Mt Gox,' usually pronounced 'mount gox,' stands for 'Magic: The Gathering Online eXchange'. *Magic: The Gathering* is a collectable card game, and the website was used initially to trade cards before it was converted to a Bitcoin exchange. Initially, you could fund your Mt Gox account using PayPal, but in October, they switched to Liberty Reserve. Mt Gox would eventually collapse in Nov 2013–Feb 2014, but in its heyday, it was the largest and most well-known and well-used exchange.

15 Aug 2010

Bitcoin's protocol got hacked. Beware the popular narrative that says, 'Bitcoin itself has never been hacked'. A potential vulnerability was discovered, and someone exploited this vulnerability in block 74,638 to create 184 billion bitcoins for themselves. This strange transaction was quickly discovered and, with the consent of the majority of the community, the whole blockchain was 'forked,' reverting it to a previous state (we will discuss forks later).

So much for the immutability of Bitcoin's blockchain: there are always exceptions.

The bug was fixed. Bruno Skvorc has written a good explanation of how it happened on his blog *bitfalls*.

com[128], and the bitcointalk forum has a thread[129] where key
developers discussed the bug.

If anyone says Bitcoin hasn't been hacked, ask them 'What
about the integer overflow bug in August 2010 where
someone sent themselves 184 billion bitcoins?'

18 Sep 2010

The first mining pool, Slush's pool, mined its first block. A
mining pool is an organisation where multiple participants
combine their hash power to give themselves a better chance
of winning a block. The participants split the rewards between
them in proportion to their hash power contributions, a
bit like a lottery syndicate. Mining pools have grown in
significance over time.

---

128   https://bitfalls.com/2018/01/14/curious-case-184-billion-bitcoin/

129   https://bitcointalk.org/index.php?topic=822.0

7 Jan 2011

12 BTC were exchanged for $300,000,000,000,000. This
is probably the highest exchange rate Bitcoin has ever
achieved. The dollars in question, however, were Zimbabwean
dollars. The Zimbabwean dollar is a good example of what
can go wrong in a failing economy, and a reminder that fiat
currencies need to be well managed.

9 Feb 2011

On the Mt Gox Bitcoin exchange, Bitcoin reached parity with
the US dollar (1 BTC = 1 USD).

6 Mar 2011

Jed McCaleb sold the Mt Gox website and exchange to a
French entrepreneur Mark Karpeles who was living in Tokyo.
Jed sold it on the premise that Mark would do a better job
expanding it. Alas Mark did not live up to these hopes. Mt
Gox filed for bankruptcy in 2014 and Mark eventually landed
up in jail.

27 Apr 2011

VirWoX, a website that allowed customers to convert between
fiat currencies and Linden Dollars (the virtual currency
for use within the computer game Second Life), integrated
Bitcoin. People could now exchange directly between bitcoins
and Linden Dollars. This was possibly the first virtual
currency to virtual currency exchange.

1 Jun 2011

WIRED magazine published a famous article, 'Underground website lets you buy any drug imaginable,'[130] written by Adrian Chen. It described a website called The Silk Road, launched in Feb 2011 and run by twenty-seven-year old Ross William Ulbricht under the nickname 'Dread Pirate Roberts,'[131]. The Silk Road was described as a kind of 'eBay for drugs'—a darknet market, only accessible through the special browser Tor[132], which matched buyers and sellers of drugs and other illegal or questionable paraphernalia. Bitcoins were used as the payment mechanism.

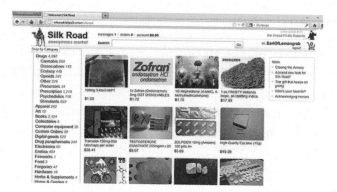

Source: stopad.io[133].

---

130   https://www.wired.com/2011/06/silkroad-2/ and I have also seen this on Gawker, http://gawker.com/the-underground-website-where-you-can-buy-any-drug-imag-30818160 but I am not sure which came first of if they were simultaneously printed.

131   This is a reference to the 1973 film *The Princess Bride*, and Dread Pirate Roberts was, it turns out, a pseudonym for a series of ruthless pirates who handed the pseudonym from individual to individual once each was wealthy enough to retire.

132   https://www.torproject.org/

133   https://stopad.io/blog/what-is-the-dark-web-and-how-it-is-different-from-deep-web

Here is how the article describes Bitcoin:

As for transactions, Silk Road doesn't accept credit cards, PayPal or any other form of payment that can be traced or blocked. The only money good here is Bitcoins.

Bitcoins have been called a 'cryptocurrency,' the online equivalent of a brown paper bag of cash. Bitcoins are a peer-to-peer currency, not issued by banks or governments, but created and regulated by a network of other Bitcoin holders' computers. (The name 'Bitcoin' is derived from the pioneering file sharing technology BitTorrent.) They are purportedly untraceable and have been championed by cyberpunks, libertarians and anarchists who dream of a distributed digital economy outside the law, one where money flows across borders as free as bits.

To purchase something on Silk Road, you need first to buy some bitcoins using a service like Mt. Gox Bitcoin Exchange. Then, create an account on Silk Road, deposit some bitcoins, and start buying drugs. One Bitcoin is worth about $8.67, though the exchange rate fluctuates wildly every day.

This was the first time Bitcoin came to the attention of a wide audience. The Silk Road was eventually taken down by US authorities in October 2013, though many copycats have taken its place.

14 Jun 2011

Wikileaks and other organisations began to accept bitcoins for donations. Bitcoin is attractive for these organisations owing to its censorship resistance. While is it relatively easy for a government to lean on traditional payment systems (banks, PayPal, etc) to monitor transactions, block assets and freeze accounts, cryptocurrencies provide an alternative funding mechanism. Whether this is good or bad, of course, is a matter of opinion...

20 Jun 2011

Possibly the first documented evidence[134] of a physical brick-and-mortar merchant accepting Bitcoin as a means of payment. Room 77, a restaurant based in Berlin, Germany sold fast food for bitcoins.

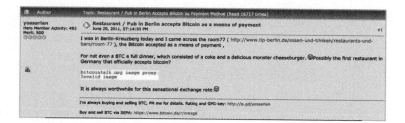

2 Sep 2011

Mike Caldwell started creating physical bitcoins which he called Casacius coins. They are physical discs of metal, each with a unique private key embedded behind a hologram sticker. Each coin's private key is linked to an address that is funded with a specified amount of bitcoins, as depicted on the coin.

---

134   https://bitcointalk.org/index.php?topic=20148.0

Source: Bitcoin wiki[135].

These Casascius coins are the physical representations used in many stock photos used for media articles about bitcoins. They are also prized as collector's items and cost much more than the value of the bitcoins contained in them, especially the first edition, which had a spelling mistake.

8 May 2012

Satoshi Dice was a gambling website launched on 24 April 2012. Users could send bitcoins to specific addresses with a chance of winning up to 64,000 times their original stake. Each address had a different payout and a different chance of winning. On 8 May, it became responsible for over half the transaction volume on the Bitcoin blockchain. Satoshi Dice was created by libertarian Eric Voorhees and was extremely popular. Early adopters seemed to have a penchant for gambling, and there wasn't much else they could do with their bitcoins.

---

135   https://en.bitcoin.it/wiki/File:Casascius_25btc_size_compare.jpg

It was an interesting gambling system. Unlike other online casinos where users have to trust that the house is not cheating, Satoshi Dice was *provably fair*, using deterministic cryptographic hashes as the random number generators. Of course, the house had an edge, but the edge was small, known (1.9%), and was demonstrably adhered to.

This development started the debate about what 'spamming' a network with transactions means when there are no terms of service. It also started the community thinking about what fair transaction fees should be.

28 Nov 2012

Bitcoin's first block reward halving day: On block 210,000
the block reward halved from 50 BTC to 25 BTC, slowing the
rate of generation of bitcoins. Transaction fees then were
insignificant, so this halving day reduced by half each block's
financial reward for miners.

2 May 2013

The first two-way Bitcoin ATM was launched in San Diego,
California. This was a machine where you could buy bitcoins
or sell your bitcoins for cash. This sparked a wave of one-way
Bitcoin vending machines (cash in, BTC out) and two-way
Bitcoin ATMs being installed around the world. Many were
found to be unprofitable, as demand didn't meet expectations.
At some stage in Singapore there were more than twenty
machines, but there are very few in evidence today.

Jul 2013

The first Bitcoin ETF (Exchange Traded Fund) proposal
was filed with the United States Securities and Exchange
Commission. Tyler and Cameron Winklevoss, twins made
famous in the film *The Social Network* about Facebook, were
responsible for this filing. An ETF could make investment
into Bitcoin more accessible to the public, as many funds
are allowed to buy ETFs but not bitcoins directly. A number
of other Bitcoin ETFs, have been filed for approval but as of
mid-2018, I am not aware of any Bitcoin ETF anywhere in

the world[136]. Other instruments exist that trade on traditional financial exchanges and provide exposure to the price of Bitcoin.

6 Aug 2013

Bitcoin was classified as a currency by a judge in Texas, USA. This was one of many arguments and determinations of what Bitcoin is: Currency? Property? A security? Some other financial asset? A New Thing? There is still no global definition, and there may never be a globally consistent one.

Bitcoin's categorisation has tax and other implications that differ by jurisdiction. The classification of bitcoins and cryptocurrencies may mean the difference between zero or punitive tax rates in any given tax regime, and therefore may have an impact on its potential adoption and usage (see below, 20 Aug 2013).

9 Aug 2013

Bitcoin's price became searchable through Bloomberg software, which is popular with traders in traditional financial markets. Bloomberg used the ticker 'XBT' to represent Bitcoin, consistent with ISO currency code standards. With ISO currency codes (e.g., USD, GBP, etc), the first two letters denote the country and the third letter denotes the currency unit. The symbol 'BTC,' if adopted, would indicate a currency of Bhutan[137]. Precious metals such as gold (XAU),

---

136   Though there are some ETFs that can contain some bitcoins, for example the ARK Innovation ETF http://www.etf.com/sections/features-and-news/barely-any-bitcoin-left-ark-etfs

137   https://en.wikipedia.org/wiki/ISO_3166-1

silver (XAG), palladium (XPD), and platinum (XPT) are
also considered a 'currency' but start with X as they are
not associated with a country. Bitcoin follows the currency
standard for precious metals.

20 Aug 2013

Bitcoins were ruled as private money in Germany[138], with tax
exemptions if held for more than a year. The tax treatment of
bitcoins and cryptocurrencies is a major point of contention,
especially in the USA where the buying and selling of bitcoins
attracts capital gains. If you bought a Bitcoin at $100, then,
after its price had risen to say $1,000, you exchanged it for
Ether, another cryptocurrency, then you would have to record
that as a capital gain of $900 and pay tax on that capital
gain, even though your assets were still in cryptocurrency
and you hadn't realised that gain in USD. So, depending on
jurisdiction, tax authorities may well consider the exchange of
cryptocurrencies as selling and buying with fiat currency and
want to see those transactions taxed.

22 Nov 2013

Richard Branson, owner of Virgin Galactic, announced
he would accept bitcoins as payment for a flight to space.
Bitcoins and space travel—what a great time to be alive!

28 Feb 2014

After a long saga of hacks, glitches, poor management
practices, lost coins, suspended withdrawals, failed banking
transactions, and other incompetence, Mt Gox finally filed for

---

138   https://www.cnbc.com/id/100971898

bankruptcy protection in Japan in Feb 2014. The company said it had lost almost 750,000 of its customers' bitcoins and around 100,000 of its own bitcoins, together worth around $473 million near the time of the filing. There are numerous theories as to what happened, the most compelling being a combination of hackers draining the Mt Gox hot wallets and management incompetence. The whole escapade, including the bankruptcy proceedings, was in such shambles and even the full creditor list (containing full names and amounts claimed) was leaked. The story of Mt Gox deserves its own book, but for a summary it is worth reading the Wikipedia entry[139] about this sorry story.

After Mt Gox's implosion, Bitfinex became the world's largest exchange for a while.

Creditors to the bankrupt estate have not yet been compensated, and if they ever will be, it will be in Japanese yen at a rate that roughly equates to $400 per Bitcoin—less than a tenth of Bitcoin's value at time of writing.

Bitcoin's Price

Like gold or oil or any other asset, bitcoins have a value that can be priced in USD or any other currency. This means there are people who are willing to exchange BTC with USD, usually using cryptocurrency exchanges, marketplaces which attract buyers and sellers. On exchanges you can see indications of supply and demand for cryptocurrencies at any price level (more on these later). You can also buy and sell bitcoins with

---

139   https://en.wikipedia.org/wiki/Mt._Gox

anyone in the world, physically on the streets or over the internet, or using brokers who mediate between buyers and sellers, or who trade on their own behalf. To trade BTC, you simply need the ability to send or receive BTC and the ability to receive or send the other asset, usually a local currency.

Like any other market-traded asset, the price of Bitcoin fluctuates with supply and demand. At any point in time, people trade at prices that they are comfortable buying or selling at. If there is more buying pressure and people want to buy more bitcoins, prices will increase. If there is selling pressure and people want to sell more bitcoins for fiat currencies, then the price at which the bitcoins change hands will drop. Later we will go into more detail about how cryptocurrencies and tokens can be priced, but here we will look at specifically Bitcoin's price.

Bitcoin's Price History

Bitcoin's price has been a wild ride. A recent price rise to almost $20,000 USD per Bitcoin and subsequent fall the $6,000 levels has caught the media's attention:

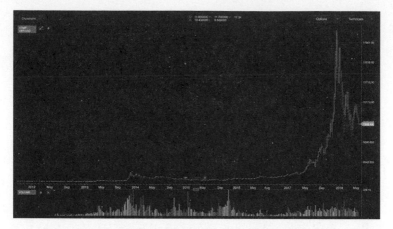

2018: $20,000 per Bitcoin and a 60% crash? That is nuts!

But this is not the first time Bitcoin has been this volatile. Bitcoin appears to be cyclically volatile, with each cycle as dizzy as the previous.

Here is the 2013/14 bubble in detail:

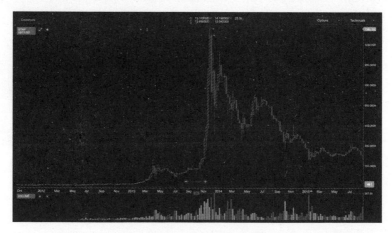

2013/14: $1,200 per Bitcoin and an 80% crash? That is also nuts!

The peak price on Mt Gox was almost $1,200 per Bitcoin, and then crashed to below $200, rebounded and then traded lower and lower over to the $200-300 range during the 'Bitcoin winter' of 2014. These were painful times for holders of Bitcoin, if good times for far-sighted buyers. There are different theories for the cause of this bubble including the activities of trading bots—programs that automatically buy and sell—and the fact that you couldn't withdraw fiat from Mt Gox. Anyone wanting to withdraw value from Mt Gox had to buy bitcoins (pushing the price up) and withdraw bitcoins. The Chinese government then announced that they were going to ban Bitcoin trading and the price crashed.

But this was by no means the first bubble. Here is early 2013, close up, when in April the price rose from $15 to a peak of $266 before crashing to around $50:

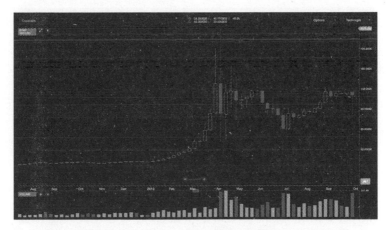

Early 2013: $266 per Bitcoin and an 80% crash? That is nuts again!

A common theory about this was that people in Cyprus were buying bitcoins. At the time, there was financial chaos in Cyprus. Some bank accounts were frozen, some ATMs were empty, and one-off taxes were applied to large bank account balances. Another theory was that some large institutional funds were buying bitcoins to build a position, buying up available supply. I am not sure how likely these theories are to have directly affected prices, but all it takes to move markets is for people to believe stories.

This bubble may seem quaint as the numbers are smaller than the range we are used to today, but an 80% drop is an 80% drop, as stressful then as it would be today.

Further back in time, we have the June 2011 bubble:

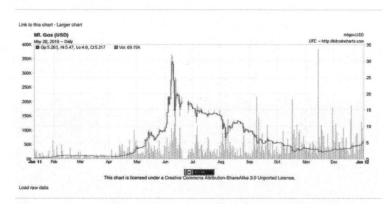

2011: $31 per Bitcoin and an 80% crash? That is more nuts!

Articles published in tech-focused online magazines *WIRED* and Gawker helped to generate interest in Bitcoin, pushing the price from about $3 to a high of about $31. Over the next 6 months the price slowly fell to below $5, more than 80% down.

And here is the first bubble in July 2010:

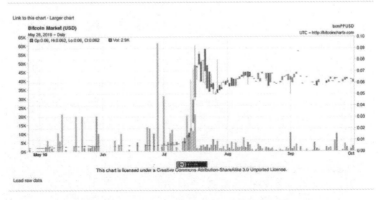

2010: $0.09 per Bitcoin and a 40% crash? Even that is nuts!

An article about a new version of the Bitcoin software was published in a popular technical magazine *Slashdot*[140] and interest was generated, pushing the price on the Bitcoin Market up from less than 1 cent per Bitcoin to almost 10 cents. The price then fell 40% and traded sideways at about 6 cents per Bitcoin for a few months before increasing again.

Storing Bitcoins

You may hear that *bitcoins* are stored in wallets. If this were true, then if you copied your wallet you'd own double the number of bitcoins. Clearly you couldn't have digital money that works this way. So no, bitcoins are not stored in wallets.

So where are bitcoins stored? Well, *ownership* of bitcoins is recorded on Bitcoin's blockchain, which is, as we have seen, the database replicated on over 10,000 computers around the world containing every Bitcoin transaction ever. So you can look at that database and see that at this time, a specific address has a specific number of bitcoins associated with it. For example, the blockchain would store the fact that the address 1Jco97X5FbCkev7ksVDpRtjNNi4zX6Wy4r had had 0.5 BTC sent to it, and that those 0.5 BTC have not yet been sent elsewhere. Bitcoin's blockchain doesn't store *balances* of accounts (it is not a list of account numbers and corresponding BTC balances), it stores *transactions*. So to get the current balance of any account, you need to look at all the inbound and outbound transactions through that account.

Bitcoin wallets store *private keys* (not bitcoins!) and their software makes it easy for the user of the wallet to see how many coins they control and to make payments. If you cloned your wallet, you would be cloning your private keys, not doubling your bitcoins.

Software Wallets

Bitcoin wallets are apps that can at least:

- Create new Bitcoin addresses and store the corresponding private keys

- Display your addresses to someone who wants to send you a payment

- Display how many bitcoins are in your addresses

- Make Bitcoin payments

Let's explore each of these capabilities.

Address Creation

Creating new Bitcoin addresses is an offline operation and involves creating a public and private key pair. You can do this, if you like, using dice[141]. This is different from any other account creation process where you have to ask a third party to create an account for you, for example asking your bank or Facebook to assign you an account.

- Step 1: Generate some randomness and use it to pick a number from 1 to 2256-1. This is your private key.

- Step 2: Do some maths on it to generate a public key.

- Step 3: Hash your public key twice to create your Bitcoin address.

- Step 4: Save the private key and its corresponding address.[142]

So you assign yourself an address without asking or checking with anyone to see if it already taken. This sounds scary. What if someone else has already chosen your private key? The short answer is that this is extremely unlikely. 2256 is a big number, 78 digits long, and you can pick any number up to that. Your chance of winning the UK lottery is 1 in 13,983,816—which only has eight digits. A number with seventy-eight digits is astronomically large. In theory

---

141   William Swanson has instructions on his blog https://www.swansontec.com/bitcoin-dice.html

142   It is recommended to encrypt the private key first with a memorable passphrase.

someone could deliberately generate millions or billions of accounts per second and check them for coins to steal, but the number of valid accounts is so humongous that they'd be doing it forever before finding a single account that has been used before. In practice, however, weaknesses can exist, and they rely on exploiting flaws in the random number generation for the private keys. If there is a flaw in the randomness when generating your private key, this flaw could be exploited to reduce the search space for a thief[143].

Address Display

When someone wants to send you bitcoins, you need to tell them your address—like telling someone your bank account number so they can send you money. There are a few ways to do this. One popular way is by showing it as a QR code.

Example Bitcoin address:
1LfSBaySpe6UBw4NoH9VLSGmnPvujmhFXV

Equivalent QR code:

QR codes are not magic. They are just text, encoded in a visual way that makes it easy for QR code scanners to read the code and convert it back into text.

---

143   As an analogy, if you used unbalanced dice that always landed on a 5 or a 6, then it would be easier for a thief to match your rolls.

Another way is just to copy and paste the address itself:

Account Balance

The wallet needs to access an up to date version of the blockchain in order to be aware of all the transactions going in and out of the addresses it is keeping tabs on. The wallet, software can do this by either storing the entire blockchain and keeping it up to date (this is called a full node wallet) or by connecting to a node elsewhere which does the heavy lifting (this is called a lightweight wallet).

A full node wallet would contain over a hundred gigabytes of data and would need to be constantly connected over the internet to other Bitcoin nodes. So in many cases, especially on mobile phones, this is not practical so the wallet software is lightweight and connects to a server which hosts the blockchain. The wallet software on the phone asks the server

'What's the balance of address x?' and 'Please give me all the transactions related to address y'.

Bitcoin Payments

As well as reading the account balances, the wallet needs to be able to make payments. To make a Bitcoin payment, the wallet generates a bundle of data called a 'transaction,' which includes references to the coins that are going to be spent (transaction inputs consisting of unspent outputs of previous transactions), and which accounts the coins will be sent to (new outputs). We saw this in an earlier section. This transaction is then digitally signed using the relevant private keys of the addresses holding the coins. Once signed, the transaction is sent to neighbouring nodes, via its server node if it is a lightweight wallet, or directly to other peers if it is a full node wallet. The transactions eventually find their way to miners who add them to blocks.

Other Features

Good wallet software has more functionality, including the ability to back up private keys (encrypted with a passphrase) either to a user's hard drive or to a cloud storage server somewhere, to generate one-time use addresses for privacy, to hold addresses and private keys for multiple cryptocurrencies. Some are even integrated with exchanges to allow users to convert between one cryptocurrency and another directly from within the wallet software.

Often wallets will allow you to split keys or set up addresses that require multiple digital signatures to spend from.

You can split a private key into several parts so that a certain threshold number of parts are needed to create the original private key. This is a process known as 'sharding' or 'splitting' a private key and a common example is 2-of-3 sharding where a private key is split into 3 parts, any 2 of which can be combined to regenerate the original key. Similarly you can have 2-of-4 or 3-of-4 or any combination of parts and total shards, generically *m-of-n*. One algorithm to do this is using Shamir's secret sharing[144]. This lets you split a key and store parts of it separately in different places, but with some resiliency in that, if you lose one or more pieces, it may not be catastrophic.

You can also create addresses that require multiple digital signatures to make payments from them. These are known as 'multi-sig' addresses[145]. Again, you can have 1-of-3, 2-of-3, 3-of-3, or generically m-of-n. This has a similar effect as sharding a single private key, but with slightly better security properties. This lets you create a transaction, sign it, send it over the internet in the clear, and let someone else sign it before it is considered a valid transaction (key splitting on the other hand only results in one signature). These addresses let you create systems where multiple people need to sign or approve a transaction, like some corporate cheques that need two signatures.

---

144   An easy way to understand a 2-of-3 key split is by considering a straight line on a graph. Let's say the point at which the line crosses the x-axis is the private key. You can pick any 3 points on the line. Any single point will not give you any information at all about where the line crosses the x-axis, but any two points will lock down the line and tell you exactly where it crosses the x-axis.

145   Technically these are 'P2SH' or 'Pay to Script Hash' addresses, but most people call them 'multi-sig'. These addresses start with the number '3' instead of the number '1'.

Software Wallet Examples

Examples of popular Bitcoin software wallets:

- Blockchain.info

- Electrum

- Jaxx

- Breadwallet

Note that I do not endorse these, and others are available. They could have bugs, and you must do your own research before picking a wallet to use. Most wallet software is open source, so you can investigate the code and see that there are no backdoors or vulnerabilities in the code, before you use them.

Hardware Wallets

Sometimes Bitcoin wallets can have a hardware component. Private keys are stored in chips on small handheld devices. Two popular hardware wallets are called 'Trezor' and 'Ledger Nano,' but there are others.

A Trezor

A Ledger Nano

These devices are specifically designed to store private keys securely and only respond to certain pre-programmed requests, for example, 'Please sign this transaction,' and not, 'Show me the private key you are storing'. Because the private key is stored on hardware that is not connected to the internet and can communicate with the outside world only via a limited set of pre-programmed interfaces, it is much harder for a hacker to gain access to the private keys.

The user interface software is run on an online machine. When it comes to the critical part of the transaction (the signing), the unsigned transaction is sent to the hardware wallet, which returns the signed transaction without revealing the private key.

Hardware wallets are more secure than software-only wallets, but nothing is infallible.

Cold Storage

The phrase 'keeping coins in cold storage' was popular in 2013-17 before hardware wallets became widely available. Remember, you don't store bitcoins, you store private keys. 'Cold storage' is keeping a note of those private keys on offline media, such as a piece of paper or a computer not connected to the internet. As private keys are just strings of characters like:

```
'KyVR7Y8xManWXf5hBj9sliFD56E8ds2Em71vxvN-
73zhT99ANYCxf'
```

There are many ways of storing them. You can memorise keys if you have a good memory, you can print them out on bits of paper, you can even engrave them on a ring that you wear, like Charlie Shrem did according to *WIRED Magazine*[146]. You could store them on an offline computer which, for increased security, should not have a modem or network card.

---

146   https://www.wired.com/2013/03/Bitcoin-ring/

You could write them down and put them in a bank's locked deposit box. These are all methods of storing your private keys offline.

If you do keep private keys on a device or printed out, you wouldn't want someone else to be able to see it and use it to steal your bitcoins. So one way of increasing security is to first encrypt the private key with a passphrase that you can remember and then store or print out the encrypted result. Passphrases are a lot easier to remember than private keys! This means that even if someone gets hold of the device or print out, they'd need to decrypt it with your passphrase before the private key is revealed. You can split keys or use multi-sig addresses for further security. This means if one part is found by a thief, it is useless without another part, and also means if one part is lost, the other two will still work. Remember, you are trying to simultaneously guard against two things: Loss of keys and theft of keys.

Hot Wallets

A hot wallet is a wallet that can sign and broadcast transactions without manual intervention. Exchanges, who control many bitcoins need to manage lots of Bitcoin payments, as we will see later. They often have a 'hot wallet' that controls a small proportion of their total bitcoins. Customers of exchanges like to withdraw bitcoins from the exchanges by clicking a button, causing an automated process to run to make and sign a Bitcoin transaction moving bitcoins from the exchange's hot wallet to the user's personal wallet. This means that somewhere, a private key belonging to the exchange must be stored on a 'hot' machine connected to the internet. There is a trade-off between security and convenience. Online machines are easier to hack than offline

machines, but can automate the process of creating and
broadcasting Bitcoin transactions. Due to this trade-off,
exchanges keep only a small fraction of BTC in hot wallets,
enough to satisfy customer demand, similar to banks that
keep a small amount of cash in tellers' tills at branches.

Buying and Selling Bitcoins

You can buy bitcoins from anyone who has them. Likewise
you can sell bitcoins to anyone who wants them. Fortunately,
there are various places where you are likely to find a group of
people willing to trade at competitive prices—exchanges.

Exchanges

Just like stock exchanges, Bitcoin or cryptocurrency
exchanges are places (usually websites) that attract traders.
However, you don't buy bitcoins from the exchange itself.
Just like a stock exchange, where you buy shares from
another *user* of the exchange rather than from the exchange
itself, a cryptocurrency exchange is the website that allows
people to buy and sell between themselves. The exchange
itself is just the location that brings together buyers and
sellers, and people go there because they know they are likely
to get the best prices there.

In financial services jargon, the exchange is an *order
matching engine*. It matches buyers and sellers. It also acts
as the *central clearing counterparty*. All matched trades
appear to be against the exchange rather than between the
customers directly, providing anonymity for customers.
Finally, the exchange is the *cash and asset custodian*. It

controls customers' fiat money in its bank account and cryptocurrencies in its wallet.

How Do Cryptocurrency Exchanges Work?

Exchanges are based in different countries and support different fiat currencies and different cryptocurrencies. They all work roughly the same way using the same four steps:

1. Create account

2. Deposit

3. Trade

4. Withdraw

Create Account

To use an exchange, just like a bank, you need to open an account. Exchanges are coming under increasing regulatory scrutiny due to the fact that they process large amounts of money. The top cryptocurrency exchanges match billions of dollars of buys and sells per day. Most legitimate exchanges follow a similar account opening procedure to banks, where new customers submit details and evidence of their identity, for example passport and utility bills[147]. The documentation needed may become more onerous in proportion to the value of fiat or cryptocurrencies you plan to transact, in a progressive risk-based approach. Exchanges are now big business and take these processes seriously.

---

147 I find that the user experience of account opening to be better with some cryptocurrency exchanges than traditional banks.

Once the exchange is satisfied, your account is created. Then you can log in and the next step is to deposit.

Deposit

Before you can attempt to buy or sell anything on an exchange, you need to fund your account. This is like funding an account with a traditional broker before being allowed to buy traditional financial assets.

Exchanges have bank accounts and cryptocurrency wallets. In order to fund your account you click on 'Deposit,' then follow the instructions. If you are funding your account with fiat currency (presumably in order to buy cryptocurrency), then the exchange will display a bank account for you to make a fiat currency transfer to. If you are funding your account with cryptocurrency, (presumably to sell for fiat currency or trade for a different cryptocurrency) then the exchange will display a cryptocurrency address for you to make a cryptocurrency transfer to.

Once exchange has detected the transfer to their bank account or cryptocurrency address, the balance will be reflected in your 'account balance' on the exchange's website, and you are ready to trade.

Trade

You can now trade up to the amounts you have deposited. For example, if you have deposited USD 10,000, then you can buy up to $10,000 worth of cryptocurrency. If you have deposited 3 BTC then you can sell up to 3 BTC for fiat or other cryptocurrency that is available at that exchange.

Prices are expressed in pairs that look something like this: BTC/USD or BTCUSD with a number such as 8,000. The way to read this is, 'One unit of BTC costs 8,000 USD'. Not all currencies can be traded for each other—it is really up to the exchange as to which pairs they enable. For example you may see BTCUSD and BTCEUR as trading pairs, meaning that you can trade BTC with USD and trade BTC with EUR, but you may not trade USD with EUR directly if you don't see EURUSD. In that case, to convert USD into EUR, you'd need to sell USD for BTC then use the BTC to buy EUR.

You will see a screen of other people's bids and offers. These are the prices at which they are willing to trade, and how much they are willing to trade at that price. You can decide either to match their prices, which will result in a matched trade, or submit your own orders which will rest in the order book until someone matches your price (if they ever do).

This is a *financial* market—this means that the larger amounts you want to buy or sell, the worse the prices will be. This is unlike a supermarket where you get a discount for buying in bulk. This is confusing for some people initially, but it is easily explained. When you buy something on an exchange, the exchange will naturally match you off with the person who is selling it at the cheapest price. When you've bought all that they have to offer, you have to find the next best price, which will be slightly higher. Selling uses the same logic: when you sell something, the exchange will match you with the person who is willing to pay the highest price for it. When you have sold as much to them as they want to buy, you will have to go to the next highest price which will be slightly lower.

Here is an example screenshot of Bitfinex, a typical exchange:

On the left-hand side is information about your balances in each currency (not shown here as this is a demonstration account). The main part of the screen shows a price and volume chart—Bitcoin's price and how many bitcoins have been traded. And the bottom third shows your open trades, i.e. your orders that haven't been matched yet, and the full order book, i.e. everyone's orders to buy and sell bitcoins and their amounts and price levels. A ticker is shown on the bottom right which streams the prices and amounts of matched trades in real-time.

Withdraw

Finally, you will want to withdraw fiat currency or cryptocurrency. To do so you have to instruct the exchange where you want it to go. If you are withdrawing fiat, you will need to tell the exchange your bank account details for them to make the transfer to you. If are withdrawing cryptocurrency, you need to tell the exchange your cryptocurrency address so that they can make the cryptocurrency transaction. Usually cryptocurrency

withdrawals are faster for the exchange to process than fiat
withdrawals because most exchanges have 'hot wallets,' as
described earlier, which automate the process of sending
small amounts of cryptocurrency back to users.

How Do Exchanges Make Money?

Exchanges make money by charging fees, just like your stock
broker. Different exchanges charge different fees in different
ways. Some charge withdrawal fees (e.g., if you withdraw
$10,000, then they might send you $9,950, and you would
receive even less than this because of bank fees). Others
charge by taking a small fraction of every trade you do,
usually by reducing the amount of whatever you are receiving.
For example, if you have $8,000 in your exchange account
and use it to buy BTC at a price of $8,000 per BTC, then you
will receive slightly less than 1 BTC, say 0.995 BTC. Trading
fees are usually determined by how much trading you do,
so if you trade more, the fee rate decreases according to a
published fee schedule.

Pricing On Different Exchanges

The price of any asset at a cryptocurrency exchange depends
on the participants using the exchange. Different exchanges
can have different prices for each cryptocurrency, because of
the different participants using the exchange and the different
levels of supply and demand on those exchanges. Usually the
prices are within a few percent of each other. If they get too
out of line, arbitrageurs step in and buy the bitcoins from the
exchange where they are cheap and sell them where they are
trading at a premium.

The extent to which arbitrageurs can keep doing this profitably affects how aligned the prices will ever become. To complete the circle of a successful arbitrage you need to move the fiat, and sometimes this will have costs and time delays. To buy bitcoins on the cheap exchange, you need to move fiat currency there, buy bitcoins, withdraw the bitcoins and send them to the more expensive exchange, then sell them, withdraw the fiat, and repeat the cycle. Each step has a financial cost and may not be instant. Some countries have currency controls, which hinder cross border exchange arbitrage. This is why there can be price differentials between exchanges for some time.

In late 2013-14, the exchange Mt Gox traded at a premium to its competitor Bitstamp, because people found they couldn't withdraw fiat from Mt Gox, so instead they had to buy bitcoins and withdraw the bitcoins instead. This created artificial demand for bitcoins on Mt Gox, and the arbitrage of buying cheap bitcoins on Bitstamp and selling them on Mt Gox didn't work because you couldn't get your fiat out of Mt Gox!

Regulation

Cryptocurrency exchanges perform activities that may be regulated in their operational jurisdictions. The fact that the instruments involved are cryptocurrencies does not necessarily mean that the exchanges escape local trading and tax disclosure requirements. However, depending on how the legislation is written, and owing to regulatory uncertainty, the classification of cryptocurrencies, exchanges currently operate in a legal grey area, especially crypto-only exchanges who allow trades between cryptocurrencies but not fiat.

Over the Counter (OTC) Brokers

When you buy on an exchange, you are buying from another customer of the exchange in quantities and prices agreed between you and the other customer. The exchange is only involved with the deal insofar as it acts as an escrow agent and has custody of *your* money and the *other person's bitcoins*, until they become *your* bitcoins and *the other person's* money. Every trade is shown to all other participants, and the order book moves in real time in response to the trading activity. One characteristic of exchange trading that a large trader may wish to avoid is that transparency. Sometimes you want to trade large amounts without other traders knowing, or without moving the market.

Enter the brokers. These are people or companies with whom you establish a relationship. Instead of showing a transparent order book of customer orders (as the exchanges do), the brokers will buy and sell directly with you, negotiating a price for the full amount that you want to transact, in what are known as 'block trades'. Trade details are not published to the public. They are private transactions in bulk and there is nothing illegal about this—this also happens in the traditional financial markets. Legitimate brokers also apply know-your-customer processes to establish your identity and may be bound by local disclosure requirements.

When you trade with a broker, there are two modes: the broker could act as *principal* to the trade, or as *agent*.

When the broker acts as *principal*, the deal is just between you and the broker. They are the counterparty to your trade. You tell them what you want to do (buy or sell) and in what amount, and they will tell you their best price and you can say yes or no. It is like a large wholesale trade, and the broker needs to have enough money or cryptocurrency to complete the deal. In accounting jargon, the trade is on the broker's balance sheet because the broker itself is trading with you. This is the case, for example, when you buy foreign currencies at an exchange desk at an airport.

When the broker acts as *agent*, the deal is between you and someone else with whom the broker is in touch. The broker acts as an intermediary who serves to provide anonymity to both parties. In accounting jargon, this is *off* the broker's balance sheet—it's not their money, they are just matching buyers and sellers. Generally the way this works is that you contact the broker and tell them what you want to do, then the broker will try to find another customer who wants to do the opposite to you (the other side of the trade). The broker will communicate price and amount information to both sides until the deal is agreed. The broker takes a fee from one or both customers for providing this service.

Due to the large amount of manual overhead and small margins, brokers usually have a minimum trade size below which, they won't pick up the phone. This can be anything from $10,000 to $100,000 per trade and seems to be increasing as the market matures.

Localbitcoins

What if you don't want to go to an exchange or use a broker or provide any sort of identification? There is a website, localbitcoins.com, which acts a bit like eBay for people wanting to buy and sell cryptocurrencies. People post prices at which they are willing to buy and sell bitcoins. You can browse the list to find someone nearby, and you then agree to send them money in return for bitcoins, either by meeting physically with fistfuls of banknotes, or by making bank transfers to their bank account. It is a bit like a bulletin board or eBay, and there is a reputation system with ratings and feedback comments. It also has an escrow function for the temporary custody of cryptocurrency.

Who is Satoshi Nakamoto?

We now come to the question, who is Satoshi Nakamoto and why does it matter?

Satoshi was the author of the Bitcoin whitepaper and was active on cypherpunk mailing lists where like-minded people discuss ways of reclaiming personal privacy in the electronic age. After publishing the original whitepaper, Satoshi continued to participate on Bitcoin forums until December 2013, and then vanished.

Satoshi also owns or controls a significant number of bitcoins, estimated in 2013 by cryptocurrency security consultant Sergio Lerner[148] at 1 million bitcoins. This represents just under 5% of the total 21m bitcoins that will ever be created, if the protocol rules don't change. At 2018, prices of around $10,000 per Bitcoin, this puts the nominal value of the bitcoins controlled by Satoshi at $10bn. If Satoshi ever moves any bitcoins thought to be associated with him/her, the community would immediately find out. The transactions

---

148   https://bitslog.wordpress.com/2013/04/24/satoshi-s-fortune-a-more-accurate-figure/

would be visible on the blockchain and addresses thought to be associated with Satoshi are monitored. This would almost certainly affect the price of Bitcoin[149].

Satoshi's real-world identity matters because, if the real person or group of people were discovered, their views and voice could dominate the future of Bitcoin. However, this centralisation is what they are trying to avoid. They would also have extremely high personal security risk. It is never a good idea for people to know (or even believe) that you have significant amounts of wealth, especially in cryptocurrency.

We have seen a number of high profile cryptocurrency owners publicly state that they have sold all their cryptocurrencies. In Jan 2018, Charlee Lee, founder of Litecoin (LTC) publicly stated that he sold or donated all his LTC[150]. In the same month, Steve Wozniak, founder of Apple, also stated that he had sold all of his Bitcoin[151]. Although they have their reasons, I suspect that the high personal risk of being known owners of high valued cryptocurrencies also feeds into this. I have had conversations with lucky Bitcoin owners who do not disclose their cryptocurrency wealth for precisely this reason.

There have been a number of high profile attempts at exposing Satoshi's identity. These are known in the industry as 'doxxings': the public revelation of an internet nickname's

---

149   Up or down? It could be either: any indication that the coins are being sold could cause a panic that Satoshi no longer believes in the project, but conversely, if the coins were sent to a 'burn' address that effectively renders the coins to be immobile, this would take the supply off the market, which could lead to increased confidence and a price increase.

150   https://www.reddit.com/r/litecoin/comments/7kzw6q/litecoin_price_tweets_and_conflict_of_interest/

151   http://nordic.businessinsider.com/steve-wozniak-stockholm-apple-seth-godin-nordic-business-forum--/

real-world identity. It is however highly unlikely that the real truth about Satoshi's identity is among these doxxings.

On 14 March 2014, a cover article for *Newsweek* magazine claimed that Satoshi was a sixty-four-year-old Japanese gentleman named Dorian Nakamoto (birth name Satoshi Nakamoto) living in California.

The article printed the suburb where Dorian lived and included a photograph of his house. This led to repeated harassment of Dorian and his family over the course of the next few weeks. Of course, Dorian was not Satoshi. To think that the privacy loving cypherpunk creator of a revolutionary unstoppable anonymous digital currency would use his own name as his pseudonym is so far-fetched as to be ludicrous. To identify his home address is unethical. Nevertheless, and despite the best efforts of the journalist concerned, anecdotal evidence suggests that after a period of great distress, Dorian is now enjoying, and I hope monetising, his newfound fame as the real fake Satoshi.

In December 2015, an article in *WIRED Magazine*[152] suggested that Dr Craig Wright, an Australian computer scientist, could be the mastermind behind Bitcoin. In March 2016, in interviews with *GQ magazine*[153], the *BBC*,[154] and *The Economist* newspaper,[155] Craig claimed to be the leader of the Satoshi team. He even published his own blog post, now taken offline, with these claims. Craig suggested that he didn't want to self-doxx, and that there may have been external pressures on him to do so. In June 2016, the *London Review of Books* published a long form article[156] where the journalist, Andrew O'Hagan, was able to spend an extended amount of time with Craig Wright. This is well worth a read in full, and my favourite part is:

> *Weeks later, I was in the kitchen of the house Wright was renting in London drinking tea with him when I noticed a book on the worktop called Visions of Virtue in Tokugawa Japan. I'd done some mugging up by then and was keen to nail the name thing.*
>
> *'So that's where you say you got the Nakamoto part?' I asked. 'From the eighteenth-century iconoclast who criticised all the beliefs of his time?'*
>
> *'Yes'.*

---

152   https://www.wired.com/2015/12/Bitcoins-creator-satoshi-nakamoto-is-probably-this-unknown-australian-genius/

153   http://www.gq-magazine.co.uk/article/Bitcoin-craig-wright

154   http://www.bbc.com/news/technology-36168863

155   https://www.economist.com/news/briefings/21698061-craig-steven-wright-claims-be-satoshi-nakamoto-Bitcoin

156   http://www.lrb.co.uk/v38/n13/andrew-ohagan/the-satoshi-affair

'What about Satoshi?'

*'It means "Ash," ' he said. 'The philosophy of Nakamoto is
the neutral central path in trade. Our current system needs
to be burned down and remade. That is what cryptocurrency
does—it is the phoenix ...'*

'So, Satoshi is the ash from which the phoenix ...'

*'Yes. And Ash is also the name of a silly Pokémon character.
The guy with Pikachu'. Wright smiled. 'In Japan the name of
Ash is Satoshi,' he said.*

*'So, basically, you named the father of Bitcoin after Pikachu's
chum?'*

*'Yes,' he said. 'That'll annoy the buggery out of a few people'.
This was something he often said, as if annoying people was
an art.*

Alas, the cryptographic proofs and demonstrations that Dr
Wright performed on and off camera were not watertight,
and the community is still undecided as to the veracity of
his claims.

A few other Satoshi suspects have been cypherpunk and PGP
developer Hal Finney, smart contract and Bit gold inventor
Nick Szabo, cryptographer and creator of b-money Wei Dai,
e-donkey, Mt Gox, and Stellar creator Jed McCaleb, and
Dave Kleiman. Coindesk has a more extensive list[157] of those
suspected to be Satoshi.

---

157   https://www.coindesk.com/information/who-is-satoshi-nakamoto/

My bet is that Satoshi Nakamoto is not an individual but a pseudonym for a group of people who have similar political views and who wish to remain anonymous. Craig Wright may have been part of that team. The team may not even know each other's real-world identities. Some of the team may have died since Bitcoin's popularisation. We may get another clue in 2020 when the roughly 1 million BTC locked in the Tulip Trust will be accessible. The Tulip Trust is a trust fund supposedly created by Dave Kleiman, an associate of Satoshi. It contains early bitcoins potentially owned by Satoshi.

If you decide to do some sleuthing, there are a few things to remember that people seem to have forgotten: A digital signature proves possession and use of a private key, but private keys can be shared among multiple people. So you cannot guarantee the mapping of private key to an individual. Private keys can also be lost. An email address can be shared. A whitepaper can be written collaboratively, so grammatical clues simply reveal the habits of the editor, not necessarily those of the author. It is very hard to tie the identity of an individual to the author of a paper.

On the other hand, it may be better if Satoshi is not found.

ETHEREUM

What is Ethereum?

The vision of Ethereum is to create an unstoppable, censorship resistant, self-sustaining, decentralised, world computer. To achieve this, Ethereum builds on the concepts we saw with Bitcoin. If you consider Bitcoin as trustless validation and distributed *storage* of (transaction) data, Ethereum is trustless validation and distributed *storage and processing* of data *and* logic.

Ethereum has a public blockchain running on 15,000 computers[158] and the token on the blockchain is called Ether, currently the second most popular cryptocurrency.

Like Bitcoin, Ethereum is also a bunch of *protocols* written out as *code* which is run as Ethereum *software* which creates Ethereum *transactions* containing data about Ether *coins* (ETH) recorded on Ethereum's *blockchain*. In contrast with Bitcoin, Ethereum transactions can contain more than just payment data, and the nodes in Ethereum are capable of validating and processing much more than simple payments.

On Ethereum, you can submit transactions that create *smart contracts*—small bits of general purpose logic that are stored on Ethereum's blockchain on all of the Ethereum nodes. These smart contracts can be invoked by sending Ether to them. This is a bit like deploying a juke machine, then putting coins in to play music. When a smart contract is invoked, all the Ethereum nodes run the code and update their ledgers with the results. These transactions and smart contracts are run by all participants using a sort of operating system called a 'Ethereum Virtual Machine'.

Ethereum's blockchain can be interrogated using websites like etherscan.io. As with Bitcoin, there are also forks of the main Ethereum, such as Ethereum Classic, which is also a public blockchain. Each fork has a separate coin (Ethereum's

---

158   https://www.ethernodes.org/network/1 in April 2018

coin is denoted ETH whereas Ethereum Classic's coin is denoted ETC). The forks have a shared history with Ethereum up to a certain point in time, after which the blockchains differ (we will discuss forks later).

Ethereum's code can also be run as a private network, starting a new blockchain with limited participants.

How Do You Run Ethereum?

To participate in the Ethereum network, you can download some software called an Ethereum client, or you can write some yourself if you have the patience. Just like BitTorrent or Bitcoin, the Ethereum client will connect over the internet to other people's computers running similar client software and start downloading the Ethereum blockchain from them to catch up with the latest state of the blockchain. It will also independently validate that each block conforms to the Ethereum protocol rules.

What does the Ethereum client software do? You can use it to:

- Connect to the Ethereum network

- Validate transactions and blocks

- Create new transactions and smart contracts

- Run smart contracts

- Mine for new blocks

Your computer becomes a 'node' on the network, running an Ethereum Virtual Machine, and behaves equivalently to all the other nodes. Remember in a peer-to-peer network there is no 'master' server and each computer is equivalent in status to any other.

How Is Ethereum Similar to Bitcoin?

Ethereum Has an Inbuilt Cryptocurrency

Ethereum's token is called Ether, shortened to ETH. This is a cryptocurrency that can be traded for other cryptocurrencies or other sovereign currencies, just like BTC. ETH ownership is tracked on the Ethereum blockchain, just like BTC ownership is tracked on Bitcoin's blockchain.

Ethereum Has a Blockchain

Like Bitcoin, Ethereum has a blockchain, which contains blocks of data (Pure ETH payments as well as smart contracts). The blocks are mined by some participants and distributed to other participants who validate them. You can explore this blockchain on etherscan.io.

Like Bitcoin, Ethereum blocks form a chain by referring to the hash of the previous block.

Ethereum is Public and Permissionless

Like Bitcoin, the main Ethereum network is a public, permissionless network. Anyone can download or write some software to connect to the network and start creating transactions and smart contracts, validating them, and mining blocks without needing to log in or sign up with any other organisation.

When people talk about Ethereum they usually mean the main public permissionless version of the network. However, like Bitcoin, you can take Ethereum software, modify it slightly, and create private networks that are not connected to the main public network. The private tokens and smart contracts won't be compatible with the public tokens though, just like private Bitcoin networks.

Ethereum Has Proof-of-Work (PoW) Mining

Like Bitcoin, mining participants create valid blocks by spending electricity to find solutions to a mathematical challenge. Ethereum's PoW maths challenge, called Ethash, works slightly differently from Bitcoin's, and allows more common hardware to be used. It is deliberately designed to reduce the efficiency edge of specialised chips called ASICs, which are common in Bitcoin mining. Commodity hardware is allowed to compete efficiently, and this allows for a greater decentralisation of miners. In practice though, specialised hardware has been created and so most blocks in Ethereum are created by one of a small group of miners[159].

Top Miners over the last 24h

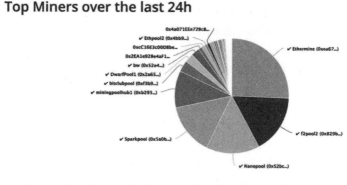

Source: https://www.etherchain.org/charts/topMiners retrieved 16 Apr. 2018

---

159   https://www.etherchain.org/charts/topMiners

On Ethereum's roadmap there is a plan to move from electricity-expensive, proof-of-work mining, to a more energy-efficient, proof-of-stake mining protocol called Casper in a future release of the Ethereum software called Serenity. Proof-of-stake is a mining protocol in which your chance of creating a valid block is proportional to the number of coins (ETH) in your mining wallet—contrast this to proof-of-work, where your chance of creating a valid block is proportional to the amount of computational cycles your hardware can crunch through.

How might this impact the community? For starters, this would dramatically reduce the energy footprint of the cryptocurrency. Miners will no longer need to consume electricity competitively in order to win blocks. On the other hand, some people think that proof-of-stake is less democratic, because those who already have accumulated a lot of ETH will have a higher chance of winning more blocks. So, the argument goes, new money will flow towards the wealthy, increasing the Gini coefficient[160] of Ethereum holders.

There are flaws in the 'less democratic' argument. With proof-of-work the high capital costs and expertise required mean that only a very small minority of people can actually make money mining, so it is not actually that democratic. Whereas with proof-of-stake, every ETH has an identical chance of winning a block, so you can get started with much less capital. Think of it as an interest rate: If you have more money you get more interest, but at least those with small amounts of money

---

160   The Gini coefficient is a metric used to describe wealth inequality in a population. It is a number from 0 to 1, where 0 means everyone has the same wealth and the number tends towards 1 as inequality increases.

can still get interest. I also think that reducing the negative externalities of pollution caused by proof-of-work is a decent and honourable goal.

How Is Ethereum Different from Bitcoin?

This is where it gets more technical, and in many ways more complex.

The Ethereum Virtual Machine can run smart contracts

When you download and run the Ethereum software, it creates and starts a segregated virtual computer on your machine called an 'Ethereum Virtual Machine' (EVM). This EVM processes all the Ethereum transactions and blocks, and keeps track of all the account balances and results of the smart contracts. Each node on the Ethereum network runs the same EVM and processes the same data, resulting in them all having the same view of the world. Ethereum can be described as a *replicated state machine* because all of the nodes running Ethereum are coming to consensus about the state of the Ethereum Virtual Machine.

Compared with Bitcoin's primitive scripting language, the code that can be deployed in Ethereum and run as smart contracts is more advanced and approachable for developers. We will describe smart contracts in more detail later, but for now you can think of smart contracts as pieces of code run by all the nodes in Ethereum's Virtual Machine.

Gas

In Bitcoin, you can add a small amount of BTC as a transaction fee that goes to the miner who successfully mines the block. This compensates the miner for checking the validity of the transaction and including it in the block they are mining. Likewise, in Ethereum, you can add a small amount of ETH as a mining fee which goes to the miner who successfully mines the block.

The complication with Ethereum is that there are more types of transactions. Different transaction types have different computational complexities. For example, a transaction performing a simple ETH payment is less complex than a transaction to upload or run a smart contract. Therefore, Ethereum has a concept of 'gas' which is a sort of price list, based on the computational complexity of the different types of operation you are instructing the miners to make in your transaction. Operations include searching for data, retrieving it, making calculations, storing data, and making changes to the ledger. Here is the price list from the ethdocs.org website,[161] but it can change over time if the majority of the network agrees:

161   http://www.ethdocs.org/en/latest/contracts-and-transactions/account-types-gas-and-transactions.html

Operation Name	Gas Cost	Remark
step	1	default amount per execution cycle
stop	0	free
suicide	0	free
sha3	20	
sload	20	get from permanent storage
sstore	100	put into permanent storage
balance	20	
create	100	contract creation
call	20	initiating a read-only call
memory	1	every additional word when expanding memory
txdata	5	every byte of data or code for a transaction
transaction	500	base fee transaction
contract creation	53000	changed in homestead from 21000

A basic transfer of ETH from one account to another uses 21,000 gas. Uploading and running smart contracts uses more gas depending on their complexity. When you submit an Ethereum transaction, you specify a gas price (how much ETH you are willing to pay per gas used) and a gas limit (the maximum amount of gas you will let the transaction use).

Mining fee (in ETH) = gas price (in ETH per gas) x gas consumed (in gas)

Gas price

The gas price is the amount of ETH you are prepared to pay per unit of gas for the transaction to be processed. As with Bitcoin transaction fees, this is a competitive market, and in general the busier the network the higher the gas price people are willing to pay. In times of great demand gas, prices spike.

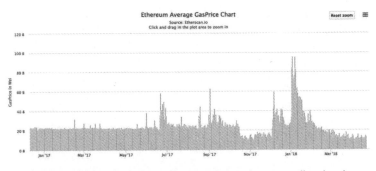

Source: https://etherscan.io/chart/gasprice. Peaks are usually related to popular ICOs where many people are attempting to send ETH to ICO smart contracts. The peak in December 2017 is related to the popular CryptoKitties Ethereum game. In 2018, the normal range for gas prices is between 0.000000005 ETH (5 Gwei) and 0.000000020 ETH (20 Gwei) per gas.

Gas limit

The gas limit you set provides a ceiling for how much gas you are prepared for a transaction to consume. This limit protects you from over-spending on mining fees and you know that the maximum mining fee will be gas limit x gas price. This stops you over-paying if you accidentally submitted a very complex transaction that you thought was simple.

Analogy time: Driving your car 10km will use up a certain amount of fuel. If you run out of fuel, your car will stop before reaching the destination. The price of fuel is dependent on market conditions and can go up and down, but the price of fuel bears no relation to how far you may drive your car with it. Gas in Ethereum is similar. When you submit an Ethereum transaction, you specify how much gas you're prepared to spend on making the transaction 'work' (this is the *gas limit*), and how much ETH you are prepared to pay the miner per unit of gas (this is the *gas price*). This results in a total

amount of ETH you're prepared to pay for the transaction to
be processed.

The miner will execute the transaction and will charge you the
amount of gas taken, multiplied by the gas price you specified.
As with Bitcoin, the mining fee is up to you, and you need to
bear in mind that you're competing with other transactions
which may have set a higher gas price.

For example, a basic transaction of a transfer of ETH from
one account to another uses 21,000 gas, so you can set the
gas limit for this kind of transaction to 21,000, or higher;
but it will only use 21,000 gas. If you set the gas limit below
the amount of gas it takes to process the transaction, the
transaction will fail and you will not be refunded your mining
fee. This is like trying to make a journey with insufficient
fuel in your tank; the fuel will be used, but you will not get to
your destination.

ETH Units

Just like one dollar can be split into 100 cents, 1 BTC can be
split into 100,000,000 Satoshi, and Ethereum too has its own
unit naming convention.

The smallest unit is a Wei and there are
1,000,000,000,000,000,000 of them per ETH. There
are also some other intermediate names: Finney, Szabo,
Shannon, Lovelace, Babbage, Ada—all named after people
who made significant contributions to fields related to
cryptocurrencies or networks.

Wei and Ether are the two most common denominations. Wei
is usually used for gas price (a gas price of 2-50 Giga-Wei per
gas is common, where 1 GWei is 1,000,000,000 Wei).

Units in Ethereum		
Unit	Number per ETH	Most appropriate uses
Ether (ETH)	1	Currently used to denominate transaction amounts (eg 20 ETH) and mining rewards (5 ETH)
finney	1,000	
szabo	1,000,000	Currently the best unit for the cost of a basic transaction, eg 500 szabo
Gwei	1,000,000,000	Currently the best unit for Gas Prices eg 22 Gwei
Mwei	1,000,000,000,000	
Kwei	1,000,000,000,000,000	
wei	1,000,000,000,000,000,000	The base indivisible unit used by programmers

Ethereum's block time is shorter

In Ethereum the time between blocks is around 14 seconds, compared with Bitcoin's ~10 minutes. This means that, on average, if you made a Bitcoin transaction and an Ethereum transaction, the Ethereum transaction would be recorded into Ethereum's blockchain faster than the Bitcoin transaction into Bitcoin's blockchain. You could say Bitcoin writes to its database roughly every 10 minutes, whereas Ethereum writes to its database roughly every 14 seconds. The history of Ethereum's block times has been quite interesting, as you can see on bitinfocharts.com:

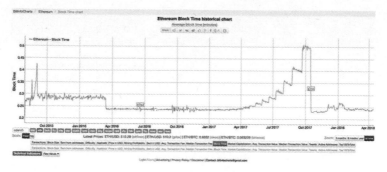

Source: Bitinfocharts[162]

Compare this with Bitcoin's relatively stable block time (note the time scale, as Bitcoin is much older than Ethereum):

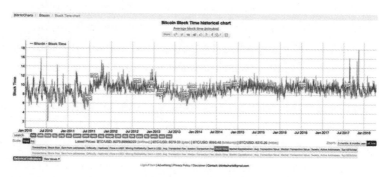

Source: Bitinfocharts[163]

Ethereum has smaller blocks

Currently, Bitcoin's blocks are a little under 1MB in size whereas most Ethereum blocks are about 15-20kb in size. However, we should not compare blocks by the amount of

---

162   https://bitinfocharts.com/comparison/Ethereum-confirmationtime.html

163   https://bitinfocharts.com/comparison/Bitcoin-confirmationtime.html

data in them: While Bitcoin's maximum block size is specified in bytes, Ethereum's block size is based on complexity of contracts being run. It is known as a gas limit per block, and the maximum is allowed to vary slightly from block to block. So whereas Bitcoin's block size limit is based on amount of data, Ethereum's block size limit is based on computational complexity.

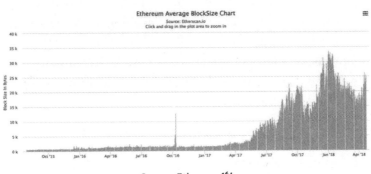

Source: Etherscan[164]

Currently, the maximum block size in Ethereum is around 8 million gas. Basic transactions, or payments of ETH from one account to another (i.e., uploading or invoking a smart contract), have a complexity of 21,000 gas; so you can fit around 380 of those basic transactions into a block (8,000,000 / 21,000). In Bitcoin, you currently get around 1,500-2,000 basic transactions in a 1MB block.

Uncles: blocks that don't quite make it

Because Ethereum's rate of block generation is much higher than Bitcoin's (250 blocks per hour on Ethereum vs

---

164   https://etherscan.io/chart/blocksize

six blocks per hour on Bitcoin), the rate of 'block clashes'
increases. Multiple valid blocks can get created at almost
the same time, but only one of them can make it into the
main chain. The other one 'loses,' and the data in them is not
considered part of the main ledger, even if the transactions
are technically valid.

In Bitcoin, these non-mainchain blocks are called orphans, or
orphaned blocks, and they do not form part of the main chain
in any way and are never referenced again by any subsequent
blocks. In Ethereum they are called uncles. Uncles can be
referenced by a few of the subsequent blocks and although
the data in them is not used, the slightly smaller reward for
mining them is still valid.

This achieves two important things:

1. It incentivises miners to mine even though there is a
    high chance of creating a non-mainchain block (the
    high speed of block creation results in more orphans
    or uncles)

2. It increases the security of the blockchain by
    acknowledging the energy spent creating the
    uncle blocks

Transactions that end up in orphaned blocks simply end up
being re-mined on the main chain. They don't cost the user
any more gas, because the transaction in the orphaned block
is treated as if it was never processed.

Accounts

Bitcoin uses the word *address* to describe accounts. Ethereum
uses the word account but technically they are also addresses.
The words seem to be more interchangeable with Ethereum.

Maybe you can say, 'What's the address of your Ethereum account?' It doesn't seem to matter[165].

There are two types of Ethereum accounts:

1. Accounts that only store ETH

2. Accounts that contain smart contracts

Accounts that only store ETH are similar to Bitcoin addresses and are sometimes known as Externally Owned Accounts. You make payments from these accounts by signing transactions with the appropriate private key. An example of an account that stores ETH is 0x2d7c76202834a11a99576acf2ca95a7e66928ba0[166].

Accounts that contain smart contracts are activated by a transaction sending ETH into it. Once the smart contract has been uploaded it sits there at an address, waiting to be used. An example of an account that has a smart contract is 0xcbe1060ee68bc0fed3c00f13d6f110b7eb6434f6[167].

---

165   Etherscan, a popular website for searching the Ethereum blockchain, uses both on https://etherscan.io/accounts

166   https://etherscan.io/ address/0x2d7c76202834a11a99576acf2ca95a7e66928ba0

167   https://etherscan.io/ address/0xcbe1060ee68bc0fed3c00f13d6f110b7eb6434f6#code

ETH token issuance

The issuance of Ether tokens is a bit more complicated than
Bitcoin. The number of ETH in existence are: Pre-mine +
Block rewards + Uncle rewards.

Total Ether Supply and Market Capitalization   Home / List Of Charts / Ether Supply

♠ ETHER DISTRIBUTION OVERVIEW	
Genesis (60M Crowdsale+12M Other):	72,009,990.50 Ether
+ Mining Block Rewards:	25,338,618.38 Ether
+ Mining Uncle Rewards:	1,708,040.75 Ether
= Current Total Supply	99,056,649.62 Ether

Data Source: Total Eth Supply API

99,056,649.62   **$61,859,887,124**

Total Ether Supply   Market Capitalization

Breakdown By Supply Types

$ PRICE PER ETHER	
In USD:	$624.49
In BTC:	0.07138

Data Source: CryptoCompare

Genesis (72009990.49948 ETH)   Block Rewards (25338618.3751 ETH)
Uncle Rewards (1708040.75 ETH)

Source: Etherscan[168]

Pre-mine

Around 72 million ETH were created for the crowdsale in
July/Aug 2014. This is sometimes called a 'pre-mine' as they
were just written in rather than mined through proof-of-work
hashing. These were distributed to initial supporters of the
project and to the project team itself. It was decided that after
the initial crowdsale, future ETH generation would be capped
at 25% of the pre-mine total, i.e., no more than 18m ETH
could be mined per year.

---

168   https://etherscan.io/stat/supply

Block rewards

Originally, each block mined created five fresh ETH as the block reward. Due to concerns about oversupply, this was reduced to 3 ETH, in a set of changes to the protocol called the Byzantium update, in October 2017 (block 4,370,000).

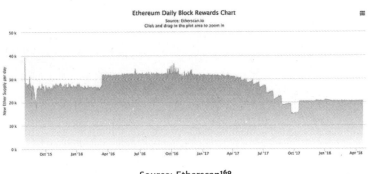

Source: Etherscan[169]

Uncle rewards

Some blocks are mined but do not form part of the main blockchain. In Bitcoin, these are called 'orphans' and are entirely discarded, and the miner of the orphaned block receives no rewards. In Ethereum, these discarded blocks are called 'uncles' and *can* be referenced by later blocks. If a later block references an uncle, the miner of the uncle gets some ETH. This is called the 'uncle' reward. The miner of the later block referencing the uncle also gets an additional small reward called an 'uncle referencing' reward.

---

169   https://etherscan.io/chart/ethersupply

The uncle reward used to be 4.375 ETH (7/8th of the full 5
ETH reward). It was reduced in the Byzantium upgrade to
0.625-2.625 ETH.

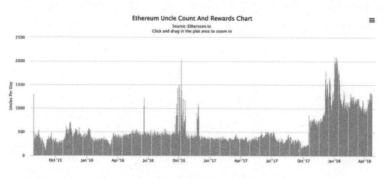

Source: https://etherscan.io/chart/uncles

The biggest difference between ETH and BTC token
generation is that BTC generation halves approximately every
4 years and has a planned finite cap, whereas ETH generation
continues to be generated at a constant number every year
indefinitely. Like any other parameter or rule, however, this
rule is subject to ongoing debate and can be changed if the
majority of the Ethereum network agrees.

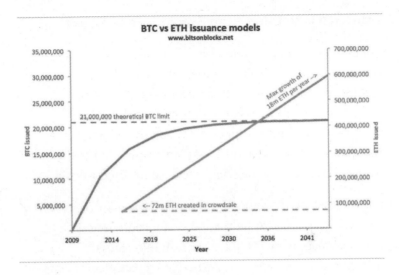

The future of ETH generation

The Ethereum community hasn't yet come to agreement about what happens to the rate of issue when Ethereum moves from proof-of-work to proof-of-stake. Some argue that perhaps the rate at which ETH is created should decrease, as the value will not have to subsidise competitive electricity usage.

Mining rewards

In Bitcoin, the miner of a block receives the block reward (new BTC), plus transaction fees for transactions mined (existing BTC). In Ethereum, the miner of a block receives the block and uncle referencing rewards (new ETH), plus mining fees (gas amount x gas price) from transactions and contracts that were run during the block.

Other parts to Ethereum: Swarm and Whisper

Computers need to be able to calculate, store data, and communicate. For Ethereum to realise its vision as an unstoppable, censorship resistant, self-sustaining, decentralised, 'world' computer, it needs to be able to do those three things in an efficient and robust way. The Ethereum Virtual Machine is just one component of the whole, the element which does the decentralised calculations.

Swarm is another component. This is for peer-to-peer file sharing, similar to BitTorrent, but incentivised with micropayments of ETH. Files are split into chunks, distributed and stored with participating volunteers. These nodes that store and serve the chunks are compensated with ETH from those storing and retrieving the data.

Whisper is an encrypted messaging protocol that allows nodes to send messages directly to each other in a secure way and that also hides the sender and receiver from third party snoopers.

Governance

Although Bitcoin and Ethereum are both open source projects and open, permissionless networks, one of the biggest differences between them is that Bitcoin doesn't have an active, identified leader, whereas Ethereum does. Vitalik Buterin, the creator of Ethereum is hugely influential, and his opinions count. Although he can't stop his creation or censor transactions or participants, his vision and commentary have a big impact on the technology. For instance, he championed a hard fork to recover funds stolen in the DAO hack (this is explained later). He also proposes changes to the protocol rules and the network economics. Bitcoin, on the other hand, has a few influential developers, but none with the clout that Vitalik has with Ethereum. Nick Tomaino argues in a blog post[170] that the governance of blockchains 'may prove to be as important as the computer science and economics of blockchains'. Whether a single influencer is good or bad for decentralised cryptocurrency networks is still be determined.

Smart Contracts

Smart contracts mean different things depending on the blockchain platform. Ethereum smart contracts are short computer programs that are stored on Ethereum's blockchain, replicated across all the nodes, and are available for anyone to inspect. There are two steps that are performed separately:

1. Uploading the smart contract to Ethereum's blockchain

2. Making the smart contract run

You upload a smart contract by sending the code to miners in a special transaction. If the transaction is successfully processed, the smart contract will then exist at a specific address on Ethereum's blockchain[171]. You may then make it run by creating a transaction that says 'Please run the smart contract found at address x'.

Here is an example of a basic smart contract. It creates a token called 'GavCoin' that initially issues 1 million GavCoins

---

170   https://thecontrol.co/the-governance-of-blockchains-5ba17a4f5da6

171   This address is not random; it is calculated deterministically using a combination of the creator's address and how many transactions that creator has ever sent.

to the creator of the smart contract, and then allows them to send GavCoins to other users[172]:

```
contract GavCoin
{
    mapping(address=>uint) balances;
    uint constant totalCoins = 100000000000;

    /// Endows creator of contract with 1m GAV.
    function GavCoin(){
        balances[msg.sender] = totalCoins;
    }

    /// Send $((valueInmGAV / 1000).fixed(0,3)) GAV from the account of $(message.caller.address()), to an account accessible
    only by $(to.address()).
    function send(address to, uint256 valueInmGAV) {
        if (balances[msg.sender] >= valueInmGAV) {
            balances[to] += valueInmGAV;
            balances[msg.sender] -= valueInmGAV;
        }
    }

    /// getter function for the balance
    function balance(address who) constant returns (uint256 balanceInmGAV) {
        balanceInmGAV = balances[who];
    }
}
```

For a real example of a smart contract, the smart contract that holds the balances of the Indorse ICO tokens can be found at address 0xf8e386eda857484f5a12e4b5daa9984e06e73705[173].

Once a contract has been uploaded, it behaves a bit like a jukebox. When you want to run it, you create a transaction pointing to the contract and supply whatever information the contract expects. You pay gas to the miner to run it. As part of the mining process, each miner will execute the transaction, which involves running the smart contract.

The miner who successfully wins the proof-of-work challenge will publish the winning block to the rest of the network. The other nodes will validate the block, add the block to their own blockchains, and process the transactions, including running the smart contracts. This is how Ethereum's blockchain gets updated, and how the state of the EVMs on each node's machine is synchronised.

Ethereum smart contracts are described, 'Turing complete'. This means that they are fully functional and can perform any computation that can be done in any other programming language.

Smart Contract languages: Solidity / Serpent, LLL (Lisp Like Language)

The most common language that Ethereum smart contracts are written in is Solidity. Serpent and LLL can also be used. Smart contracts written in these languages will all compile and run on Ethereum Virtual Machines.

- Solidity is similar to the language JavaScript. This is currently the most popular and functional smart contract scripting language.

- Serpent is similar to the language Python and was popular in the early history of Ethereum.

- LLL is similar to Lisp and was used mainly in the very early days only. It is probably the hardest to write in.

Ethereum software: geth, eth, pyethapp

The three official Ethereum clients (full node software) are all open source. You can see the code behind them and tweak them to make your own versions. They are:

- geth[174] (written in a language called Go)

---

174   https://github.com/Ethereum/go-Ethereum

- eth[175] (written in C++)

- pyethapp[176] (written in Python)

These are all command-line based programs (think green text on black backgrounds) and so additional software can be used for a nicer graphical interface. Currently, the most popular graphical interface is Mist (https://github.com/Ethereum/mist), which runs on top of geth or eth. So, geth/eth does the background stuff, and Mist is the pretty screen on top.

Currently the most popular Ethereum clients are geth and Parity[177]. Parity is Ethereum software built by a company called Parity Technologies. It is also open source[178] and is developed in the Rust programming language.

Ethereum's History

Ethereum is a highly successful public blockchain by adoption, mindshare, and the number of developers working on Ethereum smart contracts and decentralised apps. Below is a short history of Ethereum, and some difficult periods in its history that it has managed to overcome.

2013

Vitalik Buterin described Ethereum as a concept in a white paper in late 2013. This concept was developed by Dr Gavin

---

175   https://github.com/Ethereum/cpp-Ethereum

176   https://github.com/Ethereum/pyethapp

177   https://www.parity.io/

178   https://github.com/paritytech/parity/

Wood who published a technical yellow paper in April 2014. Since then, the development of Ethereum's software has been managed by a community of developers.

A crowdsale took place in July and August 2014 to fund development, and Ethereum's live blockchain was launched on 30 July 2015. You can see the very first block here: https://etherscan.io/block/0

Ethereum crowdsale

The development team was funded by an online sale of ETH tokens during July to August 2014 where people could buy ETH tokens by paying in Bitcoin. Early investors received 2,000 ETH per BTC, and this was gradually reduced to 1,337 ETH[179] per BTC over the course of about a month, to encourage investors to invest early.

Crowdsale participants sent bitcoins to a Bitcoin address and received an Ethereum wallet containing the number of ETH bought. Technical details are on Ethereum's blog[180].

A little over 60m ETH was sold this way for more than 31,500 BTC, worth about US$18m at the time. An additional 20% (12m ETH) were created to fund development and the Ethereum Foundation.

Software Release codenames

Frontier, Homestead, Metropolis, and Serenity are friendly names for versions of the core Ethereum software, a little like

---

179   This is a geek joke, the number 1337 means 'leet' or 'elite' referring to elite hacking skills.

180   https://blog.Ethereum.org/2014/07/22/launching-the-ether-sale/

Apple's OS X version names such as Mavericks, El Capitan, Sierra.

Release name	Details
Olympic (testnet)	Launched May 2015—a testing release where coins are not compatible with 'real' ETH. A testnet still runs in parallel to the main live network so that developers can test their code. The testnet operates in the same way as the live network but there is much less mining competition as the coins are not tradeable on exchanges— they are defined has having zero value.
Frontier	Launched 30 July 2015—an initial live release with a way for people to mine ETH and build and run contracts.
Homestead	Launched 14 March 2016—some protocol changes, more stability.
Metropolis	This was designed to prepare Ethereum for a move from proof-of-work to proof-of-stake. Metropolis was split into two upgrades, Byzantium and Constantinople. Byzantium was released in October 2017 at block 4,370,000. It included changes to set the stage for private transactions, sped up transaction processing (important for scalability), and improved some smart contract functionality. The most visually obvious change was reducing the mining reward from 5 ETH per block to 3 ETH. The Constantinople upgrade will be another upgrade to set the stage for the move to proof-of-stake (Casper).
Serenity	Future launch—moving from proof-of-work to proof-of-stake (Casper).

The DAO Hack

There is a concept called a 'Decentralised Autonomous Organisation'. The idea is that an automated company or entity runs itself according to some encoded charter, without human intervention or management. It just does what it says it will do. A common example is a self-driving taxi that makes money by providing a taxi service and can go and get itself repaired or filled with petrol. Call me old fashioned, but this sounds fantastical to me without a human ultimately responsible for the actions of the taxi.

Anyway, some enthusiasts seem to love the idea. In 2016, a team from a German company called Slock-it pivoted from their business model of making smart locks that can be opened using tokens on blockchains and built a sort of automated venture capital (VC) company as a smart contract deployed on Ethereum's public blockchain. They called it 'The DAO' (note the capitalisation). This is a confusing name, it is like calling a bank 'The Bank' or a company 'The Company'. Anyway, *The DAO* is an example of *a* DAO.

The idea behind The DAO is that it would be a cryptocurrency fund for funding startups. Investors who want to invest in relevant startups would send money (in the form of ETH) to the smart contract, and the smart contract would issue them DAO tokens in proportion to their investment. The smart contract would be the pot of money used to fund the startups, like a traditional VC fund.

In a normal VC fund, the investors, called Limited Partners, give money to the fund and expect the management of the VC firm to manage the funds and to generate a return by investing in successful ventures. In The DAO, the investors would have a more active role. They would receive DAO tokens in return for their investment, and use them to vote on what startups receive funding. In this way the investors would have direct input into which startups get funding, instead of devolving that responsibility to a management team. The smart contract would govern a voting process, and at the end of a vote, cryptocurrency would be released to the startups that had the most funding votes. That was the theory behind The DAO.

Of course, there *was* actually human intervention. Someone—a management team—had to curate a list of potential startups that investors could vote on, so in fact it wasn't much of a DAO after all. All it did was automate the provision of funds. Anyway, none of this really mattered because the DAO failed before it invested in a single startup.

Over a one month funding period in May 2016, The DAO managed to raise the equivalent of over $150m USD in ETH from over 11,000 separate addresses. This suggests a large number of investors, but it is hard to tell, as a single investor may have multiple ETH addresses. ETH was trading between $10 and $20 per ETH and The DAO held about 15% of all ETH in existence.

In June, a hacker managed to find a way to get the DAO to release 3,641,694 ETH, then worth about $50-60m, into another account controlled by the hacker. This sent the price of ETH down almost 50%. When the hack was discovered and investigated, some white-hat (ethical) hackers replicated the attack and drained the rest of the ETH into their own accounts. This is like the goodies stealing money from a broken vault so that the baddy can't steal it. Now remember, that smart contracts simply do as they promise they will do, and DAOs just do as they have been programmed. The user agreement is right there in the code. If you find a way to get the smart contract to do something that it has been programmed to do, and it does it, is it a hack or is it just behaving according to the rules which you all subscribed to?

Anyway, this was considered a hack and the Ethereum Foundation suggested an update for all Ethereum participants which would in effect freeze the ETH that had been drained by specifying a blacklist which would invalidate any transactions trying to spend money from the theft account. This goes against the vision of a censorship resistant world computer, but this was an emergency, and many early supporters of Ethereum were in danger of having their money stolen. So lost money took precedence over values. The pressure on the Ethereum Foundation to find a way to 'unwind' the transaction must have been huge. Just before the proposed implementation of this change, a bug was found with the proposed change, so the blacklist wasn't adopted. The Ethereum Foundation then made a proposal to unwind the specific transactions related to the theft and allow DAO investors to withdraw their invested ETH.

Again, this transgressed the very principles of a censorship resistant world computer. In cryptocurrencyland, it is apparently fine to cheer for censorship resistance, unless you've lost money.

In July 2016, a vote was taken to determine the fate of the stolen Ether, and the result was that the community decided to install an upgrade in what is known as a hard fork, that would move the stolen Ether to a new smart contract and have them returned to the original investors.

This was quite controversial. After all, an unstoppable immutable world computer was stopped and mutated to cater to a small number of people who lost a lot of money to a smart contract which functioned exactly as it specified it would.

Ethereum Classic

A small but vocal part of the community thought that unwinding contradicted the values of Ethereum and continued with the old Ethereum software. This resulted in two Ethereum blockchains, one which returned the stolen funds to the DAO investors, another which didn't. The one that didn't became known as Ethereum Classic. Ethereum and Ethereum Classic have a shared history until block 1,920,000 (July 2016) after which point the blockchains diverge. Anyone who owned ETH before the fork, now had an equal amount of ETH (tokens recorded on the Ethereum blockchain) and ETC (tokens recorded on the Ethereum Classic blockchain). This was good for anyone who had ETH before the hard fork as, to all intents and purposes, they received free money in the form of ETC[181].

The Parity Bug

Parity is a piece of Ethereum software written by Parity Technologies. It acts as a full node on the Ethereum network, storing the blockchain, running contracts, forwarding transactions, etc. At time of writing, about a third of Ethereum nodes run Parity software.

Source: Ethernodes[182]

---

181   You would think that the value of ETH should have fallen by the same value that was created by the ETC tokens. Alas, cryptocurrency markets don't work according to conventional logic.

182   https://www.ethernodes.org/network/1

Parity also contains some advanced wallet software that you can use to store ETH. The wallet has had a couple of critical bugs. On 20 July 2017, Parity's code was updated to fix a bug that had enabled a hacker to steal $32m worth of ETH from Parity multi-signature wallets. However, this update itself contained a bug: A smart contract was deployed which was relied upon for some wallet functionality, but it had a vulnerability. Anyone could convert this smart contract into a multi-signature wallet, take ownership of it, and then suicide it, destroying this particular piece of code on which multi-signature wallets created after 20 July relied, freezing the assets in the wallets.

So, someone with the Github handle devops199 'Did just that on 6 Nov 2017[183]:'

anyone can kill your contract #6995

Open   devops199 opened this issue a day ago · 12 comments

> devops199 commented a day ago · edited
>
> I accidentally killed it.
>
> https://etherscan.io/address/0x863df6bfa4469f3ead0be8f9f2aae51c91a907b4

Almost 600 wallets were affected, with a combined balance of over half a million ETH, valued at the time at about $150m. Ironically, Gavin Wood, founder of Parity Technologies, had about 300k ETH in a Parity wallet related to funds raised in an ICO called Polkadot. Those funds are frozen.

---

183   https://blog.comae.io/the-280m-ethereums-bug-f28e5de43513

The ETH are still there in the wallets, but currently can't be sent. As of early 2018, developers are still investigating if anything can be done to fix this bug.

Actors in the Ethereum Ecosystem

The Ethereum Foundation

The Ethereum Foundation is a non-profit organisation registered as 'Stiftung Ethereum' in Switzerland whose mission is to:

> Promote and support Ethereum platform and base layer research, development and education to bring decentralized protocols and tools to the world that empower developers to produce next generation decentralized applications (dapps), and together build a more globally accessible, more free and more trustworthy Internet.[184]

The Foundation's job is to manage the funds raised in the Ether pre-sale in any way that furthers Ethereum. Mainly it pays the core development team a salary, but it also offers grants to developers to tackle specific problems. For instance, in March 2018, grants were awarded to fund projects that provided scaling and security solutions to Ethereum[185]. Vitalik Buterin, known as the creator of Ethereum, sits on the council of the foundation, and the foundation has a great deal of influence into the roadmap of Ethereum. In theory, Ethereum

---

184   https://Ethereum.org/foundation

185   https://blog.Ethereum.org/2018/03/07/announcing-beneficiaries-Ethereum-foundation-grants/

participants (miners, bookkeepers) don't have to implement any software changes made by the Foundation, but in practice they do.

Ethereum Enterprise Alliance

The Ethereum Enterprise Alliance is a non-profit industry group launched in March 2017 whose goal seems to be to make Ethereum suitable for enterprise use. From their materials, it is hard to understand whether this means businesses using the public Ethereum blockchain, or if it means adapting the Ethereum code to make it suitable for industry use cases.

The website[186] says:

> *The Enterprise Ethereum Alliance connects Fortune 500 enterprises, startups, academics, and technology vendors with Ethereum subject matter experts. Together, we will learn from and build upon the only smart contract supporting blockchain currently running in real world production— Ethereum—to define enterprise-grade software capable of handling the most complex, highly demanding applications at the speed of business.*

From the website the vision of the EEA is to:

- Be an open source standard, not a product

- Address enterprise deployment requirements

- Evolve in tandem with advances in public Ethereum

---

186   https://entethalliance.org/

- Leverage existing standards

Unfortunately, I could not find any further detail as to what this means. The mission of the Alliance states:

- EEA is a 501 (c) (6) non-profit corporation.

- A clear roadmap for enterprise features and requirements.

- Robust governance model and accountability, clarity around IP and licensing models for open source technology.

- Resources for businesses to learn about Ethereum and leverage this groundbreaking technology to address specific industry use cases.

Its members are an impressive list of large established companies as well as new startups. The launch members were:

Source: https://entethalliance.org/

Members pay between \$3,000 and \$25,000 in annual dues for which they get the following benefits:

MEMBERSHIP BENEFITS

BENEFITS MATRIX	CLASS B	CLASS C
Participants	General Members	Legal Practitioners
EEA Board of Directors Seat		
Designated as Voting Member		
May chair Committees		
May chair Working Groups	X	X
May Create & Participate in Working Group	X	X
Access to Open Code	X	X
Invitation to All Member Meetings	X	X
May Host EEA Meet Up	X	X
Company logo on EEA Website	X	X
Included in New Member Press Release	X	X
Post Company Hosted Events to EEA Online Calendar	X	X
Discount on EEA Sponsorships	X	X
Annual Dues	50 employees or Less | \$3,000 / year Between 51 - 500 Employees | \$10,000 / year Between 501 - 5,000 Employees | \$15,000 / year More than 5,000 Employees | \$25,000 / year	50 employees or Less | \$3,000 / year Between 51 - 500 Employees | \$10,000 / year Between 501 - 5,000 Employees | \$15,000 / year More than 5,000 Employees | \$25,000 / year

The EEA website also explains why prospective members should join the EEA:

WHY JOIN THE EEA?

The EEA is an industry-supported, not-for-profit established to build, promote, and broadly support Ethereum-based technology best practices, open standards, and open-source reference architectures. The EEA is helping to evolve Ethereum into an enterprise-grade technology, providing research and development in a range of areas, including privacy, confidentiality, scalability, and security. The EEA is also investigating hybrid architectures that span both permissioned and public Ethereum networks as well as industry-specific application layer working groups.

In early 2018 there were 450 members according to a Coindesk article[187].

---

187   https://www.coindesk.com/enterprise-Ethereum-alliance-pledges-2018-blockchain-standards-release/

Ether Price

Like Bitcoin, the price of Ether has also been through ups and downs. Ethereum's crowdsale was at a price of 2,000 ETH to 1 BTC, and at the time (July-Aug 2014), 1 BTC was worth about $500, making 1 ETH = $0.25. At its peak in early 2018, the price of ETH almost touched $1,500. So, to date, Ether has been a highly successful cryptocurrency in terms of price.

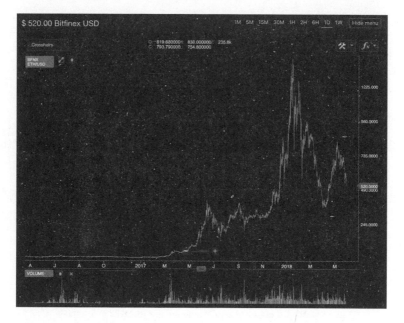

Compared to Bitcoin, Ethereum has an additional use case. Its token ETH is often used in ICOs. A company that runs an ICO will create a smart contract on Ethereum which will automatically create tokens and assign them to Ethereum addresses who have sent Ether to a related smart contract. This means you can run an automated ICO on Ethereum, as long as investors pay in ETH or another token recorded on Ethereum.

FORKS

What is a cryptocurrency fork? When people use the word *fork* they can mean two different, but related things:

1. A fork of a codebase

2. A fork of a live blockchain (a *chainsplit*)

The difference is whether you're creating an entirely new ledger, which is achieved by forking a codebase (the code behind the node software), or creating a new coin that has a shared history with an existing coin by forking a blockchain. Let's explore both of these.

A Fork of a Codebase

A fork of a codebase in general is where you copy the code of a particular program so you can contribute to it or adapt it. This is encouraged in open source software, where code is deliberately shared for anyone to tinker with.

In cryptocurrency, this means that you copy the code behind a popular cryptocurrency node software (e.g., Bitcoin Core), maybe tweak it and change a few parameters, and then run the code to create an entirely new blockchain starting from a blank ledger. You'd say you forked Bitcoin's code to create a new coin. This is how many alt-coins (alternative coins) were created in 2013-14. Litecoin for example was created using a copy of Bitcoin's code with some parameters changed, including the speed of block generation and the kind of calculations that the miners had to in the proof-of-work challenge.

The key here is that, when you run the new code, you create a new 'empty' blockchain ledger from scratch—with an entirely new Genesis block.

In the popular open source code-sharing platform GitHub, you can easily fork (copy) a project's code with a few clicks of a mouse. You then have your very own copy which you can edit. These codebase forks are common and encouraged in open source technology development, as they lead to innovation.

A Fork of a Live Blockchain: Chainsplits

A fork of a live blockchain, better described as a *chainsplit*, is more interesting. Chainsplits can happen by accident or on purpose.

An *accidental* chainsplit is when there is an uncontentious upgrade to the blockchain software and some proportion of the network omits or forgets to upgrade their software, leading to a number of blocks being produced by them that are incompatible with the rest of the network. According to BitMEX research[188], this has happened a few times in Bitcoin's history, with three identified chainsplits lasting approximately 51, 24, and 6 blocks, in 2010, 2013, and 2015, respectively. So forks can occur even when there is no contention over rule changes, creating some temporary confusion as to the 'real' state of the blockchain during the period where there is more than one candidate blockchain.

---

188   https://blog.bitmex.com/bitcoins-consensus-forks/

Accidental chainsplits tend to be resolved quickly with the small proportion of participants upgrading their software and discarding the incompatible blocks.

A *deliberate* chainsplit occurs when a group of participants of a live network thinks that things should be done a different way from the rest of the participants, and runs some new software with changes to the protocol rules to create a new coin that has a shared history with the old coin. This deliberately splits the chain at a specific block according to a well communicated plan. Deliberate chainsplits can be successful, with both assets continuing to live and develop, or fail, where there is not enough participatory interest and the value of the token drops to zero, and stops being mined.

To execute a successful deliberate chainsplit, you need to publicly rally and persuade a group of miners, bookkeepers, exchanges, and wallets that your new rules are better than the existing rules. They will need to agree to support your new coin, creating a community supporting a new coin that people can buy and sell, store and use. When the chain splits, you have created a new coin with different protocol rules but which has a shared history with the original coin. Anyone with a balance on the blockchain before the split now has a balance in two different coins after the split.

So the determination of whether something is a protocol upgrade, a failed fork, or a successful fork is really about who chooses to adopt the new rules:

- If new protocol rules are adopted by the vast majority of the community, then it is called a protocol upgrade, and those who don't upgrade have a choice to maintain the old rules as an attempted fork or to join the majority.

- If new protocol rules are adopted by very few participants, you have an unviable fork which may ultimately fail.

- If new protocol rules are adopted by enough participants to maintain a community and interest then it is a successful fork.

What's the Result of a Deliberate, Successful Fork?

The upshot is that anyone who owned some of the original cryptocurrency continues to have the original cryptocurrency, plus the same number of tokens in new forked cryptocurrency.

Quick analogy: Imagine you usually fly with an airline called CryptoAir where you earn loyalty points, and let's say you have accumulated 500 points with them. Now imagine that some staff from CryptoAir get upset and leave to create their own separate airline, NewCryptoAir. They take a copy of the customer list with them, including the record of how many loyalty points each customer has. Now you have 500 points with CryptoAir *and* 500 points with NewCryptoAir. But you can't spend your NewCryptoAir points with CryptoAir or vice versa. They are incompatible. If you then spend points with one airline, it doesn't affect your points on the other airline. Your old CryptoAir points continue to have whatever value they had, whereas your new NewCryptoAir points will need to establish their own value. Not a perfect analogy but I think it is helpful.

If coin holders had 100 tokens before a successful cryptocurrency fork, have they 'doubled their money?' In one sense, yes, they have doubled the number of tokens they have, as they now have 100 units of the old coin and 100 units of the new coin, and they can spend them independently. In reality, they haven't doubled their *money*, as the two coins (original plus new) have different fiat currency values. In practice, the old currency tends to maintain its fiat value, whereas the new one must float on exchanges with a new ticker symbol, and it will usually start trading at a lower value.

How Does a Deliberate Chainsplit Work?

Participants of a fork make changes to the protocol rules and market their philosophy to a wide audience of miners, wallet software providers, exchanges, merchants, and users. They then coordinate to switch over to the new rules at a planned time, determined by a specific block number known as a *block height*.

At that planned time, two incompatible blocks are mined, one that is valid for the incumbent participants, and the other that is valid for the rebellious participants. The blockchain splits into two, because what is acceptable on one blockchain is not acceptable on the other. Consider the very first transaction that is created that breaks the old rules but conforms to the new rules. This rebellious transaction will be rejected by the old school participants, who will not propagate it, mine it, or add it to their blocks. However, it will be treated as valid by the rebellious validating nodes, and will get mined by a rebellious miner, and the rebellious block will be added to the blockchains of the rebellious participants.

So now there are two blockchains, recording transactions of two different coins which share a common history up to the point of the split. The coins will have different symbols and names to differentiate them, wallets need to be configured to accept the new coin, exchanges need to list the new coin to create a market for it, and merchants and other participants need to accept the new coin.

Media Descriptions

Forks, or specifically chainsplits, are often described in the media as a 'stock split'. This is a poor analogy because, in a stock split, more shares are created and assigned to shareholders but the old and the new shares all represent the same thing. This is not the case in a cryptocurrency chainsplit. A 'spinoff' is a more accurate analogy because in a spinoff, shareholders of the old company get new shares of a new company. This is similar to a fork where holders of the original coin also get the new coin which has different rules from the old coin.

Hard Forks vs Soft Forks

Sometimes the terms hard and soft fork are used. These terms refer to changes in the rules about what constitutes a valid transaction and block.

A soft fork is a change in the rules that is backwards compatible, meaning that blocks created under the new changed rules will still be considered valid by participants who didn't upgrade.

A hard fork is a change in the rules that is not backwards compatible, so that if some participants fail to upgrade, there will be a chainsplit.

In practice, if changes to protocol rules are tightened or more constrained, this results in a soft fork, whereas if consensus rules are loosened, then this is a hard fork.

Case Study 1: Bitcoin Cash

Bitcoin Cash[189] is a (currently) successful fork of Bitcoin, created as a hard fork. Bitcoin Cash and Bitcoin (sometimes called Bitcoin Core to reduce confusion) had a shared history until block 478,558 when the chain split.

The philosophy of Bitcoin Cash is to more accurately reflect the vision in the original Satoshi whitepaper of fast, cheap, decentralised, censorship resistant, digital cash, and proponents believe that Bitcoin Core has not been making progress towards this vision.

So far, Bitcoin Cash has been regarded as successful, as it is supported by popular wallet software, merchants accept it, and it trades on popular cryptocurrency exchanges under the ticker symbol BCH.

Case Study 2: Ethereum Classic

Ethereum Classic is a (currently) successful fork of Ethereum. It was created, as we saw earlier, after The DAO was hacked

---

189   https://www.bitcoincash.org

and more than \$50m of ETH was drained from it. As we have seen, the Ethereum community deliberated as to what to do and the majority decided to hard fork at block 1,920,000 and restore the hacked ETH to the original holders.

But a minority of the community saw this restoration as revisionist and anti-ethical and refused to hard fork, so they continued on with the original blockchain, theft and all. So in a sense, Ethereum itself is the fork, as it had additional code to neutralise the hack of The DAO, and Ethereum Classic is the original Ethereum. But because Classic was in the minority, it is regarded as the fork.

Ethereum Classic trades on cryptocurrency exchanges under the ticker symbol ETC and is widely supported by wallets.

Other Forks

Forks are trendy. It is easier to take something that is proven to already work than to build something from scratch. And, as cryptocurrencies tend to be open source, it is legal to copy the code, tweak it, and run it. Community building with a forked chain is easier than building a new blockchain too. Anyone who had a balance on the original chain will also have a balance on the new chain, so they are more likely to support a fork where they have a balance, rather than support a new blank blockchain.

People saw that Bitcoin Cash successfully forked and retained some currency value, so this spurred many copycats to try the same. However, there is only so much energy in the cryptocurrency space, and there seems to be some 'fork fatigue'. Some commentators predict that many future forks will fail.

BitMEX research[190] provides a list of forks that have happened since the Bitcoin Cash fork:

List of Bitcoin forked coins since Bitcoin Cash

Name	URL/Source	Fork Height
Bitcoin Cash	https://www.bitcoincash.org	478,550
Bitcoin Clashic	http://bitcoinclashic.org	(Forked from Bitcoin Cash)
Bitcoin Candy	http://cdy.one	(Forked from Bitcoin Cash)
Bitcoin Gold	https://bitcoingold.org	491,407
Bitcore	https://bitcore.cc	492,820
Bitcoin Diamond	http://btcd.io	495,866
Bitcoin Platinum	Bitcointalk	498,533
Bitcoin Hot	https://bithot.org	498,777
United Bitcoin	https://www.ub.com	498,777
BitcoinX	https://bcx.org	498,888
Super Bitcoin	http://supersmartbitcoin.com	498,888
Oil Bitcoin	http://oilbtc.io	498,888
Bitcoin Pay	http://www.btceasypay.com	499,345
Bitcoin World	https://btw.one	499,777
Bitclassic Coin	http://bicc.io	499,888
Lightning Bitcoin	https://lightningbitcoin.io	499,999
Bitcoin Stake	https://bitcoinstake.net	499,999
Bitcoin Faith	http://bitcoinfaith.org	500,000
Bitcoin Eco	http://biteco.io	500,000
Bitcoin New	https://www.btn.org	500,100
Bitcoin Top	https://www.bitcointop.org	501,118
Bitcoin God	https://www.bitcoingod.org	501,225
Fast Bitcoin	https://fbtc.pro	501,225
Bitcoin File	https://www.bitcoinfile.org	501,225
Bitcoin Cash Plus	https://www.bitcoincashplus.org	501,407
Bitcoin Segwit2x	https://b2x-segwit.io	501,451
Bitcoin Pizza	http://p.top	501,888
Bitcoin Ore	http://www.bitcoinore.org	501,949
World Bitcoin	http://www.wbtcteam.org	503,888
Bitcoin Smart	https://bcs.info	505,050
BitVote	https://bitvote.one	505,050
Bitcoin Interest	https://bitcoininterest.io	505,083
Bitcoin Atom	https://bitcoinatom.io	505,888
Bitcoin Community	http://btsq.top/	506,066
Big Bitcoin	http://bigbitcoins.org	508,888
Bitcoin Private	https://btcprivate.org	511,346
Classic Bitcoin	https://https://bitclassic.info	516,095
Bitcoin Clean	https://www.bitcoinclean.org	518,800
Bitcoin Hush	https://btchush.org	1st February 2018
Bitcoin Rhodium	https://www.bitcoinrh.org	Unknown
Bitcoin LITE	https://www.bitcoinlite.net	Unknown
Bitcoin Lunar	https://www.bitcoinlunar.org	Unknown
Bitcoin Green	https://www.savebitcoin.io	Unknown
Bitcoin Hex	http://bitcoinhex.com	Unknown

(Source: BitMEX Research, Forked coin websites, findmycoins.ninja)

---

190 https://blog.bitmex.com/44-bitcoin-fork-coins/

Part 5

DIGITAL TOKENS

WHAT ARE DIGITAL TOKENS?

Terminology is evolving quickly. While bitcoins and other cryptocurrencies are all referred to as 'digital tokens' in a generic sense (as in 'a Bitcoin is a digital token'), a distinction now seems to be emerging between *cryptocurrencies*, such as BTC and ETH whose coins are tracked on their respective blockchains, and *tokens* which are usually issued by an issuer during an Initial Coin Offering (ICO) and tracked within smart contracts on Ethereum's blockchain. The word 'token' can mean different things depending on the context in which it is used[191].

What are tokens? What is a digital token? Why is it important?

It is easy to understand what a 'token' is in the physical world. Think of round plastic things like casino chips, beer vouchers, or fairground ride tokens. Essentially a token is something which is issued by an issuer (the casino, the beer festival organisers, or the fairground) and can be used in a specific context or in a specific marketplace, perhaps under specific conditions or timings. The token has value because the context gives it value, but if you take the token outside the context the value decreases or falls to zero. While a $5 casino chip is worth $5 inside a casino, it would be worth less on the other side of the world. And fairground ride tokens would not be worth much, if anything, outside the context of the fairground.

---

191   I now have a new appreciation for dictionary editors who have to battle daily with linguistic evolution versus pedantry!

But what do people mean when they talk about *digital tokens*? If you digitise a beer voucher or casino chip does it become a digital token? Is a balance in a PayPal wallet a digital token? Is a bank balance a digital token? What's special about a Bitcoin?

The characteristics of the different types of token vary widely, and generalisations lead to confusion. In this section, I hope to clarify the different types and characteristics of tokens by differentiating between *blockchain-native* tokens like BTC and ETH, *asset backed tokens* like IOUs, and *utility tokens* that can be spent on goods or services at a later date, usually recorded within smart contracts on the Ethereum blockchain as 'ERC-20' standard tokens[192], but may also be recorded on other blockchains.

Owning a Token

We can be more specific and use the term *cryptoasset*. Ownership of any cryptoasset, whether it is a cryptocurrency or a token, is vested in the person who has the private key that corresponds to the address with which the token is associated. This private key allows that person—the owner—to create and sign transactions releasing the token and assigning it to

---

192   ERC-20 is a set of technical standards for designing smart contracts on Ethereum that hold fungible tokens. Tokens compliant with ERC-20 have well-known interfaces and properties, meaning that they can be easily added by exchanges and wallets. Superior standards exist but remain compatible with ERC-20. JP Buntinx describes the idea in The Merkle: https://themerkle.com/what-is-the-erc20-ethereum-token-standard/

someone else. In some respects, cryptoassets are like bearer assets—if you hold the private key, it is yours[193].

The rules of blockchains require that if a token is to be sent (i.e., if a payment to be made), the transaction must include the digital signature related to the token's current address. This digital signature is validated by all of the blockchain network participants. The digital signature acts as a single point of authentication to signal that it really is the address owner who is making the payment instruction.

With online banking, in contrast, you prove that you are you then instruct the bank to do something on your behalf. You provide a username and password and usually a one-time PIN created on another device—a so called 'second factor'. Authenticating with a username and password has its benefits. If you forget or lose your password, you can have it reset if you supply more proof that you are the account holder.

With a cryptoasset, transactions must have a valid digital signature. If you lose your private key, you cannot access your asset and you cannot have it reset. If your private key is copied the thief can make transactions on your behalf, and you can't stop them. In this respect cryptocurrencies are much less forgiving than banks. Not even those who maintain the ledger can alter the balances, because they can't provide the necessary digital signatures. This is different to a traditional ledger maintained by a bank, which can be alter balances without any kind of cryptographic proofs.

---

193   In another respect, cryptoassets are not bearer assets, because they are recorded on a register – the blockchain! Traditionally an asset is a bearer asset (she who holds it owns it) or a registered asset (she whose name is on a list owns it). Cryptoassets are somewhere in between.

Some people say that with Bitcoin, you are your own bank. You don't instruct an entity to make a payment on your behalf: you are responsible for making payments yourself.

Categorising Tokens

New tokens are emerging almost daily. Their properties vary. While segregation and separation are difficult, I currently think of tokens in three categories:

Native blockchain tokens, which are essential for the underlying blockchain to work or be incentivised. Native tokens are usually the incentive for block-creators to do their work. Cryptocurrencies are usually native tokens.

Asset backed tokens, which represent title or ownership to some real-world asset held in trust by a custodian.

Utility tokens, which represent a claim on a service provided by the issuer of the token.

Data website onchainfx.com provides these categories for digital tokens[194]:

> **Currency Tokens:** Currency tokens are native blockchain assets intended to be used as money. Networks classified as currencies typically do not have many 'features' beyond those necessary to define and transfer the native blockchain asset.

> **Platform Tokens:** Platform tokens are required to use general purpose decentralised networks that support a wide variety of possible applications. Platform tokens

---

194   https://onchainfx.com/categories used with permission

are often used specifically to mediate use of the platform (ie, tokens are used to pay 'gas' in order to access the platform's functionality).

Utility Tokens: Utility tokens are native to decentralised networks that are designed for specific application types. That is, they are open networks but designed with a specific-use-case in mind. For example, decentralised storage and decentralised asset exchange are both use-types for which targeted networks (and their corresponding tokens) are being built. The terms 'Utility Tokens' and 'Protocol Tokens' are often used to describe the same type of token.

Brand Tokens: Brand tokens exist as tradeable digital assets for use mostly on one company/entity's platform. Some Brand Tokens may evolve into more generalised Utility Tokens over time.

Security Tokens: Security tokens represent a claim on a specific cash-flow, or off-chain asset. Networks which generate fees-for-service that accrue to token holders, explicitly grant voting rights to token holders, or where tokens are said the be 'backed' by some other asset, such as gold or company equity, are Security Tokens.

In the section on ICOs we will discuss how tokens may be classified by regulators as financial securities. For now, I will describe my own distinctions between native tokens, asset backed tokens, and utility tokens.

Native Blockchain Tokens

Here I will use the word 'token' generically to mean any units recorded on any blockchain.

Cryptocurrencies such as Bitcoin and Ethereum use native tokens BTC and ETH respectively. These units are needed to incentivise miners to create valid blocks without an external party to fund the participants. ETH is also used to pay Ethereum miners to run smart contracts. The tokens are also known as 'intrinsic' or 'built-in' tokens. They are inseparable from their blockchain systems, and are used both as an incentive for participants to keep the blockchains running, and as a payment mechanism to use the blockchains.

How do these native tokens come into existence?

Intrinsic tokens are created by the same blockchain software that keeps track of ownership of these units. They are created transparently by software in the mining process according to a schedule defined by the blockchain protocol. All participants agree to abide by the protocol rules.

What backs native tokens?

Nothing 'backs' these native tokens. They just exist and have value. The gold analogy is useful here. When you hold physical gold it is not 'backed' by anything; it is just valuable in itself. With native tokens there *is* no issuer to whom you can return a token, to redeem for an underlying asset, any more than you can go to a 'gold issuer' (mother nature?) and redeem your gold for something else.

Satoshi Nakamoto created the *idea* of Bitcoin, but is not the issuer of the BTC units. Bitcoin miners *create* BTC according to some mutually agreed constraints, but they are no more the *issuer* of BTC than a gold-prospector is the *issuer* of the gold that they discover.

Where do native tokens derive their value?

Their value comes partly from their usefulness and partly from their speculative value. Let's use the gold analogy again. Gold derives its value from two sources. Firstly, it is useful for filling gaps in your teeth, for certain technical or industrial processes, and, because it is pretty and doesn't tarnish, for wearing as jewellery. Secondly, gold has a speculative value arising from its scarcity, general desirability, and its long price history.

Native tokens are useful because they can be used in a specific context. The context for the BTC token is the Bitcoin blockchain and the context for the ETH token is the Ethereum blockchain. Bitcoins, like gold, don't *represent* an asset, they *are* the asset. As considered in our earlier discussion about different types of money, bitcoins are representative money. Native tokens also have speculative value as some people want to buy and hold them, just like any other asset that speculators can buy and hold.

Examples of native tokens

Some of the more well-known examples of intrinsic tokens:

- BTC on the Bitcoin blockchain

- ETH on Ethereum

- NXT on the NXT platform

- XRP on the Ripple network

There are many more, and they all differ slightly. Since 2018, native tokens that are not issued or backed by anyone have been increasingly described as 'cryptocurrencies'. The word 'token' is increasingly confined to those tokens issued by projects which *are* redeemable for a product or service at a later stage. But definitional boundaries are blurred. For example, ETH, although widely described as a cryptocurrency, was issued by the Ethereum Foundation during their crowdsale, whereas BTC has not been issued by anyone. EOS tokens were issued before their blockchain went live and those tokens can be swapped into native tokens that run on their blockchain. I suspect that terminology will continue to be.

What are intrinsic tokens for?

As discussed, intrinsic tokens are the incentives for miners to do their jobs. But each blockchain has its nuances. We have explored BTC and ETH in detail earlier. Ripple and NXT are two other cryptocurrencies which have some interesting twists.

The Ripple network uses tokens called ripples, with a ticker symbol XRP aligned with the ISO currency standards. On the Ripple network all, the XRP tokens were created at the beginning—all the XRP that will ever exist were *pre-mined* and shared out among key participants. Each transaction on the Ripple network needs to include a small amount of XRP as a transaction fee. Unlike Bitcoin and Ethereum, XRPs are destroyed by block makers, rather than being claimed by them as is the case with Bitcoin and Ethereum. Therefore the total number of XRPs in circulation decreases with time. The XRPs destroyed in each transaction ensures that transactions have a tiny cost, preventing transaction spam which can happen if transactions are costless to create.

The NXT network uses pre-mined NXT tokens. Each transaction on the NXT network requires a fee to be added. The fee goes to the block maker (in NXT this is called a 'forger' instead of a 'miner'). Therefore, the total number of NXT remains constant with time.

Asset Backed Tokens

Any financial asset can be recorded as a token, either directly, where the token *is* the financial asset, or as a depository receipt, where the token is a *claim on a custodian* for the financial asset. You may think of a share or a bond as a physical object, but financial assets are nothing but *agreements* between parties, usually an issuer and the owner of the asset. For example, a share of a company is a legal agreement between the issuer company and the owner of the share; a bond is a legal agreement between the issuer and the holder of the bond; a loan is a legal agreement between the borrower and lender. Money itself is an agreement between two parties. Deposits in a bank account are an agreement between the bank and the depositor, with many provisions including daily transaction limits, daily withdrawal limits, interest, etc. A banknote is an agreement between the central bank and the bearer.

These agreements can all be represented as tokens recorded on blockchains or distributed ledgers.

Asset backed digital tokens take a number of forms:

1. Depository receipt tokens

2. Title tokens

3. Contract tokens

Depository Receipt Tokens

Depository receipts are tokens that are claims on a specific entity for an underlying item. You can think of them as a digital version of a goldsmith's receipt for gold stored in their vault, or like a digital version of a cloakroom ticket or left-luggage ticket. The tokens represent ownership of the underlying item held in trust by a custodian. The receipt could be for real world physical objects, such as gold, or for a financial asset, such as a share of a company. When a token holder wants to redeem a token, they go to the issuer with the token to claim back the underlying asset. The issuer then destroys the token once they have returned the underlying asset.

Title Tokens

Title tokens are a slightly different concept. They are the digital document that represents proof of ownership of an asset, for example a digital title document to a car or house. Unlike a depository receipt token, the item is not necessarily under someone else's custody.

How Do Asset Backed Digital Tokens Work?

Let's take the example of Goldchain Inc, a fictitious entity. It stores physical gold bullion in its vault on behalf of itself and its account holders who have bought some of that gold. It issues digital tokens called GoldchainOz to the account holders when they buy that gold. Each token represents 1 oz of the gold bullion stored. These gold tokens are recorded on a blockchain. They may be recorded in smart contract on the public Ethereum blockchain, or on a private Ethereum blockchain, as assets on any number of other public blockchains or private blockchains such as Corda. It doesn't really matter for these illustrative purposes. What matters is the ability for a customer of Goldchain Inc to withdraw the tokens and keep them in a wallet where they, and only they, have the private keys.

Let's assume you want to acquire 1 oz of their gold bullion. So:

1. You create an account with Goldchain Inc by going to their website.

2. You make a bank transfer of fiat funds to Goldchain's bank account to fund your account.

3. After a period of time (hours or days depending on how long your bank transfer takes to get to Goldchain's bank), Goldchain sends you an email indicating they have checked their bank account and have received your funds. You can now buy gold tokens.

4. You log in again and click 'buy' for 1 oz of gold at $1,500 per oz.

5. The money in your Goldchain account drops by $1,500, and you see you have 1 'GoldchainOz' token in your

account. In the background, Goldchain reclassifies 1 oz of gold in its books from 'Gold owned by Goldchain Inc' to 'Customer assets'. Goldchain has sold some gold to you, but instead of shipping the physical gold to your home it has issued you a token representing that gold. The gold token is still under the control of Goldchain Inc because you haven't yet withdrawn it to a wallet entirely under your control.

6. If you wish to have the gold token completely under your control, you can withdraw the GoldchainOz token to your independent address. Goldchain will send a transaction to the blockchain transferring one GoldchainOz token from their address to your address.

7. You can keep the token, give it to your friends, sell it, or do whatever you want with it. Let's say you transfer it to Alice.

8. Eventually Alice wants to redeem the token real gold, if that is an option, or sell it for USD. She can do so by creating an account at Goldchain Inc, transferring the gold token from her blockchain address to their blockchain address, and requesting delivery of gold, or selling the token back to Goldchain Inc, assuming these options are available.

If Goldchain Inc, who controls the warehouse, is a central point of failure and control, what is the value in using tokens? Why doesn't Goldchain Inc just use an Excel spreadsheet?

Firstly, the use of cryptography in blockchain technology makes the tokens very hard to fake, and this creates more transparency over the number of tokens issued and held by customers. The warehouse can prove that there are not more tokens than they have gold in their vault. An auditor would periodically match the amount of physical gold to the number of tokens outstanding.

Secondly, existing processes of passing title documents or receipts may be manual, time consuming or operationally challenging. Transfer of digital tokens may be more efficient, and increasingly so as new software and hardware is developed to manage digital assets.

Finally, in a peer-to-peer system, the warehouse itself doesn't have to be online and participate in transactions between customers. All it has to do is issue and redeem the digital tokens. The trading of the tokens can occur on whatever digital asset exchange or exchanges are chosen rather than being managed centrally by the warehouse. The settlement of the tokens is recorded on the chosen blockchain.

This leads to a segregation of responsibilities and opens up the possibility of competition for each element of the end to end 'trade lifecycle'. The warehouse's job is to store gold, issue tokens representing that gold, and transfer gold to any party legitimately redeeming the token, as it would have done under a paper-based system of old. Trading, settlement, liquidity, collateralisation, and other functions unrelated to storage can be done elsewhere without the warehouse having to update their records or manage those functions. The title documents or receipts, by virtue of being on a blockchain, can be trusted as genuine and uncounterfeitable, and the ownership or liens on any particular lump of gold can be made more transparent, potentially reducing the confusion relating to who has what claim on which piece of gold.

Asset backed tokens are easy to transfer. Blockchains enable predictable and secure record keeping. The key risk is that the issuer must remain solvent. If the gold is stolen from the vault, or if the issuer becomes bankrupt, whether from fraud or otherwise, asset backed tokens can become valueless.

Contract Tokens

Contract tokens represent a contractual obligation between the issuer of the token and the bearer of the token, or between two parties who jointly agree to hold the token. For example, a token could represent a share of a company or an interest rate swap between two parties. Shares can be issued by a company in the form of a token, and the owner of the token is the shareholder. Two parties who agree on an interest rate swap enter into an agreement which is represented by the token.

Contract tokens are slightly different from depository receipts. In the case of a contract token, the token *is* the share; whereas with a depository receipt, the token is a *claim on a custodian* who is safekeeping the share.

Utility Tokens

The holder of a utility token can redeem the token from a specific entity for a *product or service* rather than for an *asset*. Sale of utility tokens is a popular ICO strategy.

Utility tokens represent a liability of the issuing company. Eventually, when the product or service becomes available, a token holder can redeem their token for that product or service. In this respect, ICOs that issue utility tokens are performing a pre-sale.

Transactions

A transaction is just an entry to the ledger that changes the state of the ledger. We have previously discussed transactions that change the ownership of tokens. But transactions can also represent changes to the token itself, if allowed by the rules for that particular token. For example, a token representing a share could change status from 'pre-dividend' to 'ex-dividend,' if signed by the right participant and a dividend is paid. That same token could be marked with 'voted' after a shareholder vote has taken place. A token representing a bond could change status from 'coupon due' to 'coupon paid' if accompanied by a transaction that pays the coupon. A utility token representing a service could be marked as 'partially redeemed' if the service had a number of elements to it. And so on. At this stage in the evolution of cryptoassets, we are just scratching the surface of what is possible.

TRACKING OF PHYSICAL OBJECTS

Blockchains and distributed ledgers work best when everything can be recorded on the chain, i.e. when everything is digital. So blockchains are great for cryptocurrencies or for tokens representing legal agreements between entities, whether shares, bonds, debt, or even a future claim on an entity. These tokens can be recorded digitally without any physical object being present. But problems start emerging when you want to track physical objects such as handbags, food, art, or elephants.

The interest in digital tokens for tracking ownership of
physical objects seems to have come from the fact that
bitcoins are traceable. This is true in a narrow sense. You
can trace the provenance of any specific bitcoins through all
of the previous addresses that they belonged to, all the way
back to where they were first mined. This is possible because
every transaction is recorded on the Bitcoin blockchain, and
anyone can download the full blockchain and interrogate it.
The provenance of bitcoins is traceable because that is the
way Bitcoin works. You can't make a Bitcoin transaction *off*
the chain, because the very definition of a Bitcoin transaction
is that it is recorded *on* the chain, and the UTxO model forces
you to specify which bitcoins are moving where, resulting in a
complete chain of provenance on the chain.

Can we extend that concept easily to real world objects?
According to an article published online by *Fortune* in
October 2016, 'Walmart and IBM Are Partnering to Put
Chinese Pork on a Blockchain'[195]. Apparently, blockchains
may be used to track the provenance of pork and to stop
potentially dangerous food from getting to consumers.

But stop for a second and think. How on earth would this
work? I don't know much about the pig supply chain but I
suppose you have a bunch of companies who do everything
from breeding the piglets, feeding them, slaughtering them,
cutting them up, shipping them, packing, and delivering.
Eventually, pork cutlets end up on the supermarket shelf
for people to buy or on a plate in a restaurant. So... all the
participants in the pig supply chain could have an address
on a blockchain, with PigCoin tokens, issued presumably

---

195   http://fortune.com/2016/10/19/walmart-ibm-blockchain-china-pork/

by the farmer, that represent pigs. Movement of PigCoin
is recorded immutably on PigChain. When a farmer sells
a pig to another farmer, the seller says, 'Hey, what's your
PigChain address? Let me send you some PigCoins,' and
makes a corresponding PigCoin transaction on PigChain to
represent the movement of the pig. But then, one fateful day,
the buyer is a slaughterhouse who chops the pigs up into
small bits and sends those different bits to different parties.
Ah! But of course a PigCoin, like Bitcoin, is divisible, so the
slaughterhouse splits up a PigCoin and sends fractions to
different buyers. But which fraction is which part of the pig?
Do we need a TrotterCoin and a LeftRearFlankCoin? What
happens if one party doesn't have an account on PigChain?
What if a party loses their private key and all of their
SnoutCoins end up trapped in their account while the real
underlying snouts are being distributed? What if (horror of
horrors), a bad person swaps out, in real life, a high-quality
pig for a low-quality pig, but then still sends the PigCoin to
the buyer, saying, 'Oh look at the PigCoin's provenance on
PigChain, the pig you are buying is definitely high quality, you
can download the PigChain and see for yourself?' And when a
pig becomes part of a sausage, then how would that work? We
will need BreadcrumbCoin, HerbCoin, NastyBitsOfPigCoin
and a market maker to exchange those for a WienerCoin.
And how does the restaurant or person in the supermarket
casually browsing the raw cutlets validate that the sausage
in front of them is the real deal? Do they take a photo of
the sausage and check it against PigChain? Do they scan
a QR code that takes them to a website that says in large
letters, 'This is definitely a real sausage?' Or do they pull out
their handy DNA testing kit and track the sausage's DNA
on PigChain? How do you stop an enterprising chef from

swapping out the high-quality cutlet for a cheaper one? This is all absurd.

According to the *Fortune* article, 'Information to be stored on the blockchain, where fraud and inaccuracies are much harder to get away with, includes details related to farm origins, factory data, expiration dates, storage temperatures, and shipping'. That is good then. Of course none of that can be faked before storing it on PigChain.

It is easy to make fun, but tracking real world items by using a digital overlay is difficult. Blockchains are great for tracking unique digital items that only exist on that blockchain, but not as good when digital and physical worlds collide. Blockchains don't tell the truth; they just record what someone tells them. Perhaps blockchains could increase certain aspects of transparency in a supply chain, but they are not foolproof and should not be used just because the phrase 'supply chain' has the word 'chain' in it.

Having said that, I can imagine a few cases which are interesting and, while not absolutely requiring blockchains, could use some of the same concepts. High value designer handbags could have tamper-resistant chips inserted; a buyer could then scan a bag to make sure that it is not a fake before buying it. The chip would contain a private key that would produce a digital signature when scanned. The digital signature could be validated against a list of public keys issued by the manufacturer. The chip would be embedded in the handbag such that it is obvious if it is removed or tampered with.

This system uses public and private keys but doesn't need blockchains. The system would solve the issue of a bad actor passing off a fake handbag as real. However, many people buy fake designer handbags knowing that they are fake...they buy them because they look like the real thing but are cheap. So the system would only go so far. It is important to deeply understand the fundamental problem being solved.

NOTABLE CRYPTOCURRENCIES AND TOKENS

There are many other cryptocurrencies that either exist as blockchains in themselves or as tokens recorded in smart contracts on other blockchains, usually on Ethereum's public chain.

Onchainfx.com and coinmarketcap.com do a good job in cataloguing these if they trade over a certain amount of volume per day. At time of writing, onchainfx[196] records the top[197] tokens, with my comments, as follows:

Currency tokens (Primarily used as Money/Store of Value):

- Bitcoin (BTC)—the original cryptocurrency and store of value, created by pseudonymous Satoshi Nakamoto, launched in 2009.

- Ripple (XRP)—a token used to move value across the Ripple network, designed as a currency that was

---

196   https://onchainfx.com/categories

197   Note that 'top' is roughly defined by 'market cap,' i.e., token price times number of tokens outstanding. Top doesn't mean good. I do not endorse any of these, nor do I think they are all legitimate. By the time you read this it will be out of date.

initially described to compete against banks then to be used by banks to improve foreign exchange and international payments. Created in 2012 by OpenCoin (rebranded to Ripple Inc in 2015[198]).

- Litecoin (LTC)—an early Bitcoin clone with faster blocks and a different mining proof-of-work. Called 'Silver to Bitcoin's Gold' by its founder Charlie Lee who announced that he sold all of his Litecoin in Dec 2017.

- Zcash (ZEC)—a privacy focused coin using advanced cryptography called zero knowledge proofs to shield transaction data. Created by Zooko Wilcox-O'Hearn in 2016.

- Dash (DASH)—another privacy focused coin, created as XCoin in 2014 by Evan Duffield, renamed Darkcoin, renamed DASH.

- Monero (XMR)—yet another privacy focused coin, uses ring-signatures to obscure payer and recipient addresses. Launched in 2014.

Platform tokens (i.e. those used as gas to power smart contracts):

- Ethereum (ETH)—the original smart contract enabled blockchain platform, created by a Vitalik Buterin and launched in 2015.

- Ethereum Classic (ETC)—fork of Ethereum which didn't bail out DAO investors. Proponents like immutability. Forked from Ethereum in July 2016.

---

198   http://www.businessinsider.com/ripple-link-xrp-explained-2018-3

- New Economy Movement (NEM)—a blockchain with 'smart assets'.

- EOS (EOS)—a new blockchain structure designed to be more scalable than Ethereum.

Utility tokens (Built for Specific-Use Networks)

- Augur (REP)—a token used for betting on things on a 'prediction market,' i.e. a betting platform. Launched in 2015 from San Francisco.

- Siacoin (SC)—a token used for paying for encrypted decentralised file storage. Launched in 2015.

- Golem (GNT)—a token used for paying for decentralised computations & calculations. Launched in 2016.

- Gnosis (GNO)—another prediction market coin. Launched in 2016 from Germany.

Brand tokens (Specific-Use on Single Entity's Network)

- Basic Attention Token (BAT)—Token used to make micropayments in a web browser called Brave. Launched in 2017.

- Civic (CVC)—Something to do with identity verification on the/a blockchain. I hope it solves the problem of having too many passwords. Launched in 2017.

- Steem (STEEM)—Token used for making micropayments on social media and forum sites. Launched in 2016.

This is just a short list of the many tokens and platforms
that exist today. Many more are planned. The blockchain
and cryptoasset industry in aggregate has attracted
significant interest and investment, and I would guess that
tens of thousands of developers are working to build viable
platforms. As with businesses, I expect that most platforms
will evolve and adapt, in search of long term viability. I expect
a few to succeed and many to fail due to unviable models,
insufficient interest, or insufficient network size. Those that
succeed could become as relevant to people as the internet
is today.

Part 6

BLOCKCHAIN TECHNOLOGY

WHAT IS
BLOCKCHAIN TECHNOLOGY?

You will see the phrase 'blockchain technology,' or commonly just 'blockchain,' in many different contexts, and it can be confusing because different people use the words to mean different things. Purists will have a different understanding of the word from generalists. Angela Walch, Research Fellow at University College London—Centre for Blockchain Technologies, provides some excellent commentary on the lexicon in her 2017 paper 'The Path of the Blockchain Lexicon (and the Law)'.[199] In general, technologists and computer scientists are more precise with their terminology than journalists, who write for the layman. In this chapter, I will provide a broad overview of blockchain technology and then explain some of the nuances.

By now, you should understand that there is no such thing as 'the blockchain,' just as there is no such thing as 'the database' or 'the network'. ETH is *the* Ethereum blockchain, a reference to the public Ethereum transaction database— but you can also create private Ethereum blockchains by simply running some node software on some machines and having them connect to each other. Your private Ethereum network will create its own blockchain, and the miners will mine ETH just like in the public network. Your private ETH will not be compatible with the public ETH because your private Ethereum network has a different history from the public version.

---

199   https://papers.ssrn.com/sol3/papers.cfm?abstract_id=2940335

In print, if you read 'the blockchain,' you may need to make a guess as to what the writer means. In conversation, and at the risk of coming across as pedantic, it should help your understanding to ask early on, 'Which blockchain platform?' then, 'The public chain or a private one?' As you now know, there are many blockchains, and many variations on how they work.

If you like hierarchies, blockchains fall under the broader category of 'distributed ledgers'. All blockchains are distributed ledgers, but you can have distributed ledgers that don't have blocks of data chained together and broadcast to all participants. Sometimes journalists and consultants inaccurately use the term 'blockchain' when they are describing non-blockchain distributed ledgers. I guess 'distributed ledgers' is too much of a mouthful whereas 'blockchain' is a nice memorable buzzword.

We need to differentiate between blockchain *technologies* and specific blockchain *ledgers*.

Blockchain *technologies* are the rules or standards for how a ledger is created and maintained. Different technologies have different rules for participation, different network rules, different specifications for how to create transactions, different methods of storing data, and different consensus mechanisms. When a network is created, the blockchain or ledger of record is initially empty of transactions, just as a new physical leather-bound ledger is empty. Some example blockchain technologies are: Bitcoin, Ethereum, NXT, Corda, Fabric, and Quorum.

Blockchain *ledgers* themselves are specific instances of ledgers that contain their respective transactions or records.

Think of normal databases. You may have heard of a few types or flavours of databases—Oracle databases, MySQL databases, perhaps others. Each flavour works slightly differently though they are all have similar goals: efficient storage, sorting, and retrieval of data. You can have multiple *instances* of the same type of database: a company might use more than one Oracle database. And so it is with blockchains. Some blockchain technologies operate one way, others operate a slightly different way and you can have multiple instances of any blockchain technology, in separate ledgers.

Public, Permissionless Blockchains

We've explored that cryptocurrencies and some other tokens use public blockchains as their medium of record—that is, their respective transactions are recorded in blocks on a replicated ledger. Public blockchains are also described as permissionless primarily because anyone may create blocks or be a bookkeeper without needing permission from an authority. In these public networks, there is also permissionlessness in another sense—anyone may create an address for receiving funds and create transactions for sending funds.

Private Instances of Public Blockchains

As described earlier, you can run blockchain software on a private network to create a fresh ledger. For example, you could take the Ethereum code and run it, but instead of pointing your node to some computers already running the public Ethereum blockchain, you could point it instead to a few other computers that are not on the public Ethereum network. As far as all of these computers are concerned, they are starting with a fresh ledger with no entries.

Could you set up a small private network running Ethereum, then mine some ETH and transfer them to the public network? No. Although this private network would use the same set of *rules* as the public blockchain, they have different records of account balances. Nodes on each network can only validate what they see in their own blockchain, and they are not able to see coins on the other blockchain.

Permissioned (or permissionable) blockchains

Some platforms are designed to allow groups of participants to create their own blockchains in a private context. They do not have a global public network. These are called 'private blockchains' and they are designed to only allow pre-approved participants to participate. Hence the term 'permissioned'.

Popular permissioned blockchains include:

- Corda, a platform built from scratch by R3 and a consortium of banks for use by regulated financial institutions but with broad applicability.

- Hyperledger Fabric, a platform built by IBM and donated to the Linux Foundation's Hyperledger Project. It was originally based heavily on Ethereum but between versions 0.6 and 1.0 was heavily re-architected. Fabric uses a concept of 'channels' to restrict parties from seeing all transactions.

- Quorum, a private blockchain system based on Ethereum originally built by JP Morgan. Quorum uses advanced cryptographic constructs called *zero knowledge proofs* to obfuscate data and address privacy issues.

- Various private instances of Ethereum under
  development by individual businesses.

Unlike permissionless networks such as Bitcoin and
Ethereum, permissioned blockchains don't need their own
native token. They don't need to incentivise block-creators,
and they don't need proof-of-work as the gating factor to
allow participants to write to the shared ledger. Instead,
when businesses transact, they are looking for data that
can be trusted to be up to date, agreed and signed off by the
appropriate parties. In a traditional business ecosystem,
participants are all identified, and if some try to misbehave
they can be sued. When parties are identified and have legal
agreements between them, the technical environment is
not as hostile as that of the pseudonymous world of public
cryptocurrency blockchains, where code is law and there are
no terms of service or legal agreements.

Some cryptocurrency proponents argue that permissioned
private blockchains are somehow inferior to public
cryptocurrency blockchains. An analogy commonly used is
that public cryptocurrency blockchains are like 'the internet,'
in that they are open, free, and permissionless, whereas
private industry blockchains are like intranets, which
are closed. The implication here, of course, is that public
blockchains will be very successful and disruptive whereas
private blockchains are boring, unsuccessful and not very
disruptive or game changing[200].

---

200   The conflation between success and disruption is one viewpoint that
seems to be common in technology and innovation hubs. However, there
are many routes to success. Success can equally be derived from creating
technologies that incrementally improve business-as-usual company
operations.

Nothing could be further from the truth. Intranets and private company networks are highly successful. I can't think of any significant company that doesn't use its own network. And it is equally far from the truth to regard the internet as being open and permissionless. As Tim Swanson notes on his blog in 'Intranets and the internet'[201]:

> *The internet is actually a bunch of private networks of internet service providers (ISPs) that have legal agreements with the end users, cooperate through 'peering' agreements with other ISPs, and communicate via a common, standardized routing protocols such as BGP which publishes autonomous system numbers.*

The fact is that cryptocurrencies and private blockchains are different tools deployed to address different problems. They are both fine and may happily coexist. In news articles written between 2015 and 2018, blockchain technology was commonly defined as 'the technology underpinning the cryptocurrency Bitcoin'. This conflates the two ideas and is as enlightening as defining databases as 'the technology that powers Twitter'.

Public and private blockchains run within different context and ecosystems and, as discussed, are designed to address different problems. So they will naturally operate in different ways. After all, technology is a tool, and tools exist to serve a need. If the needs are different, then it is likely that the tools will be different.

---

201   http://www.ofnumbers.com/2017/04/10/intranets-and-the-internet/

WHAT IS COMMON TO BLOCKCHAIN TECHNOLOGIES?

Blockchains usually contain the following concepts:

1. A data store (database) that records changes in the data. Up to now they have most commonly been financial transactions, but you can store and record changes to any kind of data in a blockchain.

2. Replication of the data store across a number of systems in real time. 'Broadcast' blockchains, such as Bitcoin and Ethereum, ensure that all data is sent to all participants: everyone sees everything. Other technologies are more selective about where data is sent.

3. 'Peer-to-peer' rather than client-server network architecture. Data may be 'gossiped' to neighbours rather than broadcast by a single coordinator acting as the golden source of data.

4. Cryptographic methods such as digital signatures to prove ownership and authenticity, and hashes for references and sometimes to manage write-access.

I often describe blockchain technology as 'A collection of technologies, a bit like a bag of Legos'. You can take different bricks out of the bag and put them together in different ways to create different results.

Sometimes when discussing specific potential uses for this technology, we hear this exchange:

'But, you don't need a *blockchain* to do that. You can just use *traditional* technology!'

'So how would you do it?'

'Oh, some data storage, some peer-to-peer data sharing, cryptography to ensure authenticity, hashes to ensure data tampering is evident etc'.

'But you've just described how blockchains work!'

So blockchains are not themselves a new invention, but instead, they put together existing technologies to create new capabilities.

What's the difference between a blockchain and a database?

A common database is a system which simply stores and retrieves data. A blockchain platform is more than that. It stores and retrieves existing data just as a normal database does. It also connects to other peers and listens for new data, validates new data against pre-agreed rules, then stores and broadcasts that new data to other network participants to ensure that they all share the same updated data. And it does so constantly, without manual intervention.

What's the difference between a distributed database and a distributed ledger?

Replicated databases, where data is copied in real time to multiple machines for resiliency or performance reasons are not new. *Sharded* databases, where the workload and storage are sharded, or spread around multiple machines, usually to increase speed and storage, are also not new. With distributed ledgers or blockchains, however, participants do not need to trust each other. They do not work on the assumption that the other participants are behaving honestly, so each participant individually checks everything. Richard Brown describes this in his blog[202] as a difference in trust boundaries:

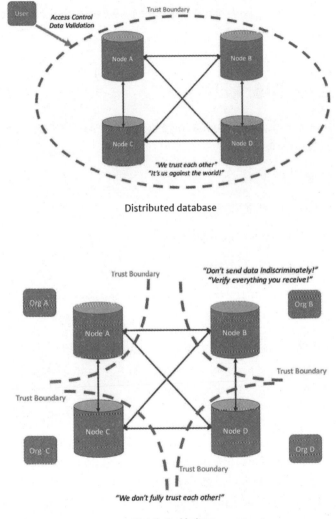

Distributed database

Distributed ledger

WHAT ARE BLOCKCHAINS GOOD FOR?

The motivations between public and private blockchains are different. Let's consider them separately.

Public Blockchains

To date, public blockchains have been used with some success in the following areas:

1. Speculation

2. Darknet markets

3. Cross border payments

4. Initial Coin Offerings

Speculation

The main use for cryptocurrencies is undoubtedly speculation. Their prices are volatile and people make and lose a lot of money trading these coins.

The fact that there are no established methods to value a cryptocurrency means that prices are likely to remain volatile for some time. This differs from traditional financial markets where pricing models help to constrain prices to within broadly understood limits. Equities have well-established pricing methodologies. Discounted forecast cashflows, book value, and enterprise value calculations can help to establish a consensus on the value of a company. Ratios such as earnings per share, price to earnings, and return on assets can help to compare share prices between similar companies. Fiat currencies trade on the basis of comparative economic data. Other traditional financial assets have other standardised pricing methodologies. Up to now, however, I have not seen credible methods for pricing cryptocurrencies or ICO tokens. This is changing—as the industry matures, pricing models are being explored, but it will take some time for these models to become widely accepted.

Darknet Markets

Cryptocurrencies have been used with some success to buy items from underground marketplaces.

Unfortunately for some, the traceability of certain cryptocurrencies makes them flawed candidates for illegal activity. In 2015, two US Federal Agents from the Drug Enforcement Agency (DEA) and the US Secret Service, sought to enrich themselves while conducting an undercover investigation of the Silk Road drug marketplace. Perhaps they believed that Bitcoin was anonymous and untraceable. They allegedly stole, bribed, blackmailed, and laundered the proceeds while under cover and were eventually charged with money laundering and wire fraud. Here is an excerpt from a press release issued by the US Department of Justice[203]:

> Carl M. Force, 46, of Baltimore, was a Special Agent with the DEA, and Shaun W. Bridges, 32, of Laurel, Maryland, was a Special Agent with the U.S. Secret Service (USSS). Both were assigned to the Baltimore Silk Road Task Force, which

---

203   https://www.justice.gov/opa/pr/former-federal-agents-charged-bitcoin-money-laundering-and-wire-fraud

investigated illegal activity in the Silk Road marketplace. Force served as an undercover agent and was tasked with establishing communications with a target of the investigation, Ross Ulbricht, a.k.a. 'Dread Pirate Roberts'. Force is charged with wire fraud, theft of government property, money laundering and conflict of interest. Bridges is charged with wire fraud and money laundering.

According to the complaint, Force was a DEA agent assigned to investigate the Silk Road marketplace. During the investigation, Force engaged in certain authorized undercover operations by, among other things, communicating online with 'Dread Pirate Roberts' (Ulbricht), the target of his investigation. The complaint alleges, however, that Force then, without authority, developed additional online personas and engaged in a broad range of illegal activities calculated to bring him personal financial gain. In doing so, the complaint alleges, Force used fake online personas, and engaged in complex Bitcoin transactions to steal from the government and the targets of the investigation. Specifically, Force allegedly solicited and received digital currency as part of the investigation, but failed to report his receipt of the funds, and instead transferred the currency to his personal account. In one such transaction, Force allegedly sold information about the government's investigation to the target of the investigation. The complaint also alleges that Force invested in and worked for a digital currency exchange company while still working for the DEA, and that he directed the company to freeze a customer's account with no legal basis to do so, then transferred the customer's funds to his personal account. Further, Force allegedly sent an unauthorized Justice Department subpoena to an online payment service directing that it unfreeze his personal account.

Bridges allegedly diverted to his personal account over $800,000 in digital currency that he gained control of

during the Silk Road investigation. The complaint alleges
that Bridges placed the assets into an account at Mt. Gox, the
now-defunct digital currency exchange in Japan. He then
allegedly wired funds into one of his personal investment
accounts in the United States mere days before he sought a
$2.1 million seizure warrant for Mt. Gox's accounts.

On 1 July 2015, Force pled guilty to money laundering with predicates of wire fraud and theft of government property, obstruction of justice, and extortion. Later, on 31 August 2015, Bridges admitted that he stole over $800,000 of Bitcoin while on the case, and pled guilty to money laundering and obstruction of justice[204]

What can we learn from this? Don't use bitcoins to perform or fund illegal activities.

Cross Border Payments

While there may have been some limited success in using cryptocurrencies as a vehicle to move fiat across borders, adoption has been limited. I personally performed an experiment in 2014 when I sent $200 Singapore dollars to my friend in Indonesia[205] using three methods: Western Union, bank transfer, and Bitcoin. The Bitcoin route was by far the worst user experience, and the most expensive. However, Bitcoin has become more usable since then, and I expect it to continue to improve further.

---

204   https://www.justice.gov/usao-ndca/pr/former-secret-service-agent-
pleads-guilty-money-laundering-and-obstruction

205   To arrive as Indonesian Rupiah

The core problem is that in a conventional fiat-to-fiat remittance, whether through a financial services agency such as Western Union or through the banking system, there is only one exchange of currencies. Using cryptocurrencies, there are now two exchanges: fiat to crypto, then crypto to fiat. More exchanges mean more steps, complexity, and cost.

Cross border payments were initially trumpeted as a 'killer app' for Bitcoin and cryptocurrencies, especially in 2014–15, but in 2018 there is less media attention for this particular use of cryptocurrency. Indeed, in June 2018, money transfer agency Western Union announced that they had been testing XRP for six months and were yet to see any savings[206]. Perhaps the industry is in the 'trough of disillusionment' in Gartner's technology hype cycle[207].

Initial Coin Offerings (ICOs)

ICOs are a new method of fundraising that became popular in 2016. Companies offer tokens to people in return for cryptocurrency. Tokens usually represent a claim on future goods or services provided by that company. We discuss ICOs in more detail in the next section.

Other

Some merchants use cryptocurrency payment processors to accept cryptocurrencies from customers as payment. In

---

206   http://fortune.com/2018/06/13/ripple-xrp-cryptocurrency-western-union/

207   https://www.gartner.com/technology/research/methodologies/hype-cycle.jsp

2014 and 2015, it was a cheap way for merchants to get press releases and seem innovative. However, since then many have quietly removed this payment mechanism due to lack of customer interest.

I have seen public blockchains being used for other 'fringe' purposes, for example the storing of hashes on a blockchain to prove that some data existed at a certain point in time. I haven't seen evidence that this use is particularly widespread.

Critics of cryptocurrencies often claim that they are widely used for money laundering. While there is undoubtedly some laundering of illicit funds using cryptocurrencies, as there is using fiat currencies, it is hard to tell at this stage what proportion of cryptocurrency transactions are used for this purpose, and what proportion of global money laundering is performed through cryptocurrencies. For serious organised crime, I suspect that the cryptocurrency markets are just too small and illiquid to satisfy their demands. Big business enterprises, high value banknotes, even banks still are more likely to be the preferred vehicles for most money laundering.

Private Blockchains

While public blockchains have enabled censorship resistant digital cash, they were not designed to solve problems that traditional businesses have. What are the challenges within existing businesses, and how might concepts borrowed from public blockchains help improve how they operate?

Business-to-business communication

Processes *within* an organisation have, over time, been made efficient by use of internal systems, workflow tools, intranets, and data repositories. However, the sophistication of technology used to communicate *between* organisations has remained low. In some advanced situations, APIs (application programming interfaces) are used for machine to machine communications, but in the majority of cases we rely on emails and pdf files. It is still common for pieces of paper with wet-ink signatures to be couriered across the world.

Duplicative data, processes, and reconciliation

Businesses trust their own data but not anyone else's. This means that businesses within an ecosystem duplicate data and processes. Digital files and records are often replicated within and between multiple organisations, with none of them being the golden source. Version control of documents and records is painful unless a third party is paid to be the golden source. Reconciliation only goes some way to solve these pain points.

Consider a digital invoice issued by company A to company B. The invoice could be a pdf file which is created by someone at company A, perhaps signed off by someone else in company A before a copy is sent from the accounts receivable department to someone at company B. Someone at company B receives it in their inbox, saves a copy on their hard drive, and forwards a copy to someone else, perhaps their manager, to sign off. Another copy goes to the accounts payable department and, when the invoice is paid, everyone needs to be updated. There could be ten or more copies of the same asset—the invoice— floating around various computers, none of which are kept in sync. When the state of the invoice changes from 'unpaid' to 'paid,' this is not reflected on all of the copies of the invoice.

Private blockchains

So it is not surprising that businesses have become interested in concepts popularised by public blockchains such as unique digital assets, trusted automation, and cryptographically secured ledger entries. However, the radical transparency of public blockchains is not attractive to businesses that quite legitimately may require a level of commercial confidentiality.

Private blockchains have been inspired by public blockchains but are being designed to meet the needs of business. They adopt some concepts from public blockchains and reject others. By relaxing the strict requirements of public blockchains around permissionlessness and censorship resistance, private blockchains do not need mechanisms such as the energy-intensive proof-of-work mining.

Some technology inspired by public blockchains do not have blocks in chains at all! They are sometimes more accurately called 'distributed ledgers'. Corda, a distributed ledger platform built by R3 and a group of banks, is an open source platform that uses many of the concepts from public blockchains, but it doesn't bundle transactions up into blocks for batch processing and distribution across the whole network. This addresses some privacy concerns as only the businesses who are involved in a transaction see it.

A key benefit of blockchains and other similar data structures that use chains of hashes is that parties have the ability to know for themselves that a set of statements is complete (not missing any) and that the statements themselves are complete and untampered. Each party can verify this for themselves without having to check with another party. This is useful in many business situations, not least banks who need to know that their list of trades is complete and the data within the trades is consistent with their counterparty.

Private blockchains aim to increase the quality and security of technology used in business-to-business communications. They allow unique digital assets to move freely and reliably between companies without the need to have a third party act as a record keeper. Private blockchains can provide transparent multilateral workflows in the form of smart contracts, and demonstrate that the agreed workflows are adhered to. This is what is meant by 'trustless automation'. Instead of having to trust a business to perform as agreed, a smart contract ensures that pre-programmed processes are followed.

Private blockchains may be useful any time a business interacts with another business to share workflows, processes, or assets. When does this happen? Pretty much all of the time! Most businesses don't operate in a vacuum; they need to interact with other businesses. The financial services industry was the first to invest, to understand, and to use this technology, specifically for wholesale banking and in financial markets. This makes sense, as the industry is dominated by business-to-business workflows, intermediaries, and digital assets; and the 'back office' had not received significant investment in decades. Perhaps the fact that Bitcoin was described as a cryptocurrency also made it interesting to banks.

Let's revisit the invoice example. Imagine now if the invoice was recorded on some sort of ledger that was kept in sync between both companies, bilaterally, and as soon as it was approved, signed, or paid, both parties would know about it. This could streamline many business processes, and the concepts could be extended to any document, record, or data.

Of course, many business-to-business workflows could be digitised and automated if you could find a party to store the data and be the golden source. In some cases, they are. SWIFT and Bolero are examples that fit this category. But in other cases, a third party may not be viable, either because everyone wants to be it or no one wants to be it, or there are regulatory or geographical reasons preventing the emergence of such a party. Industries can be suspicious of single points of power and control, and wary of the monopolistic behaviour that often emerges from this. Central repositories of data could have competitive implications if leaked or misused. So there are a number of reasons why an apparently obvious solution of having a third party may not be viable.

Non-financial industries are now becoming interested in exploring the technology for, among other things, digital identity, supply chains, trade finance, healthcare, procurement, real estate, and asset registries.

Notable Private Blockchains

Some private or permissioned blockchains are certainly gaining mindshare and traction. Current examples are:

Axoni AxCore

Axoni is a capital market technology firm founded in 2013 that specialises in distributed ledger technology and blockchain infrastructure. Among other projects, Axoni's flagship initiative is use of their technology to upgrade the Depository Trust & Clearing Corporation's trade information warehouse[208].

R3 Corda

Corda is an open source blockchain project designed to solve pain points in the financial services industry. It was designed by a consortium of banks and R3, my employer, so I declare my interest here. In Chief Technology Officer Richard Brown's own words[209]:

> *Corda is an open source enterprise blockchain platform that has been designed and built from the ground up to enable legal contracts and other shared data to be managed and synchronised between mutually untrusting organisations in any industry. Uniquely amongst enterprise blockchain platforms, Corda allows a diverse range of applications to interoperate on a single global network.*

Corda uses concepts drawn from Bitcoin and public blockchains to guarantee that digital assets are unique and data is synchronised between databases controlled by different parties, though it diverges from other blockchains in that it does not bundle unrelated transactions together and distribute them to all participants in a network for periodic processing. This means it can process higher transaction volumes and resolves the privacy issue of public blockchains. Although Corda was originally designed for regulated

---

208   http://www.dtcc.com/news/2017/january/09/dtcc-selects-ibm-axoni-and-r3-to-develop-dtccs-distributed-ledger-solution

209   https://medium.com/corda/new-to-corda-start-here-8ba9b48ab96c

financial institutions, it is now being actively explored by other industries.

Corda is being used, among other things, for trading baskets of financial assets[210], for gold trading[211], syndicated loans[212], and FX trade matching[213].

Digital Asset GSL

Digital Asset Holdings, LLC is a company founded in 2014. According to Wikipedia[214], it 'Builds products based on distributed ledger technology (DLT) for regulated financial institutions, such as financial market infrastructure providers, CCPs, CSDs, exchanges, banks, custodians and their market participants'. The technology platform is called the Global Synchronization Log (GSL).

Digital Asset has a notable contract to use DLT to modernise and replace the Australian Stock Exchange's technology systems[215]. This is regarded as a major vote of confidence for Digital Asset and the entire private blockchain industry.

---

210   http://www.hqla-x.com/hqlax-selects-corda-for-collateral-lending-solution-in-collaboration-with-r3-and-five-banks/

211   https://www.bloomberg.com/news/articles/2018-05-07/-cryptolandia blockchain-pioneers-take-root-in-hipster-brooklyn

212   https://www.finastra.com/news-events/press-releases/finastras-fusion-lendercomm-now-live-based-blockchain-architecture

213   http://www2.calypso.com/Insights/press-releases/calypso-r3-and-five-financial-institutions-develop-trade-matching-application-on-corda-dlt-platform

214   https://en.wikipedia.org/wiki/Digital_Asset_Holdings

215   http://sjm.ministers.treasury.gov.au/media-release/128-2017/

Hyperledger Fabric

Hyperledger Fabric is a blockchain technology originally developed by IBM and Digital Asset, and incubated under the Linux Foundation's Hyperledger Project. It seems to have some traction in supply chains and healthcare.

JP Morgan Quorum

Quorum is a blockchain technology originally created by US bank JP Morgan Chase and is based on the Ethereum platform. It is interesting because it uses advanced cryptographic techniques called *zero knowledge proofs* to obfuscate transaction data. In March 2018, the *Financial Times* reported that JP Morgan was considering spinning off the project into its own entity[216].

BLOCKCHAIN EXPERIMENTS

Many experiments using blockchain technology have been announced by startups and incumbents alike. Thy are often described as 'use-cases,' a term that implies, optimistically, that a blockchain would be a *good use* for the particular problem described. This selection of experiments collated by Peter Bergstrom[217] gives a flavour of the scope of interest in blockchain use:

216   https://www.ft.com/content/3d8627f6-2e10-11e8-a34a-7e7563b0b0f4

217   https://www.linkedin.com/feed/update/activity:6257098564841852928/

Blockchain use cases list by industry

Financial
Trading
Deal origination
POs for new securities
Equities
Fixed income
Derivatives trading
Total Return Swaps (TRS)
2nd generation derivatives
The race to a zero middle office
Collateral management
Settlements
Payments
Transferring of value
Know your client (KYC)
Anti money laundering
Client and product reference data.
Crowd Funding
Peer-to-peer lending
Compliance reporting
Trade reporting & risk visualizations
Betting & prediction markets

Insurance
Claim filings
MBS/Property payments
Claims processing & admin
Fraud prediction
Telematics & ratings

Media
Digital rights mgmt
Game monetization
Art authentication
Purchase & usage monitoring
Ticket purchases
Fan tracking
Ad click fraud reduction
Resell of authentic assets
Real time auction & ad placements

Computer Science
Micronization of work (pay for algorithms, tweets, ad clicks, etc.)
Expanse of marketplace
Disbursement of work
Direct to developer payments
API platform plays
Notarization & certification
P2P storage & compute sharing
DNS

Medical
Records sharing
Prescription sharing
Compliance
Personalized medicine
DNA sequencing

Asset Titles
Diamonds
Designer brands
Car leasing & sales
Home Mortgages & payments
Land title ownership
Digital asset records

Government
Voting
Vehicle registration
WIC, Vet, SS, benefits, distribution
Licensing & identification
Copyrights

Identity
Personal
Objects
Families of objects
Digital assets
Multifactor Auth
Refugee tracking
Education & badging
Purchase & review tracking
Employer & Employee reviews

IoT
Device to Device payments
Device directories
Operations (e.g. water flow)
Grid monitoring
Smart home & office management
Cross-company maintenance markets

Payments
Micropayments (apps, 402)
B2B international remittance
Tax filing & collection
Rethinking wallets & banks

Consumer
Digital rewards
Uber, AirBNB, Apple Pay
P2P selling, craigslist
Cross company, brand, loyalty tracking

Supply Chain
Dynamic ag commodities pricing
Real time auction for supply delivery
Pharmaceutical tracking & purity
Agricultural food authentication
Shipping & logistics management

And here are is a beautiful infographic from Matteo Gianpietro Zago[218]:

218 https://medium.com/@matteozago/50-examples-of-how-blockchains-are-taking-over-the-world-4276bf488a4b

I include these lists as examples of the sharable but ultimately misleading hype that is propagated in the mainstream and social media. These are not actual use cases. They are experiments to apply blockchain technology to a variety of industries and business workflows, appropriately or not.

Use case for a computer: Door stop

Just as you could draft a letter using spreadsheet software, you can use a blockchain in almost any business situation that involves data. After all, a blockchain is a database with some additional features. In my view, many of these experiments will not deliver the promised benefits because more appropriate software and tools are available. However, some may succeed or evolve and get traction.

It is still unclear which processes will be significantly improved as a direct consequence of the technology, and which are improved simply by digitising the workflows.

Does it matter? In many cases a project might not *need* a blockchain, but using one might trigger interest and management enthusiasm, and even unlock a budget which might not have been available if the project was just a boring old digitisation project. This is fine, and in this case, I think the ends justify the means. Without some amount of hype to spark the imagination there would be less money to spend on innovating, and therefore potentially less innovation.

Questions to Ask

With so many attempts to use blockchain technology, how do you attempt to understand the use and value of blockchain technology in these experiments?

There are certain questions that can be useful to ask. Earlier we asked, 'Which blockchain?' and, 'The public one or a private one?' From there, the questions depend on the answers to the original questions. Here are a few to get started.

For public blockchains, it is useful to understand:

- Will all parties run nodes or will some trust others?

- If the blockchain is backlogged, what impact might have this have on users?

- How will the project deal with forks and chainsplits?

- How will data privacy be achieved?

- How will operators comply with evolving regulations?

For private blockchains, it is useful to understand:

- Who will run the nodes? Why?

- Who is going to write blocks?

- Who is going to validate blocks and why?

- If this is about data sharing, why can't a web server be used?

- Is there a natural central authority whom everyone trusts, and if so why aren't they hosting a portal?

For any type of blockchain:

- What data is represented on the blockchain and what data is 'off-chain?'

- What do the tokens represent?

- When a token is passed from one party to another what does this mean in real life?

- What happens if a private key is lost or copied? Is this acceptable?

- Are all parties comfortable with the data that is being passed around the network?

- How will upgrades be managed?

- What's in the blocks?![219]

---

219   A special thanks to Dave Birch (www.dgwbirch.com) for popularising this question.

Depending on the project, some of these questions may be more relevant than others. Some of the solutions may come from network-wide innovations. For example, public chains can currently become congested but innovations such as payment channels may enable much higher throughput. There are many more questions to ask, depending on the project.

The point is that you should not take the breathless media announcements at face value, but take a more investigative approach to uncover if there is value in these experiments or not. At this stage of the innovation cycle, an honest 'I don't know' is an acceptable answer for some of these questions, and it is more important to understand the trade-offs than to immediately pass judgment on the solutions.

Part 7

INITIAL COIN OFFERINGS

What Are ICOs?

Initial Coin Offerings (ICOs), sometimes called 'token sales' or 'token generation events,' are a new way for companies to raise money without diluting ownership of the company or having to pay investors back. ICOs are a combination of existing forms of fundraising with a few twists, and the phrase 'ICO' seems to have been coined (ha) to evoke connotations with IPOs or Initial Public Offerings of equities. According to icodata.io,[220] over 11 billion US dollars was raised between 2014 and mid-2018 using some form of ICO. Early ICOs were Mastercoin (July 2013) and Maidsafe (July 2014) though they used the term 'crowd sale'. ICOs became popular in 2017.

Traditionally, a company can raise money in any of three ways: equity, debt, or through the pre-ordering of specific products. They can raise money from a small group of investors as is typical in early venture funding, or from a large number, a style of raising money typically called 'crowdfunding' that has become increasingly popular.

In an equity raise, investors pay money to the company in return for a share of ownership of the company. Investors receive a share of company profits in the form of dividends and may get voting rights at shareholder meetings, among other privileges. In a debt raise, investors loan money to the company and may get periodic interest payments in the form of coupons. Debt holders expect to get their capital back at the end of the lifetime of the loan. In a pre-fund or pre-order,

---

220   This is the USD value of the fundraises at the time of fundraise. As we will see later, the funding currency is usually cryptocurrency, usually bitcoins or ether. It is up to the projects to decide how they manage their received funds, and most balance between keeping some in cryptocurrency and some in fiat.

customers (note, they are customers, not investors) pay money for a product that they will receive later. Often the product isn't yet ready for distribution. Sometimes there are discounts for ordering early.

Crowdfunding is a recent phenomenon using the power of the internet where a project or company can be funded by raising small amounts of money from large numbers of people, often through a web or app-based platform that brings together the projects and the investors, or customers. All types of funding can be raised from the 'crowd'. Examples of equity crowdfunding platforms are Seedrs, AngelList, CircleUp, and Fundable. Debt crowdfunding platforms include Prosper, Lending Club, and Funding Circle. Sometimes these are called 'peer to peer lending' platforms. Pre-funding platforms include Kickstarter and Indegogo, and work on pledge basis, where a project only goes ahead if a certain target amount of money is pledged. This is popular for products that appeal to a niche. Pre-ordering is popular for book and computer game sales.

Raising money					
Method	Characteristics	Potential upside	Potential downside	Small group	Large group
Equity	• Investors become shareholders of the company • Most highly developed regulation	• Value of the company can increase many multiples	• Value of the company can fall to zero	• Seed round / Series A / Series B etc	• IPO if publicly listed • Equity crowdfunding if the company remains private • Eg Seedrs, AngelList
Debt	• Investors are creditors to the company	• Upside is limited to the interest rate (coupon) on the bond	• Company can default on bonds • If the company becomes bankrupt, bond holders get their money before equity holders	• Bond issuance • Syndicated loans	• Debt crowdfunding is known as "P2P lending" or "Microfinancing" • Eg Lending Club, Funding Circle
Pre-funding	• Participants pay to receive something later • Least regulated	• Participants lock in the price, perhaps at a discount • Participants get to access the product first	• Product fails to meet expectations due to timelines or quality		• "Rewards-based crowdfunding" • Eg Kickstarter, Indegogo
Pre-ordering	• Participants pay to receive something later • Not regulated as investment	• Participants get to access the product first • Participants reduce risk of missing out on the product	• Product distribution is delayed		• Eg Pre-ordering a book or game on Amazon with an expected delivery date

Different ICOs have different characteristics, and the generalisations I make in this chapter serve to provide a broad overview, but there will be exceptions. The industry is moving quickly, and regulators are starting to clarify their views on this new form of fundraising.

How Do ICOs work?

Companies[221] describe a particular product or service in a document called a whitepaper and announce their ICO. Investors[222] send funds, usually cryptocurrencies, to the company in return for tokens or a promise of tokens in the future. The tokens can represent anything, but usually represent either financial securities linked to the success of the project (and described as security tokens) or access to a product or service created by the venture (and described as utility tokens). At some stage, tokens may become listed on one or more cryptoasset exchanges. Eventually, a product or service is created, and in the case of utility tokens, holders may redeem their tokens for the product or service.

Whitepapers

According to Wikipedia[223], a white paper is an authoritative report or policy paper. The term was originally used by the British government and the earliest well-known example

---

221   NB Sometimes there is no company, there is just a project or venture that controls a cryptocurrency address that can receive funds. Whereas with banks you have to be explicit with the owner of the bank account, there is no such requirement for creating cryptocurrency addresses on public networks.

222   We can argue about what to call participants who contribute to ICOs. I call them investors, because at the very least they are invested in the success of the project, whether they hope to financially profit from their investment, or hope to be able to use the eventual product or service.

223   https://en.wikipedia.org/wiki/White_paper

was a 1922 paper commissioned by Prime Minister Winston Churchill, entitled 'Palestine. Correspondence with the Palestine Arab Delegation and the Zionist Organisation'. As we will see, the term whitepaper is now no longer exclusively used for these types of documents.

Bitcoin's ideas were documented in a whitepaper by Satoshi Nakamoto[224]. Ethereum was initially described in a whitepaper[225] written by Vitalik Buterin, followed by a technical yellow paper[226] written by Dr Gavin Wood. Since then, most ICO projects have included a whitepaper, though over time the whitepapers seem to have become less technical and have become a combination of a marketing document and investor prospectus.

Today's ICO whitepapers usually describe commercial, technical, and financial details of the project, including:

- The goal of the project, including the current problem and proposed solution

- Milestones for the development of the product or service

- The project team's background and experience

- The expected total fundraise value

- How the funds will be managed and spent

- The purpose and use of the tokens

---

224   https://bitcoin.org/bitcoin.pdf

225   https://github.com/ethereum/wiki/wiki/White-Paper though this version is periodically updated

226   https://ethereum.github.io/yellowpaper/paper.pdf

- The initial and ongoing distribution of the tokens

You can see some examples of ICO whitepapers on whitepaperdatabase.com, though it should be noted that inclusion in that website doesn't mean legitimacy of the project. You have been warned!

The Token Sale

Although ICOs operate differently, there seem to be two routes emerging for the token sale. A conservative route may be taken by projects whose tokens have a chance of being classified as securities in relevant jurisdictions, and another route is used by projects who are confident that their tokens are not likely to fall under securities regulations.

Those projects whose tokens may fall under securities regulations behave as if they are fundraising in a traditional way. This means that they may not widely advertise their offering, and they may only offer tokens to rich people or those with experience in complex and higher risk financial instruments. In the USA, these investors are called 'accredited investors' and other jurisdictions use 'sophisticated investors' or similar terminology[227]. Individual accredited investors are self-declared, and the criteria are usually based on some combination of net worth, annual income, and experience in complex financial instruments. The country of residence or citizenship of the investor is sometimes relevant, and some ICOs will not sell tokens to American citizens, or people living in certain countries. These ICOs will have private sales

---

227   In the European Union retail clients may request treatment as 'elective' professional clients.

but no public sales or pre-sales, at least until the project has delivered a useful product and the tokens could be re-defined as utility tokens.

Those projects who sell tokens that are likely to be classified as non-securities have more freedom to sell their tokens to a global audience and will usually engage in a private sale, one or more pre-sales, and a public sale.

Usually projects offer discounts or bonuses to encourage investors to invest, with more attractive deals for those participating in earlier rounds. This can be achieved by creating limited investment opportunities, either based on time, where the price gets worse over time, or based on amount raised, where the price gets worse as the amount raised increases. For example, in Ethereum's initial crowdsale, early investors received 2000 ETH per 1 BTC whereas later investors received only 1337 ETH per 1 BTC. Today, it is not uncommon for early investors to get up to an 80% discount on the intended public sale price.

This has similarities to funding rounds for startup companies, though the time scales and investor demands are different. ICOs can go from the first funding round to having their tokens listed on a cryptocurrency exchange in a matter of months with no product or commercial traction, whereas a traditional startup would usually take years between angel investment and IPO, and investors require demonstrable commercial success or potential.

ICO Funding Stages

Private sales

In private sales, the investments, discounts, and bonuses are negotiated bilaterally between the project and each investor. The process is similar to a traditional startup raising a round of angel or seed funding.

There is usually, but not always, a contract that details the legal agreement between the project and the investor. A popular template is the Simple Agreement for Future Tokens, or SAFT,[228] which was devised and popularised by digital currency lawyer Marco Santori[229] among others, in an effort towards industry self-regulation. The SAFT is an agreement that is modelled on a Simple Agreement for Future Equity[230], a template popular with startups. A SAFT document is an agreement that says that an investor pays money now (the

---

228   https://saftproject.com/

229   https://www.marcosantori.com/

230   https://en.wikipedia.org/wiki/Simple_agreement_for_future_equity_ (SAFE)

form of money is irrelevant and can be fiat or cryptocurrency)
and will receive tokens at a later date. The SAFT is a type
of convertible note, or more generally a forward contract.
The SAFT itself is a financial security, irrespective of the
classification of the token.

Public token sales

Increasingly, public sales are avoided by those whose
tokens may be classified a security. However, they are still
popular with some projects due to their global reach, ease of
fundraising, and hype-ability.

The project usually creates an Ethereum smart contract[231] for
receiving funds and displays the address on their website.
Investors send money to the smart contract and receive
tokens in a process automated by the smart contract or a
series of smart contracts.

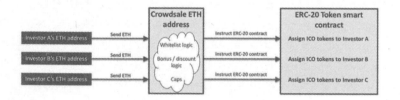

For some projects, the tokens may be ERC-20 compliant
tokens recorded on the Ethereum blockchain. For others,
especially projects that are creating new blockchain
platforms, the tokens may be initially recorded as ERC-20
tokens on Ethereum, to be redeemed later for tokens on

---

231   Sometimes other cryptocurrencies such as Bitcoin are used, but Ethereum
has become the default due to the number of templates that can be used for
creating the smart contracts.

the new blockchain, when the new blockchain is up and running[232].

Ethereum's own crowdsale accepted bitcoins as the funding currency and the Bitcoin address used was 36PrZ1KHYMpqSyAQXSG8VwbUiq2EogxLo2.

Public sales tend to be well-hyped. Countdowns and widgets displaying amounts raised are popular and often displayed prominently on the project's website. Social media, chat rooms, and bulletin boards are used to promote upcoming public sales.

Token pre-sales

Pre-sales are the 'sale before the public sale,' usually at a discounted price per token or with bonuses available to investors depending on the amount invested. They encourage investors to invest at a cheaper price and form part of the hype for an ICO. An over-subscribed pre-sale is a great psychological draw for investors in the main public sale.

Whitelisting

Both public sales and pre-sales may have some address 'whitelisting' as part of a project's efforts to identify their investors. Before the token sale, potential investors click through a series of web pages, declare their identity information, perhaps upload a picture of their passport, agree that they do not live in certain countries, accept terms

---

232   EOS is an example of a token initially recorded on Ethereum, then later redeemable for EOS-coins on the EOS platform.

and conditions, and provide the cryptocurrency address they intend to send funds from. During the actual token sale, the smart contract receiving funds will only accept funds from those cryptocurrency addresses that have been whitelisted.

Funding Caps

ICOs will declare funding caps in their whitepapers. These are floors and ceilings to the amount of funds the projects are willing to accept at any stage of the sales processes. A soft cap usually represents the minimum amount of funds needed for the project to go ahead (similar to Kickstarter's 'funding goal'), and a hard cap usually represents the maximum the project will accept. Not every ICO will have a hard or soft cap, and some may change them according to demand.

Treasury

Projects will often create more tokens than are sold in token sales, keeping some proportion behind in reserve. These reserves may be used to reward founders, pay staff or contractors, or to stabilise the price of the tokens on exchanges. The project may self-impose limits on how fast the reserves can be spent, a sort of vesting schedule, which offers investors some confidence that the project is not going to sell a large number of tokens held in treasury immediately after a sale and cause downward pressure on the price.

Once a token is listed, the project will have some idea as to the value of the tokens they hold in treasury. In accounting terminology, these tokens are held on the company's balance sheet, and so they impact the equity valuation of the company. Shareholders, particularly venture capitalists, may like ICOs because they can create value on the company's balance sheet out of nothing!

Exchange Listing

Some investors may buy tokens at ICO to use the eventual product, service, or blockchain, but often investors want to make money by selling the tokens at a higher price than they bought them for.

So the ability to easily sell the tokens is important to investors. Although tokens are immediately transferrable between people once they are assigned to investors, and therefore tokens may be bought and sold 'over the counter,' the listing of the token on cryptoasset exchanges is a key event in the lifetime of an ICO because exchanges make the tokens more liquid. The transferability of the token makes the token different from rewards-based crowdfunding, such as Kickstarter, where participants are not able to easily resell their rewards to others.

Listings may be positive or negative for the price of the token and price volatility can be high in the first few days of a token listing. If the project is popular, the listing can create an opportunity for new investors to accumulate the tokens, causing a rapid increase in price. If the project is unpopular, early investors may use the listing as an opportunity to sell their tokens, causing a rapid fall in price.

Token listings are such an important event in the project that exchanges can charge projects significant amounts of money to list their token. Listing fees of over a million US dollars are not uncommon. The exchange may also provide liquidity services, creating a market for the coins. When a token is listed, the project will monitor the price carefully, and some have strategies of buying tokens back when the price is low. The ethics and legality of this is a popular source of discussion. Traditional companies may issue shares when stock markets are high and perform share buybacks when prices are attractive, however, this is not an exact parallel of what happens in ICO-land, and traditional companies pay more attention to regulations about disclosure and trading activities.

The number of exchanges, reputation of exchanges, and liquidity on those exchanges is important for the project and for investors. Investors prefer to see a token listed on multiple reputable exchanges with large numbers of customers and lots of liquidity.

Despite the importance of exchange listing, projects tend to avoid discussing exchange listing timelines, especially those who are trying to keep their tokens from being classified as securities. This is because discussion of exchange listing adds weight to classification of the token as a security, since there is arguably more of an expectation of profit from investors.

It's worth noting that while traditional stock exchanges impose requirements on the companies they list, such as periodic public disclosure of financials, cryptoasset exchanges usually do not have such listing requirements, nor are the exchanges obligated to perform any due diligence on projects whose coins they are listing. Some cryptocurrency exchanges are happy to list any token, even those with a low likelihood of success (known colloquially as 'shitcoins') because the exchanges make revenues from trading fees, and so are indifferent to the quality of the project or the absolute value of the tokens they list. The exchanges make money as long as there is price volatility.

When Is a Token a Security?

Earlier, we discussed that projects take different actions based on whether they think their token is, or could be classified as, a financial security. The classification of a token as a security is important as it impacts who can do what with the token, because activities relating to financial securities are regulated in most countries. Note that tokens themselves are not regulated, but activities relating to them are.

So how do we decide if a token may be classified as a security or not? In the USA, the 'Howey Test' is a well-known test that was created by the United States Supreme Court in 1946 during a case 'SEC vs. Howey'. According to the FindLaw website[233]:

> In Howey, two Florida-based corporate defendants offered real estate contracts for tracts of land with citrus groves. The defendants offered buyers the option of leasing any purchased land back to the defendants, who would then tend to the land, and harvest, pool, and market the citrus. As most of the buyers were not farmers and did not have agricultural expertise, they were happy to lease the land back to the defendants.

---

233   https://consumer.findlaw.com/securities-law/what-is-the-howey-test.html

The SEC sued the defendants over these transactions, claiming that they broke the law by not filing a securities registration statement. The Supreme Court, in issuing its decision finding that the defendants' leaseback agreement is a form of security, developed a landmark test for determining whether certain transactions are investment contracts (and thus subject to securities registration requirements). Under the Howey Test, a transaction is an investment contract if:

1. It is an investment of money

2. There is an expectation of profits from the investment

3. The investment of money is in a common enterprise

4. Any profit comes from the efforts of a promoter or third party

Although the Howey Test uses the term 'money,' later cases have expanded this to include investments of assets other than money.

So each token offering could be checked against the Howey Test to determining whether the tokens qualify as 'investment contracts'. If so, then under the Securities Act of 1933 and the Securities Exchange Act of 1934, those tokens are considered securities and so activities relating to them are subject to certain requirements *in the USA*.

In February 2018, the Swiss financial regulator FINMA issued guidelines[234], saying that tokens can fall into one or more of the following categories, described below:

Payment tokens are synonymous with cryptocurrencies and have no further functions or links to other development projects. Tokens may in some cases only develop the necessary functionality and become accepted as a means of payment over a period of time.

Utility tokens are tokens which are intended to provide digital access to an application or service.

Asset tokens represent assets such as participations in real physical underlyings, companies, or earnings streams, or an entitlement to dividends or interest payments. In terms of their economic function, the tokens are analogous to equities, bonds or derivatives.

FINMA suggests the following framework[235], for determining whether a token is a financial security or not, and this seems reasonable in the current stage of industry development:

---

234   https://www.finma.ch/en/news/2018/02/20180216-mm-ico-wegleitung/

235   https://www.finma.ch/en/~/media/finma/dokumente/dokumentencenter/ myfinma/1bewilligung/fintech/wegleitung-ico.pdf?la=en

	Pre-financing and pre-sale / The token does not yet exist but the claims are tradeable	The token exists
ICO of payment tokens	= Securities ≠ subject to AMLA	≠ Securities = means of payment under AMLA[3]
ICO of utility tokens[4]		≠ Securities, if exclusively a functioning utility token = Securities, if also or only investment function ≠ means of payment under AMLA if accessory
ICO of asset tokens[4]		= Securities ≠ means of payment under AMLA

In June 2018, William Hinman, Director, Division of Corporate Finance at the United Stated Securities and Exchange Commission (SEC) said in a speech[236],

> '*Based on my understanding of the present state of Ether, the Ethereum network and its decentralized structure, current offers and sales of Ether are not securities transactions. And, as with Bitcoin, applying the disclosure regime of the federal securities laws to current transactions in Ether would seem to add little value*'.

He differentiates the manner in which something (a token) is originally sold, and the later use and sale of the token. A token

---

236   https://www.sec.gov/news/speech/speech-hinman-061418

can have utility and also be offered as an investment contract, i.e., a financial security. He explains,

> 'The oranges in Howey had utility. Or in my favorite example, the Commission warned in the late 1960s about investment contracts sold in the form of whisky warehouse receipts. Promoters sold the receipts to U.S. investors to finance the aging and blending processes of Scotch whisky. The whisky was real—and, for some, had exquisite utility. But Howey was not selling oranges and the warehouse receipts promoters were not selling whisky for consumption. They were selling investments, and the purchasers were expecting a return from the promoters' efforts'.

This means that, irrespective of what a token represents, the manner in which it is offered and the utility of the token at the time of offering is important. We will see over the coming years how this important speech impacts the manner in which ICOs are conducted.

Conclusion

Although we are in the early stages of the token industry, we can see that it is already beginning to mature.

In early ICOs, projects would write disclaimers in small print stating that the tokens are not an investment or a security, hoping that this would be enough to protect them. These investment rounds were sometimes described by the projects as 'donations' or 'contribution rounds' in order to disassociate with legally sensitive terminology. There was a clear disconnect between investor expectations of the tokens and the wording in the investor documents. Unfortunately for those with that view, wording matters less than the economic realities, as projects are finding out.

In 2017, there was a wave of attempts to self-regulate and create industry standards. Projects trying to do the right thing looked for regulatory clarity. Today, the amount of money at stake is significant, and regulators and policymakers are catching up with token sales. This is a good thing for the maturity of the industry, as regulatory clarity can attract investment and allow projects the opportunity to focus on business rather than legal uncertainty.

Regulators are now clarifying what they will and won't accept, and in light of clarifications, projects are moving to comply with or avoid regulation. Different regulators may take different approaches, creating opportunities for projects to select the most favourable operational jurisdictions. I am looking forward to the next few years when more projects deliver products and we learn how to quantitatively put a value on tokens. The economics of tokens, or *tokenomics*, are yet to be fully described or understood.

Part 8

INVESTING

In this section, I describe some considerations to help you decide whether investing in cryptoassets is right for you. There are many risks, but the markets are exciting and people have made and lost fortunes in the these markets.

PRICING

How do you put a value on cryptocurrencies or cryptoassets? For tokens that are a claim on an underlying asset such as 1 oz of gold, the price of the token should more or less track the price of the underlying asset. However, as previously discussed, cryptocurrencies are not a claim on any asset, nor are they backed by an entity. Is there a way to calculate a fair value for them?

We can ask three independent questions:

1. What is the current price of the cryptoasset?

2. What causes prices to change?

3. What should the price be?

What is the current price of the cryptoasset?

The current price of any asset is determined by the market. Cryptoassets trade on one or more exchanges, and both prices and liquidity can differ between exchanges. Exchanges that report the most trade volume provide a good measure of the price, as they are the most active and should have the most liquidity. Other exchanges may have higher or lower prices.

Coinmarketcap.com is one of many websites that provide data about the current price of tokens and which exchanges they trade on. If you click on the name of a token and then click on 'Markets,' you can see where that token trades and how much volume the exchange says it has traded. Note that some exchanges have been caught faking trade volume in order to generate business, and I am not confident this practice has been eliminated... beware!

What causes prices to change?

The prices of cryptocurrencies and tokens behave like any other financial asset, driven by buyers and sellers who make trading decisions based on various factors:

1. Sentiment (how traders feel about the asset)

2. Gossip and chatter on forums and social media sites

3. Technical successes (e.g., when blockchains successfully implement technical upgrades that make them more useful, or when an ICO makes progress on its roadmap)

4. Technical failures (e.g., if transactions slow down or a weakness is found in the way the blockchain operates)

5. Celebrity endorsements (e.g., Paris Hilton's endorsement of LydianCoin in Sept 2017, or John Mcafee's occasional promotional tweets)

6. Founders getting arrested (e.g., when the founders of Centra token were arrested in the USA, and the price of the tokens fell by 60%[237])

7. Orchestrated Pump & Dumps where people coordinate to all buy a coin together to make the price go up and persuade others to buy it at a higher price, then sell the coins to unsuspecting new buyers

---

237 http://www.coinfox.info/news/9186-centra-founders-arrested-in-us-token-dips-by-60

8. Manipulation by large holders of any particular token

Paris Hilton ✓
@ParisHilton

Follow ⌄

Looking forward to participating in the new @LydianCoinLtd **Token!** #ThisIsNotAnAd #CryptoCurrency #BitCoin #ETH #BlockChain

2:28 PM - 3 Sep 2017

819 Retweets **2,183** Likes

A celebrity endorsement[238].

238   https://www.forexlive.com/news/!/china-gets-it-right-on-the-ico-market-20170904

What should the price be?

There have been a number of attempts to create models to find a fair value for cryptocurrencies and tokens. A common but flawed model for putting a value on a Bitcoin is the 'if the money in gold went into Bitcoin' model:

> *'If x% of the money in gold (or other asset class) moved into Bitcoin, a single Bitcoin should be worth $y'.*

The argument is as follows: The total value of gold in circulation is estimated at 8 trillion US dollars. If some small proportion of the people holding gold, say 5% (but you can use any number from 0-100% here), sold their gold for dollars, it would release a large amount of money, in this case $400 billion. If the dollar proceeds were used to buy bitcoins, the total value of bitcoins in circulation, commonly referred to as 'market capitalisation' or 'market cap,' would increase by the same amount, $400 billion. As we know, the total number of bitcoins in circulation, 17 million or so, then this must increase the price of *each Bitcoin* by $23.5k ($400bn / 17m).

But this logic is wrong. That is not how financial markets work at all. The 'money going into Bitcoin' doesn't simply drop into the 'market cap'. The reason is simple: When you buy $10,000 worth of Bitcoin, someone else is selling those bitcoins for $10,000. So any money 'pumped in' is also exactly equal to money 'pumped out' (excluding exchange fees, to keep things simple). The only thing that happens when you buy a Bitcoin is that the Bitcoin changes ownership and some cash changes ownership. There is no mathematical relationship between how much money you spend buying bitcoins from someone else and the market cap of Bitcoin.

Let's put numbers to this and demonstrate the flawed logic
with a counterexample... Let's say the last price paid for
BTC was $10,000. So the 'market cap' of Bitcoin, assuming
17 million Bitcoin outstanding, is: $10,000 x 17m =
$170,000,000,000 ($170bn)

Now, let's say you want to buy a tiny amount of BTC (say $10
worth), and the best price that you can see is $10,002. So you
pay $10 and buy 0.0009998 BTC ($10 divided by $10,002
per Bitcoin). What has happened to the 'market cap?' It is
now: $10,002 x 17m = $170,034,000,000.

The market cap has increased by $34 million just because
of your measly $10 trade! You didn't 'pump in' $34 million,
but the market cap increased by that amount. So clearly the
earlier argument is wrong.

Having said that...of course if there are more buyers with a
greater desire to buy and pay whatever it takes to accumulate
BTC, then the prices will increase. Likewise, if there are
sellers who will sell bitcoins at any price, then prices will fall.

I also hear variations on, 'cost of creation' argument: The
price of Bitcoin should be at least the cost of mining them, so
the cost of mining puts a floor under the price of Bitcoin, and
as difficulty increases, it costs more to mine bitcoins, so the
price should rise. Alas, this is also false. The cost incurred by
a miner (or even all the miners in aggregate) bears no relation
to the market price of Bitcoin. The price of Bitcoin affects
the *profitability* of miners, but there is no rule dictating that
miners need to be profitable. If a miner is unprofitable, they
will eventually stop mining, but this doesn't affect the price
of bitcoins. If it costs me $5,000 to dig up 1 oz of gold, this
doesn't mean the price of gold should be at least $5,000/

oz. User ihrhase explains this with salmon and sauerkraut smoothies in a forum post[239] in 2010:

Unfortunately, I have not yet come across a reasonable fair value model for cryptocurrencies.

ICO tokens *should* be easier to price. These tokens are redeemable for a certain good or service in the future, so putting a price on the token should be a case of figuring out what that good or service is worth. Right?

Alas, it is never that easy. The fact is that ICOs who issue tokens want the price of their tokens to go up, as do their investors. Redemption is always described generically and not *quantified*. For example, they say, 'Tokens will allow you access to cloud storage,' rather than, 'One token will give you 10 GB of cloud storage for 1 year starting in 2020'. This is a deliberate strategy. If the issuers *quantified* the goods or services, you could figure out an appropriate ballpark price for the token. But this would constrain the price, preventing the price of the token from massively increasing (which is really what ICO issuers and investors really want). I have never seen an ICO whitepaper *quantify* exactly what a token will be redeemable for.

---

239   https://bitcointalk.org/index.php?topic=20.0

Who Controls the Price of Utility Tokens?

The simple answer might seem to be 'the market' or 'buyers
and sellers,' but this is not the full picture as we have an
issuer who can pull some tricks to affect the value of a token.
Initially, the quantity of goods/services that the tokens can
buy is unspecified, so the price of the token is subject to
normal cryptocurrency market forces, and there is no way to
do fundamental analysis on what a fair market price should
be (you can't price 'cloud storage' without quantifying how
much, for how long). During this period, some ICOs exert
some influence on the price of their tokens by buying them
up when the price falls. Some ICOs even discuss this strategy
in their whitepapers. ICOs often retain a significant amount
of tokens in their treasury, so they can sell some if the price
rallies too aggressively. Essentially, they may act like a central
bank of their tokens, managing the price.

Later, there comes a point when the project has to make a
decision: Do they set prices in fiat or in tokens? Should 1
GB of cloud storage for 1-year cost $10, payable in tokens at
market rate, or should 1 GB of cloud storage for 1-year cost
one token?

Let's explore the options.

1) Priced in fiat, paid in tokens

If this is the case, then at first you'd think that the price
of tokens should be irrelevant. Customers hold fiat, then
when they want to use the service, they buy the tokens then
quickly redeem them. This process could be automated so the
customer doesn't know it is going on in the background. This
is the same argument that remittance-by-Bitcoin companies

use when they say that the price of Bitcoin is irrelevant to
their business.

In this case, are tokens a good investment? Perhaps. As
tokens are redeemed against the issuer, fewer and fewer
of them exist in circulation, so long as the project does not
re-issue them and sell them for fiat to pay their staff. Fewer
tokens may mean a higher price due to scarcity. So a project
in good financial health, not reliant on reselling redeemed
tokens to pay their costs, can allow tokens to become more
scarce over time, perhaps putting upwards pressure on their
price. Perhaps. But a project in poor financial health will need
to keep reselling their tokens to cover their costs. So actually,
the financial health of the company may impact the pricing
pressures on the token.

2) Priced in tokens, paid in tokens

This is wonderful: if the company sets the price of the goods
or services in tokens, the company will have control over
the value of their tokens, just as an airline controls the value
of the air miles they issue. How does this work? Unless the
product or service is unique, customers will have some idea
about how much they are willing to pay for it. Imagine that a
competitor sells a similar product for $10. If the project wants
their tokens to be worth $10, then they set their product at
a price of one token. If they want their tokens to be worth
$20, then they set their product at a price of 0.5 tokens! The
competitor's pricing helps to peg the token's price and as long
as the products are somewhat substitutable, the project can
make their tokens worth whatever they want. They should
understand that as they do this, their liabilities change. Their
liabilities are the outstanding tokens in circulation, and by
changing the price of one product from one token to 0.5

tokens, existing tokenholders can redeem tokens for twice as many products.

If the company decides to price their product in tokens, are tokens a good investment? Probably. The founders of the project, provided they haven't done a quick exit scam, also hold tokens and are financially incentivised to keep the price of tokens high and relatively stable.

So, projects have more control over their token price if they price their services in tokens, and I would expect that, as projects come to maturity, we will see projects priced in tokens, providing that the projects haven't been shut down for violating securities regulations first.

Anshuman Mehta attempted to price a fictional utility token on his blog[240] and concluded that, 'In a fiat currency world, the market or traded price of the token is completely de-linked with the usage and velocity of the token'.

RISKS AND MITIGATIONS

Market Risk

Cryptoasset prices are volatile and many have fallen to zero. At time of writing, deadcoins.com[241] lists over 800 coins whose price has fallen to zero. I expect this number to increase. The price of any cryptoasset can potentially fall to zero or near zero. This scenario may seem less likely

---

240   https://medium.com/@anshumanmehta/futility-tokens-6b8283c977a9

241   https://deadcoins.com/

for popular cryptocurrencies; time, a significant hack, or exploited vulnerability could cause a fatal loss of confidence in the asset at any time.

Liquidity Risk

Liquidity risk is the risk that the market cannot support your transaction at the price you expect. Liquidity comes and goes, as with all markets. Less popular coins are less liquid, meaning that a large buy or sell can move the market against you more than expected.

With less popular coins or coins of regulatory uncertainty, there is also a risk that they are de-listed by exchanges, which reduces their liquidity. For example, in May 2018, Poloniex announced that they were de-listing seventeen tokens:

Poloniex Exchange ✔
@Poloniex

On May 2, 2017, the following will be delisted: BBR, BITS, C2, CURE, HZ, IOC, MYR, NOBL, NSR, QBK, QORA, QTL, RBY, SDC, UNITY, VOX, XMG

8:08 AM - 19 Apr 2017

389 Retweets **399** Likes

💬 289   ↻ 389   ♡ 399   ✉

Exchange Risks

It is convenient to keep assets on exchanges because you don't have to deal with private keys, and you can quickly trade

between assets. However exchanges have had an extremely
poor track record of keeping customer assets secure.
Nearly all exchanges have been hacked in the past. Michael
Matthews published a list[242] of a selection of cryptocurrency
exchange hacks between 2012 and 2016:

Date	Bitcoin Service Targeted	Attack Details	BTC Stolen	USD Value
2016 Aug	Bitfinex (exchange)	user wallets/ inside job	119,756	$66,000,000
2016 May	Gatecoin (exchange)	hot wallet	multicurrency	$2,000,000
2016 Mar	ShapeShift (exchange)	inside job	multicurrency	$230,000
2016 Mar	Cointrader	hot wallet	81 BTC	$33,600
2016 Jan	Bitstamp (exchange)	hot wallet	18,866	$5,263,614
2015 Feb	Bter (exchange)	cold wallet/ inside job	7,000	$1,750,000
2015 Feb	Exco.in (exchange)	cold wallet/ inside job	n/a	n/a
2015 Feb	Kipcoin (exchange)	cold wallet/ inside job	3,000	$690,000
2015 Feb	796 (exchange)	cold wallet/ inside job	1,000	$230,000
2015 Jan	Bitstamp (exchange)	hot wallet	19,000	$5,100,000
2015 Jan	Cavirtex (exchange)	user database stolen	n/a	n/a

242   https://steemit.com/bitcoin/@michaelmatthews/list-of-bitcoin-
hacks-2012-2016

2014 Dec	Blockchain.info (wallet)	user wallets (bug, R values)	267	$101,000
2014 Dec	Mintpal (exchange)	inside job	3,700	$3,208,412
2014 Aug	Cryptsy (exchange)	inside job	multicurrency	$6,000,000
2014 Mar	Flexcoin (wallet)	hot wallet	1,000	$738,240
2014 Mar	CryptoRush (exchange)	cold wallet/ inside job	950	$782,641
2014 Jan	Mt.gox (exchange)	hot & cold wallets/inside job	850,000	$700,258,171
2013 Dec	Blockchain.info (wallet)	2-factor authentication breach	800	$800,000
2013 Nov	Inputs.io (wallet)	cold wallet/ inside job	4,100	$4,370,000
2013 Nov	BIPS (wallet)	cold wallet/ inside job	1,200	$1,200,000
2013 Nov	PicoStocks (exchange)	cold wallet/ inside job	6,000	$6,009,397
2012 Mar	Linode (webhosting)	inside job	46,703	$228,845

From this analysis, we can see not only that exchanges have been successfully hacked by external parties, but it is not unknown for staff at exchanges to steal cryptocurrencies from their customers.

On his website, Blockchain Graveyard[243], Ryan McGeehan manages a list of security breaches and thefts with their causes, based on public information. The root cause

---

243   https://magoo.github.io/Blockchain-Graveyard/

analysis shows that there are multiple ways for exchanges to be hacked:

ROOT CAUSE ESTIMATES

The data below is roughly gleaned from publicly available data about **56** incidents. This should assist estimation during threat modeling.

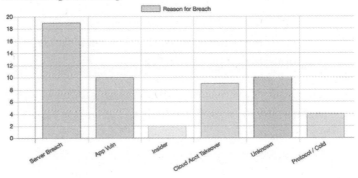

Being hacked is an existential threat to exchanges. So the top exchanges take security extremely seriously. Nevertheless, prudence suggests that you should use exchanges only when necessary, and to withdraw funds as soon as possible after trading. Only keep as much on an exchange as you are willing to lose.

Exchanges and users of exchanges may also engage in illegal or unethical activity. Tricks, borrowed from the wholesale financial markets industry, include:

- Painting the tape: Artificially increasing trading activity by having parties controlled by the exchange repeatedly trade with each other. This 'fake volume' encourages other customers to trade.

- Spoofing: Submitting orders with the intention of cancelling them before they are matched. This trick can be used to drive prices up or down.

- Front-running: An exchange can see a customer order and use the information to trade before the customer's order is accepted.

- Running stops: A certain type of customer order, called a 'stop loss,' is not visible to other customers of the exchange but is visible to the exchange. Insiders who can see customer stop loss orders can use this information to trade against their own customers. This is a popular trick in FX markets.

- Fake liquidity: Exchanges can publish 'unfillable' orders that disappear, or only partially fill, when a customer tries to match them. This makes it look like there is more liquidity on the exchange than there actually is.

There are many other tricks that may be used either by exchanges or by customers of exchanges while the management of the exchange looks the other way. Different exchanges behave with different levels of professionalism. Many exchanges are dodgy. Do your own research!

Wallet Risks

With wallets, there is a trade-off between security and convenience. Wallets that run online on computers or smartphones are convenient because it is easy to make cryptocurrency payments. However, storing private keys on a device exposed to the internet is not advised. Some people keep a small amount of cryptocurrency on their phone wallet so they can make payments instantly, but the advice, again, is to keep only as much in them as you are willing to lose[244].

In the past, it was common for people to print private keys onto bits of paper, a technique known as cold storage, discussed previously, but this is troublesome for making payments. Now, hardware wallets are the best compromise between security and convenience. But the risk remains with any wallet type that the software contains bugs or vulnerabilities that can be exploited. Many wallets open source their code to allow developers and security professionals to understand exactly how the wallet works, and to take comfort that there are no weaknesses, but this also provides transparency to hackers.

Regulatory Risks

Regulation around cryptocurrencies and tokens is evolving. It is worth understanding as fully as possible the nature of the assets you are considering. ICOs are operating in a legal grey area in many jurisdictions, and there is a risk that some are deemed to have been illegally performing regulated activities.

Depending on the jurisdiction and classification of cryptoassets, and what you are doing with them, tax also needs to be considered. You are not excused from complying with tax regulations just because the assets are recorded on blockchains!

---

244   Note: I have slipped into 'keeping few coins in wallets' terminology rather than 'keeping private keys that control few coins' but by now I think you know what I mean.

Scams

Finally, due to the nature of the cryptocurrency industry, many scams operate. Hype, technical complexity, regulatory uncertainty, and naïve investors hoping to make a quick buck all make for an environment ripe for fraudsters. Some popular scams are:

- Ponzi schemes: Investors are promised good returns and old investors are paid with new investors' money.

- Exit scams: Founders of a project, wallet, exchange or investment scheme run off with customer money.

- Fake hacks: Project gets hacked by an associate who shares profit with the project team.

- Pump & Dumps: Illiquid coins are bought cheaply by fraudsters then hyped on social media and sold at a higher price to new investors.

- Scam ICOs: ICO raises money with no intention of delivering a product. Sometimes they will list well known industry experts as advisors or as part of the team to get credibility, without the knowledge or approval of the expert.

- Spoof ICOs: Clones of real ICO websites made with the scammer's deposit address instead of the legitimate deposit address.

- Scam mining schemes: Claims that investors will earn lots of cryptocurrency but key information such as difficulty increases is not disclosed.

- Fake wallets: Wallet software that allows the scammer to access private keys, so the coins can be stolen from the user.

And so on. There are many variations to these, and scammers are proving increasingly innovative!

I hope this chapter has given you some food for thought. People have made and lost fortunes trading cryptocurrencies and investing in ICOs, but there are many risks. If you do decide to get involved, be careful and do a lot of research before committing your money.

Part 9

CONCLUSION

CONCLUSION

In this book, I set out to explain the basics of bitcoins and blockchains, and I hope that it has been easy to follow. At the very least, I have provided some ideas about concepts and terms for you to research further, and perhaps ignited a curiosity that you may not have had before.

Amid the hype, it is important to understand that the blockchain industry, including cryptocurrencies, business blockchains, and tokenisation of assets is very much in its infancy. Two important things seem to have been created:

1. New censorship resistant financial assets, methods of value transfer, and transparent automation

2. New technologies for business-to-business data and asset transfer

We can call these, respectively, a 'crypto' story and a 'blockchain' story.

The crypto story

Public blockchains are creating a new wave of censorship resistant digital assets and unstoppable automated computations. For the first time in history, people can transfer value electronically worldwide without needing specific third parties to approve the transaction. Payments can be sent to transparent smart contracts that guarantee certain outcomes without manual steps or needing to trust a third party to do what they have promised. Public blockchains are being explored for a wide range of uses from online micropayments through to remittances, fundraising and record keeping.

The blockchain story

Businesses are investing in private and public blockchains to see if they can reduce costs and risks, increase revenues, or create new business models. Private blockchains are a more recent idea than public blockchains, and are rapidly evolving and improving. These multi-party database systems promise to remove duplicative processes and allow digital assets and records to move freely between businesses, reducing reliance on expensive intermediaries.

THE FUTURE

Are these blockchains a bubble or fad? In my view, no. Both public and private blockchains have their roles and will continue to evolve and deliver value in ways we might not even be able to envisage today.

In the public cryptocurrency industry, Innovation will continue to accelerate as tokens create financial incentives that attract developers and other staff. The speed and intensity of innovation will increase if popular cryptoassets increase in price. Many developers personally hold cryptocurrencies and tokens, and so are directly financially incentivised to make their projects successful, even more so than staff at traditional startups who often only have a tiny sliver of equity.

We will continue to see the tokenisation of assets, products, and services. Computer game items are a good candidate for this. Imagine being able to own the unique sword that a famous gamer used to defeat an opponent. Imagine owning the signed digital football that was used in an e-sports

World Cup final. Or owning the digital shirt that a popular character wore during the match. There is an entire market of digital collectables that will be opened up. The confluence of e-gaming and cryptoassets is going to create some extremely exciting opportunities and new markets. E-sports and cryptoassets are a trend, not a fad, and it would be unwise to bet against them[245].

ICOs will continue to be popular, and the industry will begin to standardise with best practices and common investor expectations. Perhaps one day we might figure out a way to value tokens. Regulations will become more clear, and this will enable those currently on the side-lines to participate.

Whether bitcoins, Ether, and other cryptocurrencies become more price-stable or not, we will see cryptoassets that have a stable price with respect to fiat currencies[246]. We can call these *stablecoins* or *crypto-fiat*. Fiat currency, or a near equivalent, will be tokenised and recorded on blockchains. Whether these crypto-fiat tokens are best issued by central banks, banks, e-money businesses, or somehow managed by smart contracts is still to be determined. There are a number of initiatives to create these price-stable tokens on both public and private blockchains. Stable cryptoassets will enable another cycle of innovation.

However, public blockchains are suffering growing pains as they grow in transaction volume and throughput. In recent

---

245　On the subject of e-sports, some people mock or bully those who watch other people playing computer games, or those who dress up for fun as their favourite characters. Often these same people will themselves watch other people kick a ball around on some grass, dress up as their favourite footballer, sing songs, and pretend to be them.

246　For example, a token that trades close to 1 dollar.

years both Bitcoin and Ethereum have had periods of stress
where miners couldn't process transactions quickly enough,
causing backlogs. Engineers are working on solutions to these
problems, and concepts such as sharding and state channels
can allow public blockchains to scale.

Forks and chainsplits will become more problematic due to
the confusion that they create (which is the 'real' blockchain
and which is the fork?). Proof-of-work is energy intensive and
is polluting the planet. Ethereum may move from proof-of-
work to proof-of-stake, a much less energy intensive block-
writing mechanism, and if successful, other blockchains may
follow suit.

As the amount of value recorded on blockchains increases,
governance will too become increasingly important.
Platforms with no formal governance may not be acceptable
to some users. A public ledger called Hadera Hashgraph is
experimenting with having a formal governance structure
over a public and accessible distributed ledger.

Private blockchains will be adopted by businesses, perhaps
first in small groups for specific uses, and then sooner or later
they will come together to form larger networks, just as the
internet was formed from individual private networks.

Assets and records represented digitally will change
ownership at the speed of email with fewer steps and costs.
We will learn how to use this technology to move documents
across organisational boundaries—invoices, purchase orders,
packing lists, certificates of origin, certificates of guarantee,
health records, rental agreements... the list goes on. These
documents are assets that can all be represented as tokens
on distributed ledgers, with much stronger authenticity

guarantees due to the use of digital signatures. Many digital documents should only be represented once, with the right parties having visibility into the latest version.

Whether between or within organisations, when data sets need to be passed from one system to another, the receiving system needs to be confident that it has the complete set of data, and the data hasn't been corrupted in the process. This situation happens a lot in banking—often huge lists of trades need to be sent from one system to another. Often, there is a process, called a control process, that reconciles the data between the sending and receiving system. This reconciliation is yet another process that needs to be set up and monitored. But if the trades can be recorded and sent with a reference, a hash, to a previous trade in the set, then the receiving system can know for sure both that it has the *complete set* of trades, and that the data *within the trades* has not been altered by accident or malice. This means that a receiving system may be confident about the completeness and accuracy of data received, without performing a reconciliation against the sending system.

In the future, it will make little sense to manage any document or data set that needs to cross organisational boundaries using anything other than a blockchain.

These improvements will increase the velocity of business done within countries and across borders. This has a huge impact not only for the financial services industry, which is mostly about the movement of assets, but also for the real economy.

Smart contracts will enable business-to-business automation in a guaranteed way that hasn't been possible before.

Automation has tended to stop at the boundaries of businesses, with each business checking that the other one has performed according to the rules of the particular deal. With smart contracts, these rules can be automated and validated automatically, so duplicative processes can be made much more efficient, even eliminated.

Blockchains enable *atomic* transactions, transactions that make multiple changes to the ledger simultaneously or not at all. Atomic, because the changes are bundled together and indivisible. If two banks are engaging in a trade, perhaps one is buying a bond from another, two things happen: the bond changes ownership and the cash changes ownership. These transactions currently occur on separate ledgers, and one leg can fail while the other succeeds. This creates an operational risk that can lead to financial disaster[247]. On a blockchain, an atomic transaction can be created that includes both changes of ownership, the cash and the bond. That transaction is committed in its entirety, and either succeeds as a whole or fails. In finance this concept is called 'delivery vs payment,' and historically we have paid agents to guarantee this. Blockchain technology now provides the *technological* means to do this. This itself has the capacity to make entire business ecosystems operate more smoothly with less risk, while removing the need to pay third parties to perform the escrow service.

---

247   A famous case was that of Bank Herstatt. Bank Herstatt was a German bank that engaged in foreign exchange trades. On 26 June 1974 it received Deutsche marks from a number of trading counterparties, who expected US dollars in return later in the day when the US markets operated. However, the bank went bankrupt before the US dollars were transferred, so the counterparties were left short of US dollars having paid out Deutsche marks. This led to the creation of the Basel Committee on Banking Supervision, famous for 'Basel requirements,' and CLS.

There are some potential uses for 'special purpose money,' for example, grants or charity contributions that may legitimately end up in only certain pre-agreed accounts. This has social and economic implications and we will need to learn how to use these tools ethically.

At first, private blockchains will be used to do the same kind of business as today but better, faster, and cheaper. They will improve *how* businesses interact. Later, there will be a shift, and industries will start to evolve their processes. They will improve *what* businesses do. Intermediaries who were once necessary will be sidestepped and their business models made irrelevant. This will drive down transaction costs and return value to the real economy. This will follow a similar curve to the adoption of desktop computers in businesses in the 1980s. First they were used to automate existing processes for individuals, then people began to see a whole new world of potential opening up.

The financial services industry is particularly at risk of disruption from this technology. Before blockchains, third party intermediaries were needed to keep track of digital assets. The ledger containing your money is controlled by your bank; the ledger containing your shares is in the hands of your share custodian. You've never been able to digitally own and directly control a financial asset: it has always been kept by a third party. The financial services industry is full of intermediaries who hold your assets. They are the ones who keep track of who owns what, and it is their job to prevent double spending. And they are rewarded handsomely for doing so, a cost you bear. However, with cryptoassets you really can hold and control your assets, though this has its risks. The blockchain is the ledger. So this technology *must* result in fewer intermediaries, and that is probably a good thing overall. Fewer financial intermediaries means fewer businesses that extract profit from the real economy.

There is a possibility that the distinction between public and private blockchains fades away, or that assets can jump between one blockchain and another with such ease that the blockchains themselves become a matter of preference and matter as little as which device you use to check your email.

We have already seen the start of disintermediation. In ICOs, huge sums of money are being transferred around the world without a bank in sight. In June 2016, I personally helped to arrange the custody of almost 25,000 bitcoins seized as proceeds of crime, worth $16m Australian dollars at the time[248]. The bitcoins were held in custody by EY, a professional services firm, for a month before being transferred to winners of a global auction. No bank was paid. No bank *needed* to be paid.

Financial intermediaries are scrambling to adopt blockchain technology to figure how they can evolve their business models to work in the new environment. Far-sighted companies at risk of disruption are already jostling for a position to adopt new roles in the new ecosystem.

Whether you are a proponent of public blockchains or private, whether you believe in the long-term viability of specific cryptocurrencies or not, and whether you think that decentralisation is a good thing or not, this industry is certainly delivering for society the most interesting and potentially radical instruments of change. Whether these

---

248   https://www.ft.com/content/7353e8a0-2638-11e6-83e4-abc22d5d108c

tools will be used for good or for bad depends on how the technology is adopted, by whom, and for what purpose.

APPENDIX

The Fed

The Federal Reserve is not a single central bank. It is a central banking *system*. The system is comprised of three main parts: twelve regional Federal Reserve Banks, the Federal Reserve Board, and the Federal Open Market Committee (FOMC). According to Wikipedia:[249]

> *The Federal Reserve System is composed of several layers. It is governed by the presidentially appointed Board of Governors or Federal Reserve Board (FRB). Twelve regional Federal Reserve Banks, located in cities throughout the nation, oversee the privately-owned U.S. member banks. Nationally chartered commercial banks are required to hold stock in the Federal Reserve Bank of their region, which entitles them to elect some of their board members. The FOMC sets monetary policy; it consists of all seven members of the Board of Governors and the twelve regional bank presidents, though only five bank presidents vote at any given time: the president of the New York Fed and four others who rotate through one-year terms.*

People talk about the 'big' Fed and the 'little' Feds. When they talk about the 'big' Fed, they are usually talking about either the *Board of Governors of the Federal Reserve System* ('The

---

249   https://en.wikipedia.org/wiki/Federal__Reserve__System

Board of Governors') or the FOMC. The 'little' Feds are the twelve regional Federal Reserve Banks.

Big Fed

Board of Governors

According to the St Louis Fed[250], the Board of Governors guides the Federal Reserve's policy actions, and consists of up to seven governors, appointed by the president of the United States and confirmed by the Senate. As of Jun 2018, there are only three governors guiding the Fed[251].

Federal Open Market Committee

The FOMC is the body that raises or lowers interest rates. The St Louis Fed describes the committee as:

> *... the Fed's chief body for monetary policy. Its voting membership combines the seven members of the Board of Governors, the president of the Federal Reserve Bank of New York, and four other Reserve Bank presidents, who serve one-year terms on a rotating basis with the other Reserve Bank presidents.*

---

250   https://www.stlouisfed.org/in-plain-english/federal-reserve-board-of-governors

251   https://www.federalreserve.gov/aboutthefed/bios/board/default.htm
retrieved 5 Jun 2018

According to the Chicago Fed:[252]

The monetary policy goals of the Federal Reserve are to foster economic conditions that achieve both stable prices and maximum sustainable employment.

What does a stable price mean? The target goal for the FOMC is to set monetary policy to create a 2% per year CPI. 2% seems small but has a significant effect over a lifetime. The maximum stable employment rate is targeted at 95.4% employment, or 4.6% unemployment.

The FOMC oversees and sets policy on open market operations, the principal tool of national monetary policy. The committee meets eight times a year, approximately once every six weeks. As of Jun 2018, out of a maximum of twelve voting members, only eight committee members were appointed[253].

Little Feds

The 'Little Feds' are the twelve separately incorporated regional Federal Reserve Banks (regional FRBs). They are based in the cities of Boston, New York, Philadelphia, Cleveland, Richmond, Atlanta, Chicago, St. Louis, Minneapolis, Kansas City, Dallas, and San Francisco.

---

252   https://www.chicagofed.org/research/dual-mandate/dual-mandate

253   https://www.federalreserve.gov/monetarypolicy/fomc.htm retrieved 5 Jun 2018

Federal Reserve Banks

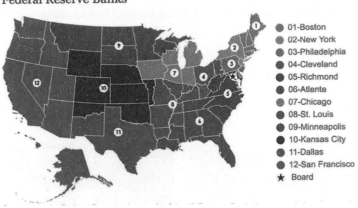

- ● 01-Boston
- ● 02-New York
- ● 03-Philadelphia
- ● 04-Cleveland
- ● 05-Richmond
- ● 06-Atlanta
- ● 07-Chicago
- ● 08-St. Louis
- ● 09-Minneapolis
- ● 10-Kansas City
- ● 11-Dallas
- ● 12-San Francisco
- ★ Board

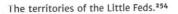

The territories of the Little Feds.[254]

The regional FRBs are responsible within their territory for supervising and examining state member banks, lending to depository institutions, providing key financial services (e.g., interbank payment systems), and examining certain financial institutions[255]. They also provide the US Government with a ready source of loans and serve as the safe depository for federal money[256].

The regional FRBs are not part of the federal government of the USA, but are set up like private corporations, according to the St Louis Fed[257]. The shareholders are banks from the private banking sector, who receive a tax-free 6% dividend

---

254 https://www.federalreserve.gov/aboutthefed/structure-federal-reserve-banks.htm

255 https://www.federalreserve.gov/aboutthefed/structure-federal-reserve-banks.htm

256 https://en.wikipedia.org/wiki/Federal_Reserve_Bank

257 https://www.stlouisfed.org/In-Plain-English/Who-Owns-the-Federal-Reserve-Banks

from the regional FRBs in any year that the regional FRB
makes money. In fact, nationally chartered banks must
purchase some amount of this stock, with the amount based
on their size. It is nice to be a bank and be forced to own the
central bank and receive guaranteed dividends risk-free[258]!

This diagram[259] shows how it all fits together today:

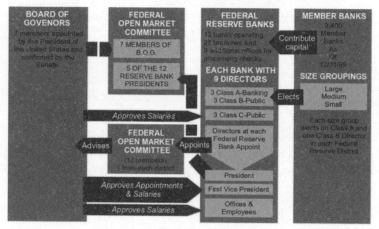

Source: Board of Governors of the Federal Reserve System

258   https://newrepublic.com/article/116913/federal-reserve-dividends-most-
outrageous-handout-banks

259   Atrtribution: By Kimse84 - I made this diagram, CC BY-SA 3.0, https://
commons.wikimedia.org/w/index.php?curid=25448710

Acknowledgments

This book would not have been possible without the support of a large number of people.

Along this journey, and although I may not agree with all of them all the time, I have been influenced by people with a wide range of perspectives. I am grateful to them for sharing their knowledge and opinions with the world, online for free. I have particularly enjoyed content from[260] Gavin Andresen, Andreas Antonopoulos, Richard Gendal Brown, Vitalik Buterin, Gideon Greenspan, Ian Grigg, Dave Hudson, Izabella Kaminska, Rusty Russell, Tim Swanson[261], Robert Sams, Emin Gun Sirer, and Angela Walch.

Other friends have been generous with their time and expertise: Drew Graham and Varun Mittal have been at the end of Whatsapp, responding quickly when I have needed help or inspiration, and industry experts in various crypto-related chat rooms have consistently made themselves instantly available to contribute with a quick insult or flippant comment—thank you.

I am immensely grateful to the team at Mango Publishing for their work in making this book a reality: Ashley, Hannah,

260   I am acutely aware that there are only two women in this list—it reflects the gender balance of the early years of the industry. Today, the number of talented women in the industry is growing and I am looking forward to learning from these experts too.

261   I'd like to thank Tim especially both for passing me detailed feedback on a number of sections in this book, and for his mentorship over the years.

Mario, Michelle, Natasha, Roberto, Chris, and the others working behind the scenes. Thank you, Hugo, for taking a risk and having confidence in me.

Sarah, thank you for looking after our children while I sat for many hours writing in coffee shops, and for occasionally reminding me of my real-life responsibilities as husband and father too.

Finally, I'd like to thank my father Kevin, who spent many hours diligently editing my drafts despite having minimal prior interest or experience in cryptocurrencies! Papa, you are now a Bitcoin expert.

It takes a decentralised village to raise a book on cryptocurrencies.

ABOUT THE AUTHOR

Inspired by a Bitcoin conference in 2013, Antony left a conventional banking career in Singapore to join a little startup called itBit. A Bitcoin exchange, itBit is a website where clients can buy and sell bitcoins, and was one of the first wave of venture capital funded companies in the nascent cryptocurrency industry.

In 2015, after itBit raised another round of venture funding and moved its headquarters to New York, Antony left and privately consulted to clients, writing papers and running workshops to explain this new technology to curious professionals.

In 2016, Antony joined R3, a financial industry consortium created to collaboratively explore the benefits of blockchain technology. As Director of Research, he explores explains the evolving concepts and technologies to clients, policymakers, and the public.

Before becoming obsessed with bitcoins and blockchains, Antony was a technologist at Credit Suisse in London and Singapore, having started his banking career as an FX spot trader at Barclays Capital in 2007.

Antony studied Natural Sciences at Gonville & Caius College, Cambridge University where he gained two full Blues for sailing and graduated in 2004 with a 2:1.

Antony lives in Singapore with his wife Sarah and their two children. He tweets from @antony_btc and blogs at www. bitsonblocks.net.